General Editors: J. R. **MULRYNE**
and J. C. **BULMAN**
Associate Editor: Margaret Shewring

Macbeth

Published in our
centenary year
❦ **2004** ❧
MANCHESTER
UNIVERSITY
PRESS

Already published in the series

Geraldine Cousin *King John*
Anthony B. Dawson *Hamlet*
Jay L. Halio *A Midsummer Night's Dream* (2nd edn)
James Loehlin *Henry V*
Scott McMillin *Henry IV, Part One*
Lois Potter *Othello*
Hugh M. Richmond *King Henry VIII*
Margaret Shewring *King Richard II*

Of related interest

Kate Chedgzoy *Shakespeare's queer children:
sexual politics and contemporary culture*

Jonathan Dollimore and Alan Sinfield, eds *Political Shakespeare:
new essays in cultural materialism, 2nd edition*

Alison Findlay *Illegitimate power: bastards in Renaissance drama*

John J. Joughin *Shakespeare and national culture*

Michele Marrapodi, A. J. Hoenselaars, Marcello Cappuzzo
and L. Falzon Santucci, eds *Shakespeare's Italy*

Ann Thompson and Sasha Roberts *Women reading Shakespeare
1660–1900: an anthology*

Macbeth

Second edition

BERNICE W. KLIMAN

Manchester
University Press

Manchester and New York

Distributed exclusively in the USA by Palgrave

Published by Manchester University Press
Oxford Road, Manchester M13 9NR, UK
and Room 400, 175 Fifth Avenue, New York, NY 10010, USA
www.manchesteruniversitypress.co.uk

Distributed exclusively in the USA by
Palgrave, 175 Fifth Avenue, New York NY 10010, USA

Distributed exclusively in Canada by
UBC Press, University of British Columbia, 2029 West Mall,
Vancouver, BC, Canada V6T 1Z2

British Library Cataloguing-in-Publication Data
A catalogue record for this book is available from the British Library

Library of Congress Cataloging-in-Publication Data
A catalog record for this book is available from the Library of Congress

ISBN 13: 978 0 7190 6229 2

First published by Manchester University Press 1992
Published in paperback 1995
Second edition first published 2004
First digital paperback edition published 2008

Printed by Lightning Source

Dedicated to the memory of
Eve Widgoff Shapiro, a bright light in the world

CONTENTS

LIST OF ILLUSTRATIONS

Every effort has been made to obtain permission to reproduce copyright material in this book. If any proper acknowledgement has not been made, copyright holders are invited to contact the publisher.

SERIES EDITORS' PREFACE

Recently, the study of Shakespeare's plays as scripts for performance in the theatre has grown to rival the reading of Shakespeare as literature among university, college, and secondary-school teachers and their students. The aim of the present series is to assist this study by describing how certain of Shakespeare's texts have been realised in production.

The series is not concerned to provide theatre history in the traditional sense. Rather, it employs the more contemporary discourses of performance criticism to explore how a multitude of factors work together to determine how a play achieves meaning for a particular audience. Each contributor to the series has selected a number of productions of a given play and analysed them comparatively. These productions – drawn from different periods, countries and media – were chosen not only because they are culturally significant in their own right but also because they represent something of the range and variety of the possible interpretations of the play in hand. They illustrate how the convergence of various material conditions helps to shape a performance: the medium for which the text is adapted; stagedesign and theatrical tradition; the acting company itself; the body and abilities of the individual actor; and the historical, political, and social contexts which condition audience reception of the play.

We hope that theatregoers, by reading these accounts of Shakespeare in performance, may enlarge their understanding of what a playtext is and begin, too, to appreciate the complex ways in which performance is a collaborative effort. Any study of a Shakespeare text will, of course, reveal only a small proportion of the plays's potential meaning; but by engaging issues of how a text is translated in performance, our series encourages a kind of reading that is receptive to the contingencies that make theatre a living art.

J. R. Mulryne and J. C. Bulman, General Editors
Margaret Shewring, Associate Editor

ACKNOWLEDGEMENTS

For help with the first and second editions of this study, thanks to Toby Bird, Kathleen Campbell, Kent Cartwright, Joe Costa, H. R. Coursen, James Daybell, Allen Dessen, Joe Dowling, Kathryn Feldman, Paul A. Fideler, Richard France, Barry Gaines, Jeffrey Horowitz, James Lusardi, Arthur F. Kinney, Merwin Kliman, Margaret Knapp, Nati H. Krivatsy, Jill L. Levenson, Cary Mazer, Jean Miller, Melinda Mullins, Thomas Pendleton, Marion Perret, Kenneth S. Rothwell, Alicia Sanchez, June Schlueter, Alexander Sin, J. L. Styan, Betsy Walsh, Mildred Widgoff, Richard Alan Wilson, and Georgiana Ziegler; also to the staffs of the Library at the Shakespeare Birthplace Trust of Stratford-upon-Avon (which provided xerox copies of reviews from its extensive scrapbooks); The Special Collections Library at the University of California at Los Angeles; The Library of Congress Federal Theater Project Collection, formerly at George Mason University Library, Fairfax, Virginia, and now largely in Washington, DC; The Billy Rose Theatre Collection at the New York Public Library at Lincoln Center and the Theatre on Film and Tape (TOFT) Archive there; The Folger Shakespeare Library, without which this study would not have been possible; The Furness Library and Special Collections Library at the University of Pennsylvania. Thanks also to Nassau Community College for a sabbatical leave and for constant support for my research activities, to the State University of New York for a sabbatical grant, and to the National Endowment for the Humanities for a Travel to Collections grant. Deep appreciation to Manchester University Press for its support and to James Bulman, one of the general editors of the Shakespeare in Performance Series, for his patience and helpful suggestions for this second edition. Thanks to Joanna G. H. Jacobs for help with the index.

For the staged version of the Trevor Nunn productions, I am indebted to Sue Dommett for her extensive notes, production stills and drawings that indicate blocking and action of the production in several performances on the main stage at Stratford in 1977. Page references to Dommett refer to her apparatus; references by act, scene and line refer to the promptbook that she reproduces. Thanks to Ron Daniels for allowing me to sit in on rehearsals and for showing me his production notes.

Above all, thanks to Paul Harvey and Graham Bradshaw. The extensive research that Harvey has done on Ninagawa and his reception in Japan and elsewhere has allowed us to expand and clarify the shorter essay that appeared in the first edition. He would like to acknowledge the assistance of Kaori Ashizu, Ryuta Minami and Point Tokyo (Tadao Nakane and his staff). Bradshaw kindly agreed to extract from his work in progress on opera and Shakespeare a section suitable for this book. Both the Ninagawa and the Verdi versions of the play enrich the conception of what *Macbeth* is and whom it is for.

Although I have usually examined primary sources, I refer to secondary sources where possible because they are more likely to be available in college libraries. Where excerpts from sources are syntactically complete or interwoven into my sentences, I have suppressed ellipses and adjusted case without notice.

Citations to the Folio text are from *The Norton Facsimile* edition, prepared by Charlton Hinman, and to the through line numbers in that text, used here by permission. Other references to *Macbeth* are to the Arden text edited by Kenneth Muir.

INTRODUCTION

Macbeth is Shakespeare's experiment in unity of focus. In its concentrated interest on the protagonists, this play differs from the other major tragedies, which from beginning to end offer sharp and distinctive portraits of many secondary and minor characters. Its chief appeal arises from the struggles of the central characters with each other and with the infernal powers that inspire or govern them. Macbeth and his wife awaken powers of darkness to seek supremacy and sway, or those powers find in the pair ambitions ready to be awakened, or those powers corrupt what could have continued wholesome. Whatever evil or pathos the protagonists convey in performance, audiences can be attracted by Macbeth's poetry, his energy, his capacity for love, his inability to deceive himself completely and above all his imagination and courage – by all these attributes and more from which actors can draw their inspiration. Lady Macbeth excites at least as much interest, with her indomitable spirit, single-minded ambition and overweening desire to advance either her husband's interests or her own. An actor can make her the nerve centre of at least the first half of the play.

Macbeth and his lady often retain their ascendance in spite of attempts by some directors to intensify other aspects of the play. The productions considered in this volume fall, mainly, into two categories: actor-dominated, sometimes with little attention to the production as a whole; or director-dominated, with interest diffused among the protagonists, the setting, other characters such as Malcolm, Banquo or Macduff, and the production concept. With a miracle, equally strong actors and directors might balance their sometimes dissonant concerns, the former primarily for character, the latter for coherence, spectacle and unity. Each of the productions in this study illuminates the balancing act.

The Folio script (1623), the sole source for the play since no quartos were published during Shakespeare's lifetime, leaves open many issues for actors and directors to exploit. Their answers to the play's questions and opportunities are determined largely by their placement of Macbeth and Lady Macbeth within a social setting. Though there is overlap and categories cannot be rigid, four possibilities emerge. (1) In the earliest and still the predominant interpretation,

Macbeth and Lady Macbeth stand alone because their struggle is within themselves. One or both of these characters, whose psychology is rendered as transparently as possible, control the tragedy. Often when two strong actors share the centre, the script allows first Lady Macbeth and then Macbeth to dominate, a structure we might call a 'chiasmus', or crossover. They are larger than life; other characters— even the three Sisters—tend to be less important and the prophecy a catalyst only, symbolising a conflict already in the characters. David Garrick, Sarah Siddons, Laurence Olivier with Vivien Leigh are exemplars of this interpretation, which galvanised performers for the first three hundred years—and which continues to be compelling today. The interpretation coincides with the text's concentration on the protagonists. (2) To shape a controlling supernatural sphere or a complex social world, however, directors sometimes rechannel the text's energies. In one such interpretation, a large, external force such as Fate or Evil controls events, making Macbeth and Lady Macbeth small grains in a cosmic scheme. Orson Welles's 1936 stage version, echoed to some extent by his 1948 film, concentrates the power in Voodoo manipulations within a corrupt society. (3) In another vision, Macbeth and Lady Macbeth are governed by their individual relationships, both with each other and with their peers; the tragedy is familial and intimate, and minor characters rise above the anonymity accorded them by the text. Trevor Nunn's version with Ian McKellen and Judi Dench is one example; Ron Daniels's for Theater for a New Audience is another. (4) In another variation, the structure of the society as a whole is the determining force; Macbeth and Lady Macbeth behave as their world has shaped them, acting on its assumptions and values. Akira Kurosawa's and Roman Polanski's films have the spatiality and the supernumeraries to widen the play's scope and embrace a whole political and social realm. Few of these productions, and the others considered in this volume, solve all the problems the play poses, but all invite the reader to join in the privilege of capturing, if only in the mind, the multifarious work of art that is *Macbeth* in performance.

The choices of actors and directors can best be appreciated by being set against the backdrop of the original performances of *Macbeth* and its early revivals.

CHAPTER I

The protagonists and the production

1606-23

Though the purpose and audience of Shakespeare's production in or around 1606 are debatable, something can be inferred about staging, especially lighting, blocking, theatrical use of language and, to some degree, casting and characterisation. The purpose of trying to understand these aspects of the early seventeenth-century *Macbeth* (or, more likely, *Macbeths*) is not to insist that modern productions should attempt to resurrect them but simply to unfold potentialities and pitfalls.

The events of *Macbeth* give it the effect of darkness, but on the Globe stage the play always would have been presented during daylight hours, with sunlight, in fact, sometimes full in the faces of the audience (Orrell, pp. 92–5), or possibly, as newer evidence suggests, fully on the characters. Darkness – night, early dawn, late twilight – is specified in several scenes. But where dialogue or imagery does not call for darkness or where torches do not an-nounce it, in scenes throughout the play, we may assume that the audience thought of the scene as taking place in daylight. Even the witch scenes with songs and dances (III.v and IV.i) could have been considered daylit, though the sound of thunder called for in the stage directions would have suggested overcast skies. Modern productions, in contrast, are likely to make many if not all of the early scenes dark and then, deploying light symbolically, intro-duce it for Malcolm's scenes. No such clear message is suggested by the possibilities for Shakespeare's stage at the Globe. As for other venues, candles could have been the principal light source in the enclosed Blackfriars Theatre, in use after 1608, while a daylit production is a very good possibility for such court theatres as Whitehall, with its many windows (see Orrell, pp. 104–5).

[1]

On the very deep Globe stage, the style of entrances and exits from the doors leading to the tiring room or rooms seems to demand that each scene be complete unto itself, and thus, as Bernard Beckerman asserts in *Dynamics of Drama*, we can look within each scene for structure rather than finding it in the Aristotelian scheme of action rising to a climax and then falling (pp. 183, 192, 205–7). Still, Shakespeare paid careful attention to the way one kind of scene dynamic plays against another. It is not so much that the structure of the scenes has meaning in itself (though sometimes it does: Macbeth never joining or joined by Lady Macbeth after the banquet scene; Macbeth deserted and isolated by the end of the play). Rather, Shakespeare seems to contrive the greatest possible variety of movement and spatiality in a play that singlemindedly concentrates attention on one or two characters. Most scenes of *Measure for Measure*, in contrast to those of *Macbeth*, take place among a limited number of characters until the large, swelling last scene; *Romeo and Juliet*, to cite an early play, has more stark contrasts between crowd scenes and intimate encounters of two characters. Compared to these plays, *Macbeth*'s singleness of focus is intense; in every scene of its twenty-seven (as marked by the Folio), no matter what its structure, either Macbeth is on stage or he and his deeds are the topic of others' concern. Lady Macbeth is present in nine scenes and discussed or mentioned in four more.[1] Shakespeare, however, complicates this unity of attention by varying the numbers of actors in each scene. Only two scenes have the same number of characters on stage throughout: the electrifying 'fair is foul' scene (I.i) – the shortest opening scene of any of the plays, twelve lines – and the scene of Lenox's disaffection with Macbeth (III.vi). More often scenes expand and contract. Several scenes begin either with Lady Macbeth or Macbeth alone, then joined by the other (I.v, I.vii, II.ii, III.ii). The Globe Theatre, with its two entrance doors, is especially apt for scenes so structured; the lone actor is far downstage (that is, near the stage edge), very close to the audience, speaking, perhaps, directly to them. As another or others enter, there is time for the actors to react and respond, while they move downstage too.

Some scenes, often in counterpoint to scenes with only a few characters, start with or build to include potentially large numbers on stage – *potentially* because in production a few can stand for many, and Shakespeare's troupe may have had as few as fifteen actors for the twenty-eight named roles (in Muir, p. 2) as well as for all the supernumeraries. As the scenes with Macbeth in Act V become more constricted, as he is more alone (in V.iii, V.v. and parts of Folio V.vii), the scenes with the opposing forces swell (V.ii, V.iv, V.vi). Within these large scenes, however, there is usually a time when focus rests on one or two characters as others observe and react. Beckerman's analysis of such concentrations within larger scenes seems particularly appropriate to *Macbeth* (see 'Shakespeare's Dramaturgy,'). Still other scenes vary similarly in a smaller compass: the three Sisters alone are joined by Macbeth and Banquo, who are then left alone and finally are joined by Rosse and Angus (I.iii); Macbeth also has occasion for solitary reflection in a long aside (I.iii.130–42).

Other scenes in *Macbeth* function as choral commentary (see Beckerman, *Dynamics*, p. 208). The Old Man and Rosse comment on the shudder in Nature at the events of the murder night (II.iv, the end of the second act). Lenox and an unnamed Lord put the proper moral construction on Macbeth's doings (III.vi, the end of the third act). Lady Macduff comments on correct behaviour and political reality (IV.ii.73–8), and Malcolm examines the nature of good kingship in the person of the English king in what seems to be a digression in an already long scene (IV.iii.147–59), near the end of the fourth act. Though the play seems to hurtle forward, action stops to allow for meditations that return the audience to right thinking – that is, to social norms. When Macbeth hesitates to kill Duncan, the audience, entirely for theatrical reasons, wants him to get on with it and so sides with Lady Macbeth in persuading him. When Macbeth seems paralysed with fear and anguish after the murder, with the knocks at the gate sounding ever more imperative, the audience joins with Lady Macbeth in urging him to escape detection. The choral segments, which affirm a moral society, readjust the audience's values. Moved one way in exciting (dramatic) scenes and then wrenched back again to ordinary social values in static (choral) scenes, the audience could feel dislocated, suspended from its usual standards for evaluating moral life. Such textual hints yield fruitful results in Polanski's *Macbeth* and other modern productions.

For Shakespeare's shifting of dynamic focus – visually, psychologically and morally – the bare thrust stage of the Globe, with the audience on three or possibly even four sides, was particularly apt. And though the Globe was not small, accommodating up to three thousand people, the arrangement seems intimate. Now that the Bankside Globe has been reconstructed, we are able to see *how* intimate. Theatres modelled on Renaissance theatrical spaces, such as the new Swan at Stratford-upon-Avon or the Shenandoah Shakespeare's Blackfriars Theatre in Staunton, Virginia, also suggest the experience of Renaissance staging. The audience is close to the action, practically 'in' the play because audience members from every perspective see audience members beyond the players. Only a few of the modern productions described here – most notably Nunn's Other Stage production – have attempted anything like the intimacy of the Globe staging.

Jill Levenson in *Shakespeare in Performance*: Romeo and Juliet (p. 12) advances the proposition that an audience of the period would have been more attuned than are current audiences to the nuances of speech, to the shifts from blank verse, to rhymed tetrameters, to prose. In *Macbeth* the shifts are well marked, with prose only for Macbeth's letter, the Porter's soliloquy, the conversation between the Porter and Macduff, and Lady Macbeth's sleepwalking scene (except for the doctor's closing lines). At the other extreme, the three Sisters' and Hecate's verse rhythms differ from the blank verse of everyone else. Macbeth's language is full of fantastic metaphors that may not, however, be readily deciphered by a listening audience. What can listeners make of the language of Macbeth's hesitancy about murdering Duncan?

> And Pity, like a naked new-born babe,
> Striding the blast, or heaven's Cherubins, hors'd
> Upon the sightless couriers of the air,
> Shall blow the horrid deed in every eye,
> That tears shall drown the wind. (I.vii.21–5)

Readers have difficulty untangling the metaphoric layers to understand Macbeth's state of mind. Sensitive to and appreciative of metaphor as Shakespeare's audience may have been, it is hard to believe that, even were the speech spoken with studied deliberation, they would grasp more than flashes of images and the emotive content, conveyed largely through intonation, gesture and expression. Richard Burbage, the actor likely to have played Macbeth, was, according to contemporary accounts, a master at expressing thought and feeling. But without grasping the specific meaning, audiences would perceive that Macbeth's language is difficult, convoluted, even tortured.

In contrast, Lady Macbeth's language, especially after Macbeth enters in the letter scene, is much more colloquial than his. One cannot imagine Macbeth saying 'O proper stuff!' as she does in the banquet scene (III.iv.59). Although she is given to word play – 'what thou wouldst highly, / That wouldst thou holily' (I.v.20–1) and 'I'll gild the faces of the grooms withal, / For it must seem their guilt' (II.ii.55–6) – her vocabulary and her images are direct and clear. Most of Shakespeare's characters are similarly distinguished by their speech; such signals *had* to be built in before rehearsals were routine, when actors did not work with a director or with each other to explore meaning.

In *Macbeth*, only the thanes are not characterised by speech patterns; by not giving them individualised language, Shakespeare reinforces concentration on the protagonists. But if attention is paid to the stage directions in the Folio, he does subtly characterise them by the scenes in which they enter and exit. By having every one of them appear in all the large scenes, modern productions often obscure the contrasts among them. Audiences familiar with the actors in a small troupe such as Shakespeare's would be more aware of particular actors than most audiences today are of actors playing minor roles. Shakespeare's audience might have noticed that Angus does not speak in the presence of Duncan or Malcolm – which establishes his rank as beneath that of other thanes who do – that he and Rosse are somewhat competitive about who will give Macbeth the good news about his promotion to Thane of Cawdor, that Rosse wins, and that Angus is never part of Macbeth's court, while Rosse is. Since Menteth and Cathness appear only in Act V, they too are not in Macbeth's court. Because these thanes and Angus are not members of Macbeth's circle, Macduff in absenting himself is not merely an aberration in the body politic but a man who makes the same choice as other men. Rather than exhibiting adherence and then faithlessness to Macbeth (like Rosse and Lenox), these thanes appear to be loyal *Scots*. And though loyalty to a nation-state rather than to the Crown was a concept that in general entered European politics with the revolutions of the seventeenth century, this was very early a particularly Scottish way of positioning oneself – at least from the time of John Barbour's *The Bruce*, written about 1375 (which became a source for the Scottish chronicles). Whether or not Shakespeare's audience would have distinguished between loyalty to a king and to the State, they would have 'read' the thanes Angus, Menteth and Cathness by noticing dramatic signals detached from language content, separable from acting ability, and determined instead by presence and absence, speech and silence.

The more important thanes who associate with Macbeth are characterised by similar signals rather than by specific language, but each of them is much more ambiguous than the three minor thanes who absent themselves. Lenox and Rosse, the latter the only minor thane specifically mentioned by name in the dialogue, are like Banquo and Macduff in attaching themselves to kings – to Duncan, to Macbeth and, in the case of Rosse at least, to Malcolm. Lenox particularly could have the political stature of Banquo or Macduff, and he can be compared to both. In the discovery scene he is especially serviceable to Macbeth, for he seems to corroborate Macbeth's version of his killing of the grooms, saying 'Those of his chamber, as it seem'd, had done't: / Their hands and faces were all badg'd with blood' (II.iii.99–100). To his witness we can impute Macbeth's election as king, for it is otherwise not conceivable in view of Macduff's suspicion about Macbeth's precipitous action ('Wherefore did you so?', II.iii.105) – though Banquo, of course, also must have played a role in Macbeth's election. While Lenox, like Banquo, remains with Macbeth after he indicates that his loyalty has shifted elsewhere (III.vi), his speech with Macbeth after the show of kings (IV.i.135–56) is limited to a few brief phrases. Thus, it is his presence more than what he explicitly says that informs the audience about his nature. Some productions shift Lenox's disaffection in III.vi to a point after IV.i, but that does not work without cuts because he knows less in III.vi than he does in IV.i. Productions that give his part in IV.i to someone else obscure the fact of his treachery – treachery we may call it to pretend loyalty after conspiring to destroy his king.

The script allows for even wider latitude in interpreting Rosse. He appears in eleven scenes and speaks in six, most volubly when he is giving messages. He declines to remain with and protect Lady Macduff (presumably out of loyalty to or fear of Macbeth), yet when we next see him he has defected to Malcolm. In modern productions, the interpretation of the roles of Lenox and Rosse depends very much on the characterisation brought by the actors. Still, the fact that they come as close as they can to kings suggests they are political creatures, rising stars through their attachment to great men, with not too much daintiness about the nature of those they support. Again, when and where and to whom they appear or speak contributes to an audience's understanding of their roles, more especially so when Macduff, Angus, Menteth and Cathness serve as contrasting figures. Shakespeare's Macbeth may not have been as isolated in his ambition as he seems in modern productions where thanes are little more than scene fillers and where audiences are seldom encouraged to think about them at all. The Polanski and Kurosawa films and the Ninagawa stage production, in contrast, make sense of the thanes as part of the warrior community.[2]

Banquo is especially ambiguous and most importantly so, since he is the thane closest to Macbeth. Knowing the prophecy, hearing Macbeth, before the murder, adopt the royal *our* and *we* (II.i.18, 22–3), he should be suspicious, but he does not prevent Macbeth's election. Either by remaining silent or by speaking for him, Banquo responds, it seems, as Macbeth had circuitously asked before the murder of Duncan: to 'cleave to my consent, when 'tis' (II.i.25). And Banquo benefits as Macbeth had promised: 'It shall make honour for you' (II.i.26). He does become a councillor in Macbeth's court: 'We should have else desir'd your good advice ... In this day's council' (III.i.20–2), and he is the 'chief guest' (III.i.11). Banquo's power as king-maker in Macbeth's election is implicit, for he is the one thane who mobilises all to act after the terror of the assassination freezes them (II.iii.123–30). What happens offstage is not part of the play, of course, unless, as here, we see the effect of what must have occurred between the scenes. Banquo's soliloquy after Duncan's murder (III.i.1–10) could imply almost anything at all about his intentions. Certainly, evil thoughts assail him (as he says in II.i.6–9), and he is struggling against them—whether successfully or not he does not live long enough to determine. The most telling facts about Banquo are that he, a sensible friend, warns Macbeth against heeding sweet-sounding prophecies (I.iii.122–6) and that immediately after voicing suspicions about Macbeth in soliloquy (III.i.1–3) – suspicions that he obviously did not raise in the (offstage) council following Duncan's death – Banquo considers how the prophecy could affect him (3–10). He then pledges his allegiance to Macbeth (III.i.15–17). He does not, like Macduff, absent himself from Macbeth's court. The character's ambiguity allows a production to emphasise his goodness, his complicity or his wrenching struggle with both. All productions have to decide what to make of Banquo, and, though many early productions chose to characterise him as the noble foil to Macbeth, recent productions often highlight the ambiguity available in the text. The choices made for Banquo may then affect those for Lenox, Rosse and Macduff.

Aside from familiarity with the actors, Shakespeare's audience would have had another advantage over modern audiences. At least some among them would have been aware, as few audiences since, of the irony of Macbeth's fear of Banquo's progeny. The play's Scottish content Shakespeare derived, either directly or through Holinshed's histories, from Hector Boece's Latin *Chronicles of Scotland* translated into Scots by John Bellenden in 1531, which in turn was translated into English by William Harrison (see Paul, pp. 204–25; see also Bullough, VII, 423–527). These sources were available to the audience as well. Those familiar with broadsides of the Stuart genealogy (see illustration in Evans, *Riverside Shakespeare*, p. 1021) or with Holinshed's *Chronicles* would have known that many generations would pass before a descendant of Banquo (Robert Stuart, grandson of King Robert Bruce) would attain the throne of Scotland in 1371. Holinshed interrupts chronology to introduces the story of Banquo's descendants after his story of Banquo's murder (*Chronicles*, V, 271–3). The audience's knowledge enhances dramatic irony: Macbeth's anxiety about Banquo's heirs who, it seems he imagines, will push him off the throne, is baseless. The Sisters do not prophesy a fruitless crown for Macbeth; he simply assumes so (III.i.60), just as he and his Lady assume that their mere prediction bodes their 'metaphysical aid' (I.v.29). Oracles, as Macbeth recognises, equivocate – lying though they tell some truth – something he knows but refuses to take into consideration in his megalomaniac self-deception. The irony must be all but lost in modern productions, which may indeed present Banquo and Fleance as a threat to Macbeth's (and Malcolm's) dynastic ambitions.

Another point to recall about early performances is that all Shakespeare's women including the witches were played by males, the most tender females (the gentlewoman, Lady Macduff) by boy apprentices, perhaps the others by young men. The masculinity of the actors playing the Sisters would have been useful, for their sex is doubtful: 'you should be women', says Banquo, 'And yet your beards forbid me to interpret / That you are so' (I.iii.45–7). If, however, a Jacobean actor were to portray Lady Macbeth as excessively masculine, her feminine nature could have been called into question; that is, audiences might not have been willing to 'believe' they were seeing a woman. Therefore, I suspect that the Jacobean

Lady Macbeth played by a male appeared feminine; later, when women played the role, an actress like Mrs Pritchard could dare to minimise her feminine side.

Lady Macbeth is Shakespeare's unique creation, a strong woman whose worth to her husband lies in 'the valour of [her] tongue' (I.v.27), a non-silent woman whom the audience certainly is led to condemn for murder and regicide but not for her outspokenness and her control. Like a Senecan heroine, Lady Macbeth through her passion is raised above common notions of womankind. Emilia in *Othello* says that it is proper for a wife to be silent (V.ii.194–225), and possibly this represents the more ordinary early modern view of things – a perspective Shakespeare subverts by making the audience desire Emilia to speak. Nothing, however, in *Macbeth* says that Lady Macbeth is wrong to speak. Her husband encourages her to do so. While manifestly she is ambitious for her husband and possibly for herself, and while she suffers death, presumably for her sins, no one within the play except Malcolm (who describes her as a 'fiend-like Queen', V.ix.35) faults her behaviour. And, though Shakespeare's wicked characters sometimes hoodwink others into approval (Iago, Richard of Gloucester), the difference is that Macbeth approves of Lady Macbeth as she is, not as she seems. She is not depicted as the type of outspoken woman who must be controlled by a man, who feminises the man who does not control her. She is, rather, like the woman of heroic Old English poetry and of the Germanic tradition whom Shakespeare could have found in Tacitus, the woman whose words are valued and who encourages her husband in heroism. Significantly, a new English edition of Tacitus's *Germania* was printed in London in 1604 in *The Annales of Cornelius Tacitus* (for the description of Germanic women see pp. 259–60, 263). Medealike in her forcefulness, Lady Macbeth never falters from loyalty to Macbeth, nor he to her. Her persistent questions about his manliness ('Are you a man?' III.iv.57) exhort him to greater forcefulness; he is not psychically weakened by her words nor made to take up the distaff, the typical result of listening to a woman in the popular culture of Shakespeare's time. Her passionate energies, expressing and magnifying his, lift them beyond the immediate domestic and political sphere. She has no paltry motives.

Her complicity rather than agency, however, is important if Macbeth is to be a responsible, tragic subject (though productions, by cutting many lines, have certainly given her the dominant role). Shakespeare, in Macbeth, delineates the man of valour whose moral sensibilities are alert, who knowingly violates a code of obligations as kin, as host, and as the king's subject:

> He's [Duncan's] here in double trust:
> First, as I am his kinsman and his subject,
> Strong both against the deed; then, as his host,
> Who should against his murtherer shut the door,
> Not bear the knife myself. (I.vii.12–16)

> He hath honour'd me of late; and I have bought
> Golden opinions from all sorts of people,
> Which would be worn now in their newest gloss,
> Not cast aside so soon. (I.vii.32–5)

He also knows what good kingship is, as Duncan has practised it, but is unable to emulate it:

> this Duncan
> Hath borne his faculties so meek, hath bin
> So clear in his great office, that his virtues
> Will plead like angels, trumpet-tongu'd, against
> The deep damnation of his taking-off. (I.vii.16–20)

In contrast to Duncan, Macbeth admits, 'There's not a one of them, but in his house / I keep a servant fee'd' (III.iv.130–1). An archetypal tyrant, he ruthlessly crushes or attempts to crush all potential opposition. (Macbeth is referred to as a tyrant fifteen times in the play.) Certainly, Shakespeare's production would have emphasised Macbeth's valour coupled with his consciousness that, to achieve an unearned eminence, he has sold his eternal jewel for a worthless trifle. He brings upon himself sleepless nights and fills himself with a sense of life's emptiness, a consciousness expressed in imagery that could sweep the audience into a shared feeling for Macbeth's painful recognition (see Donohue, *Dramatic Character*, p. 28).

Shakespeare's intentions for Macbeth can be inferred from the differences between the character and the historical figure. The Macbeth of the Chronicles had some justification for claiming the crown and indeed seemed fit to be king because of Duncan's weakness and inability to rule. Shakespeare does not allow his Macbeth any mitigating circumstances to justify his crime, but neither does he make him the totally evil beast of most of the Chronicles. For one thing, unlike the historical figure, Shakespeare's Macbeth has seductive verse – not the ironic, taunting language of an Iago or a Richard of Gloucester and not the pellucid logic of a Claudius but verse so evocative of sensibility that it affects us as ambiguously as does Caliban's, whose language collides with Prospero's view of him and with Caliban's view of himself.

Central to an audience's appreciation of Macbeth as a character, the question 'What does Macbeth want?' is answered in part by Lady Macbeth's persuasion: he wants what she considers the 'ornament of life' (I.vii.42), which is in her view 'solely sovereign sway and masterdom' (I.v.70). He does not refute her and earlier he had himself referred to the 'imperial theme' (I.iii.129). His behaviour as a king, his demand that Macduff should come at his bidding, his Machiavellian strategy of killing the whole family of someone he does not like – all these suggest that Shakespeare created in Macbeth not only a regicide but an absolutist king, who wants all power for himself. Shakespeare, who in Macbeth suggests Machiavelli's portrait of the ruler whose success is the result of courage wedded to villainy (on Machiavelli in England see Raab), may condemn absolutism itself – just as contemporary works such as those of Edward Coke, whom King James 'fired' because of his views, condemned absolutism (see Pinciss and Lockyer, pp. 149–52). From such hints of anti-absolutism in the play, offshoots such as Tom Stoppard's *Cahoot's Macbeth* and Barbara Garson's *Macbird!* draw their inspiration, but 'straight' productions, such as Nunn's also explore this subtext.

Some infer what Shakespeare intended in his *Macbeth* and how his audience might have perceived the production from the fact of the ascension of James VI of Scotland to the English throne in 1603 (as James I), from Shakespeare's troupe's commission as the King's Men soon after and from the hypothesis that the play may have been presented at court. This narrative suggests that in the character of Banquo and in the witches Shakespeare may have meant to compliment the king, who probably regarded Banquo as his ancestor and whose interest in witchcraft is evidenced by an early work of his own about it, *Daemonology*, reprinted in England in 1603. Certainly the show of kings in the cauldron scene (IV.i.112–24) seems a flattering reference to James's Stuart line. But Leeds Barroll in 'A New History' warns against crafting a single narrative on the basis of selected facts. Into the smooth narrative of compliment, other valid inferences from the known details intrude. The allusions to James could have another function:

simply to bring James to mind during the play, for Shakespeare's intention in Banquo and in the play as a whole may have been subtly subversive. As Alfred Harbage points out in the Pelican edition of the play (1956), if Shakespeare had meant to compliment James, he might have chosen more flattering episodes of Scottish history and rendered Banquo with more definite approbation (p. 18; see also Bullough, VII, 428–9). If James saw the drama at all, which is doubtful given his difficulty understanding the English accent and his general avoidance of plays, he may not have liked being reminded that his putative ancestor had conspired with the historical Macbeth to kill Duncan, for, though Shakespeare carefully eliminated the overt connivance of Banquo, it was there in the Chronicles (V, 269) and hinted at even in Bellenden's Scots translation of Boece's Latin (II, 150–1).

Aside from the problem of Banquo, James probably did not like plays about killing a king (especially in light of the fact that his mother had been convicted of regicide and that the recent Gunpowder Plot made James's own assassination all too uncomfortable a possibility). In this play two kings are dispatched; though the play gives a nod to the lawful issue that Macbeth thrust aside (Macduff refers to Malcolm as 'the truest issue of thy throne', IV.iii.106), there can be little doubt that Macbeth was a legally invested king. Nor does it seem particularly complimentary to show that right rule returns to Scotland through the power of ten thousand English soldiers (IV.iii.134). The audience for whom Shakespeare wrote, therefore, may not have been James at all, but others, some of whom would have delighted in seeing James subtly attacked and compared covertly to Macbeth. Still others would, likely, have noticed neither compliment nor attack. One can imagine Shakespeare taking some pleasure in equivocating (equivocation being an important theme in the play) in the presentation of the 'compliment' to James. All of this is conjecture, of course, but Arthur F. Kinney, too, in his recent study theorises that *Macbeth* may have been a subversive play, undercutting the absolutist pretensions of James, who was increasingly unpopular after 1605, by comparing him to the eponymous hero (p. 99). Stephen Orgel points out that *The Shakspere Allusion-Book* records very few references to the play (p. 148) and that there are no records of performance except Simon Forman's in 1611. Orgel's conclusion is that the play needed beefing up with songs and dances, but an alternative inference is that it was not performed because James did not like it. The performance, then, of *Macbeth* in Shakespeare's time could have been for his audience, whether in a public or private theatre, full of urgent ideas that were being discussed and debated. The play could be a pattern for action in the face of absolute rule and at the same time an ambivalent portrait of the amalgam of valour and injustice in an absolute prince. Though after the Restoration an audience might not have felt absolutism a compelling concern, members of Shakespeare's audience in 1606 were likely to have been deeply interested in such issues and may have, indeed, brought that interest to bear in responding to the play.

While political currents offer hints of interpretation, they do not yield details of the enactment of Macbeth's character. Dr Forman, the one who might have provided just those details, betrays no political *or* dramaturgical awareness. Author of the only extant description by a playgoer of a performance of *Macbeth* during Shakespeare's life, the quack astrologer, unfortunately, seems interested in plot alone (and the moral to be derived from it) and apparently conjures up his images of the play as much from the Chronicles and his own imagination as from memories of a performance. For example, he describes Macbeth and Banquo 'Riding thorowe a wod' (I.iii); such a scene is unlikely – if not impossible – in a public theatre. Though Dennis Bartholomeusz refers to several plays that call for a horse (pp. 4–5), the fact that in III.iii Banquo and Fleance, returning from their ride, leave their horses offstage suggests that no horses were available or used in the theatre (see Rosenberg, *The Masks of* Macbeth, p. 425n). The excellent arguments *against* Forman's reliability as a witness should be accepted (see Scragg). Forman's account helps to establish a date – the performance he may have seen cannot be dated after 1611 – but Forman says little to elucidate staging, costuming, method of acting or substantive interpretation. The one exception, perhaps reliable, is the information that the ghost of Banquo sits in Macbeth's chair when the king rises to toast the absent thane (see Forman, p. 13). Another contemporary reference, dated 1607, to a ghost who in a 'white sheete sit at upper end a' th Table' may provide a clue to how Banquo was dressed in the banquet scene so that the audience would be aware of him as a ghost (from *The Puritan*; see *Shakspere Allusion-Book*, I, 168). Other than that bit of possible costuming, not much else is known about the production in the early seventeenth century.

[13]

The most tantalisingly elusive aspect of the staging is the nature of the Sisters, something that productions today are still trying to fathom. Even if they appear only in the three scenes now generally allotted to them (I.i, I.iii and IV.i), productions must deal with their function as agents or witnesses. The woodcut of the three women in the 1577 edition of Holinshed's *Chronicles* shows three young, respectable women and seems to emphasise their ordinariness (a contrast to Holinshed's description). Shakespeare may or may not have known the 1577 edition; he usually used, it seems, the 1587 edition, which did not have the illustration (see Evans, *Riverside Shakespeare*, p. 1390). In any case, the illustration does not match Banquo's description:

> What are these,
> So wither'd and so wild in their attire,
> That look not like th'inhabitants o'th'earth,
> And yet are on't? Live you? or are you aught
> That man may question? You seem to understand me,
> By each at once her choppy finger laying
> Upon her skinny lips: you should be women,
> And yet your beards forbid me to interpret
> That you are so. (I.iii.39–47)

There are many clues here – old age, unearthliness, chapped fingers, thin lips, and hairy faces. Only the wild attire is a direct link to Holinshed's description. Stage directions refer to the three women as witches, one of them reports being called a witch by someone else, and Macbeth speaks in the abstract of witchcraft and Hecate. They, however, refer to themselves as 'Sisters'. They are supernatural beings, or they are women who have gained supernatural foresight or powers through witchcraft. The powerful and compelling idea of *weird* sisters, so familiar from modern editions, appears nowhere in the Folio but is Lewis Theobald's 1733 emendation of the Folio's *weyward* and *weyard*. Theobald's emendation is based, understandably enough, on the chroniclers' use of the word *weird*. Bellenden applies such terms to them as 'weird sisteris or wiches' and 'werd sisteris' (II, 149–50); Holinshed describes them as 'thrée women in strange and wild apparell, resembling creatures of the elder world ... either the weird sisters, that is (as ye would say) the goddesses of destinie, or else some nymphs or feiries, indued with knowledge of prophesie by their necromanticall science' (V, 268–9). But since Banquo's description differs in part from Holinshed's verbal and visual pictures, Shakespeare might have wanted to avoid the adjective *weird*, with its connotations. Thus the nature of the Folio's 'weyward sisters' is not transparent; they are not only mysterious and uncanny but also the creatures of 'vulgar spite' that A. C. Bradley long ago described (p. 272), whose occupation is 'Killing swine,' who weave spells for the sake of chestnuts, and who beg to see a pilot's thumb: 'Show me, show me' (all from I.iii). A long performance history of spectacular, and often silly, but hardly terrifying witches notwithstanding, today's critics and reviewers, possibly influenced by that adjective *weird*, persist in demanding their vision of the powerful supernatural and fateful creatures that make of the fall of Macbeth something enigmatic and inexplicable or at least otherworldly. Productions have a difficult time meeting those expectations.

Their depiction is further complicated by the problematic Hecate segments, which, though they introduce a frivolity unfitted to Sisters viewed as mysterious beings, were part of the drama in the seventeenth century, perhaps as early as 1606 (III.v, IV.i.39–43). Through excising songs, dances and Hecate, modern productions achieve unity of tone. But it is not certain that Shakespeare preferred classical decorum to medieval disjunction – the evidence, in fact, seems to point the other way. The juxtaposition of Macbeth thrown into despair by the show of kings (IV.i.112–24) and dancing witches from the world of Hecate breaking into this mood, tripping before him (IV.i.130), might seem improbable, but perhaps not: Ron Daniels's production included the dance to excellent effect. Without the dances, without Hecate, the three Sisters are more mysterious than comedic; with her scenes, paradoxically, the witches are less important. Hecate's presence suggests that supernatural powers are real, but only as Titania (another embodiment of Hecate) and Oberon are, that is, with the solidity of mythical figures who come alive in a dramatic performance. If the Hecate scenes are genuine, Shakespeare's production avoided the unified greyness of tone of modern productions. Janet Adelman's contention that 'we are entrapped in Macbeth's head as claustrophobically as he is until ... the scene in England' (p. 11) would not hold were we given a respite in III.v, lifted by the bouncing tetrameters to a more distant vantage point, ready to hear the faint drum sounds from England spoken of in III.vi by Lenox and another lord. The Hecate scenes, also, develop the three Sisters as characters. Their beginning as prophets and their ending as palterers 'in a double sense' (V.viii.20) are mediated by Hecate's comical, romping criticism of their free gifts to Macbeth and by her determination to 'draw him on to his confusion' (III.v.29). Furthermore, as Charlotte Stopes points out, Shakespeare's strange introduction of Hecate may have been meant to evoke the Parcae (the Fates), with whom Proserpina, Diane or Hecate were often associated (p. 668).

If what we call 'Shakespeare' is the text we have, the identity of text and author argues that envisioning *Shakespeare* means including dances and Hecate, however she may have been depicted. Since actors and producers who had played in or had seen plays performed before the theatres were closed in 1642 when the Civil War brought the Puritans to power were alive in 1660 when Charles II was restored to the throne and theatres reopened, some shadow of the original conception of the witches and Hecate may be discernible in the later productions. In fact, it may have been the witches' potential for spectacular effects that made *Macbeth* an acceptable play after the Restoration, when, in emulation of continental practices, the bare thrust stage of the Globe gave way to the proscenium stage with scenic elements. If the Restoration depiction of Hecate and the witches does mirror to some extent Jacobean practices, they are worth investigating for that reason alone. In their own right, moreover, Restoration practices influenced performances for years and, to some extent, still do: for example Davenant's introduction of Seyton, first named in the Folio in Act V, as the universal servant and messenger; the sound of an offstage army for Macbeth's first entrance; a second *never* for Lady Macbeth's line 'O never (never) / Shall sun that morrow see' (I.v.60–1); and much more.

Davenant and Betterton

'When the vogue for opera emerged', say Avery and Scouten, speaking of the early Restoration, 'plays like *Macbeth* and *The Tempest* were ... natural choices for adaptation' (p. cxxx). This assertion would be news to people familiar with modern productions of *Macbeth*, who do not see it as anything like 'opera' (though *opera* then meant a play with some musical interludes rather than a Verdian grand opera). But if the Restoration saw it as *already* operatic, at least in the two scenes including Hecate, then Avery and Scouten's point makes sense. Apparently, operatic enhancement was necessary to make the plays palatable to Restoration audiences, who favoured new plays. Sir William Davenant's operatic interpolations, which made *Macbeth* popular in his own day, have possibly influenced scholars to see the Folio songs and dances and the scenes surrounding them as interpolations also. Even with operatic enhancements, however, Davenant may have come closer, at least in one of his versions of the play, to the Folio witches than do the modern directors who eliminate the Hecate scenes.

As leader of the Duke's company, Davenant revived *Macbeth* in 1664, and Pepys, who wrote in his diaries of attending a performance on 5 November 1664, was in that first audience (see *Shakspere Allusion-Book*, II, 91). While a woman played Lady Macbeth, the witches remained men impersonating women and thus were able to engage in the energetic 'flytings' that prompter John Downes described years later:

> The Tragedy of *Macbeth*, alter'd by Sir *William Davenant;* being drest in all it's Finery, as new Cloath's, new Scenes, Machines, as flytings for the Witches; with all the Singing and Dancing in it: The first compos'd by Mr. *Lock*, the other by Mr. *Channell* and Mr. *Joseph Preist;* it being all Excellently perform'd, being in the nature of an Opera, it Recompenc'd double the Expence; it proves still [1708] a lasting Play. (*Roscius Anglicanus*, p. 33, quoted in *Shakspere Allusion-Book*, II, 439)

Davenant's operatic enhancements held the stage for many years. David Garrick's immediate predecessors (before 1744) appear to have used a Davenant text of 1674 for their productions, a text that is as different from Shakespeare as Shakespeare from Holinshed. But something more like a 1673 text that may represent a more modest revision by Davenant was played from Garrick in the eighteenth to Henry Irving in the late nineteenth century; it is a Folio text with the Davenant-expanded witch scenes in Acts III and IV and with, at least until the mid nineteenth century, a new scene of predictions, songs and dances in Act II. For the first two hundred years of revivals, then, whether based on the 1673 or the 1674 text, *Macbeth* was Shakespeare with Hecate and with more songs and dances than are found in the Folio. The appeal of operatic embellishments to audiences from the seventeenth to nineteenth centuries is as mysterious to us as our preference for

Shakespeare 'pure' would be to them. Contemporary opinion, however, was hardly monolithic; all along some critics found the dancing and singing witches too silly to countenance. Yet the rise in popularity of Shakespearean plays must have been owing, at least in part, to the ability of producers such as Davenant to detect what audiences would find appealing and from the ability of actors such as Thomas Betterton to embody the characters.

Partly because Davenant's Sisters were spectacular, they also smacked less of the supernatural than more austere witches might have done. The eighteenth-century critic Francis Gentleman, in the John Bell edition, faulted Betterton for the innovation of having the witches deliver the prophecies and thus making the claptrap totally superfluous and unmagical (quoted by Rosenberg, *The Masks of* Macbeth, p. 501). Gentleman seems to have missed the point: making the apparitions unmagical may have been precisely Betterton's aim – to heighten an effect already begun by Davenant. On the one hand, Davenant may have felt he was relieving the play of its superstitious elements by introducing the merely fantastical; and on the other hand, Shakespeare, as we have seen, may have already undermined the supernatural elements with his triple-crowned Hecate, a figure from the world of *A Midsummer Night's Dream*, with Davenant simply administering the *coup de grâce*. Davenant's operatic enhancements, intentionally or not, scattered rather than intensified the effect of supernatural power over Macbeth.

However spectacular the added material of flying witches and Hecate lifted by car to the heavens may have been, it certainly was brief, for the musical additions extended this short play by only about fifteen or twenty minutes (see Fiske, p. 117). There is no doubt that, in spite of Davenant's efforts to expand the focus, the principal characters retained their hold on the play – else why would Pepys, a spectator inordinately fond of 'divertisement', have disliked the play only when Betterton, his favourite, was unable to perform? In his diary for 16 October and 6 November 1667, Pepys notes his dissatisfaction when an inferior replaced Betterton, who was ill (*Shakspere Allusion-Book*, II, 93, 94). While today some commentators consider certain passages from the Folio non-Shakespearean because their tone does not match the rest of the play, Pepys's comment about the mystifying variety in the play may be an apt reminder of a prior taste for disjunctive diversity:

[I] saw 'Macbeth', which though I saw it lately, yet appears a most excellent play in all respects, but especially in divertisement, though it be a deep tragedy; which is a strange perfection in a tragedy, it being most proper here, and suitable. (7 January 1666–7, quoted in *Shakspere Allusion-Book*, II, 92–3; see also 19 April 1667)

Pepys was conscious that he was seeing something unprecedented in its combination of effects, but he found a 'strange perfection' in the mingling. He recorded attending *Macbeth* more often than he did any other single play – nine times (Odell, I, 22) – though his attendance at Shakespeare plays in general is far overshadowed by attendance at other plays.

Much of Davenant's influence depended, of course, on the success of the production with Betterton. Although the general shapes of the Davenant productions are reasonably clear from the performance editions of 1673 and 1674, much less is known about Betterton's specific interpretation. Pepys is full of approbation for Betterton but short on detail, for this was not yet an age that valued minute analyses of acting. The production can be inferred, however, from the illustration taken from the show of kings of IV.i in Nicholas Rowe's edition of 1709 (see illustration). Rowe, a man of the theatre, saw Betterton perform in old age and praised him in his introduction. The one engraving Rowe's publishers provided for each play often suggests theatrical practice, and who better to represent *Macbeth* than Betterton, still playing Macbeth at the time? He played the role in 1707, 1708, both at the Queen's and Drury Lane Theatres (from 1708), and as late as December 1709, just months before his death at seventy-five (Hogan, I, 268–70). Further support for Betterton's connection to the illustration comes from Anthony Aston, an actor in Betterton's latter days, because his description of Betterton – the rounded shape, the short arms – matches the figure in the illustration (II, 299).

The setting in the illustration could, it seems, have been managed in any of the three theatres in use then. It appears to be a cave, popular for the apparitions scene for many years (used in the 1955 Olivier and in the 1971 Polanski productions, among others). Downstage right, three 'women' of varying ages, robed nondescriptly and with hair-covering shawls, hold wands and gesture with their right hands to Macbeth, dressed as a seventeenth-century beau. Not until the next century would there be an attempt to correlate costume with dramatic time period. The

1   Frontispiece to *The Tragedy of Macbeth* from *The Works of Mir William Shakespeare*, 1709 Rowe edition

'great cauldron', between Macbeth and the Sisters, appears to be sinking into the earth (as called for by Macbeth's description in IV.i.106), while four shadowy figures of kings, with conventional ermine robes, crowns and sceptres, parade in the background from stage right to stage left. Banquo, following the procession, stands facing Macbeth diagonally across the playing space from upstage right. Dressed as a ghost, with flowing gown and hair, the stern-faced figure holds up his left forearm in admonition, and with his right hand points to his bloody wounds (as George Walton Williams asserts, *Shakespeare Newsletter* (Spring 1993): 3; see also Kliman, 'Rowe Again'). Macbeth's pose in the picture, with the left toe placed forward, the bent right arm just raised to rib level and the left arm just reaching under the short coat for the sword, hints at a rhetorical approach to acting. The picture is full of motion, yet strangely static as well because it catches all the actors in what appear to be highly stylised gestures. It is also awash with light, especially concentrated on the floor and on the apparitions, with light reflected against the front of the Sisters and Macbeth, as if the light were emanating from the cauldron itself. Flames extending above its rim represent or are fire. And, in corroboration, a preface to the anti-Garrick satire *Hecate's Prophecy* – of 1758, to be sure – states that

> During a Performance of Macbeth some time ago, in the Cave Scene ... the Cauldron, after a loud Crack, burst under the Stage; ... extinguished all the Lights; and would (as 'tis supposed) have spread Effects more fatal, had not a neighb'ring Rivulet, of real Water ... play'd full upon the INCANTATION-FLAME, and quench'd it of its own Accord. (*Briefe Remarks on the Original and Present State of the Drama: To which is added Hecate's Prophecy ...* pp. 21–2)

This parody validates the theatrical relevance of the Rowe illustration, for its flames are not in the text. Still, since the Betterton script featured Hecate very prominently and she is absent from the frontispiece, it is not a complete record.

At the time, scenery foregrounded acting, literally and figuratively. In general, flat paintings at the back of the set indicated place (though the Rowe illustration suggests the proscenium's capacity for establishing a picture frame, with scenic elements enhancing the arch). The scene paintings were placed in position, Odell claims, in the audience's full view at least into the nineteenth century and the latter times of Sarah Siddons. The Restoration was not an age that attempted to create an illusion of spatial reality; rather, producers decorated a stage that was remarkably similar to the non-illusionistic thrust stage of Renaissance public theatres (Odell, I, 100). Actors, as in the Renaissance, played well to the front of a stage (Nicoll, pp. 29–30). Costume, props and emblematic gestures were more important than scenery, and spectacle was effected by supernumeraries rather than scenery (Odell, I, 179–81).

As for the acting on this stage, there is little to go on. Legend has it that Betterton was taught the art of Shakespearean acting by Davenant, who knew it from the old pre-Restoration players, and who claimed to be Shakespeare's illegitimate son. Bartholomeusz refers to Colley Cibber's and others' descriptions of Betterton as Hamlet, and probably their claims about his excellence can be extended to his Macbeth: Cibber says Betterton 'could vary his spirit to the different characters he acted' and had the 'requisite Variations of Voice' (p. 14). Aston says that Betterton 'was the most extensive Actor, from *Alexander* to Sir *John Falstaff*' (II, 300). Furthermore, said Aston, he completely inhabited his role: 'Betterton, from the Time he was dress'd, to the End of the Play, kept his Mind in the same Temperament and Adaptness, as the present Character required' (II, 301). Bartholomeusz's descriptions of Betterton as an actor, drawn largely from contemporary commentary and recollection, often include the term 'Nature' (pp. 25, 38), a term that does not fit, it seems, the stance of the actor in Rowe's frontispiece. Obviously, *natural* in 1664 would not look natural in 2004. By *natural* early writers meant expressing the emotion that one would expect in a person under such circumstances. The word *believable* may be the operative one. Betterton's acting was, doubtless, strong enough to withstand Davenant's efforts to expand the play's operatic effects. He had those qualities still esteemed today: range of impersonation, variety of voice and compelling believability. Busy as he was as actor-manager, teacher of fledgling actors and writer-adapter, it is not surprising that Betterton, when he became manager, did not try to rework the play but retained Davenant's successful script, presenting it no more than a few times each year during his whole career.

David Garrick

Macbeth with music, with choruses of singing and dancing witches, was the second most popular Shakespeare play in the eighteenth century (Hogan, II, 716–17). But the more fantastic the supernatural, the less it affects the protagonists' character development, which unfolds in a different plane. The recruitment of the supernatural elements for the purpose of entertainment, therefore, allows for the characterisation of the terrible Lady who bends Macbeth to do evil, acting out her own ambitions through him. For, if Macbeth is conceived as the noble warrior, something or someone must divert him from his natural course; when it is not the witches it can be the wife (or it can be both in concert). The heroic Macbeth and the powerful Lady are best exemplified by David Garrick (1717–79), who played Macbeth from 1744 to 1768, and Sarah Siddons (1755–1831), who played her famous Lady Macbeth in London from 1785 to 1819, including some post-retirement performances. These two serve as types of the honourable Macbeth and the awe-inspiring, terrifying Queen. Since *Macbeth*, with its emphasis on the protagonists (unlike *Antony and Cleopatra*, *Romeo and Juliet* and other plays that divide attention among many), is an obvious vehicle for star actors who merit undivided attention from an audience, it is not surprising that both Garrick and Siddons, with their preeminence, excelled in this play.

Garrick was, in addition to being the foremost tragic and comic actor of his time, a playwright, poet, theatre manager and text adapter. Though he boasted of restoring Shakespeare's language, he cut many lines from *Macbeth*, retained Davenant's singing and dancing witches, and to some minds ruined the effect of the whole with a pious confession by the dying Macbeth – a confession that stated Macbeth's own understanding of his motive more unambiguously than did Shakespeare (see Rabkin, pp. 104–5), more fulsomely than did Davenant. Garrick had Macbeth say,

> 'Tis done! the scene of life will quickly close. Ambition's vain delusive dreams are fled, And now I wake to darkness, guilt, and horror; I cannot bear it! let me shake it off – it will not be; my soul is clog'd with blood – I cannot rise! I dare not ask for mercy – It is too late, hell drags me down; I sink, I sink, – my soul is lost for ever! – Oh! – Oh!

Finally, he dies (see Furness, *Macbeth*, p. 345). In spite of such lapses, it is not easy to dismiss Garrick's textual innovations.

Indeed, his extensive correspondence with members of his audience illustrates the thoughtfulness of his decisions. (Excerpts from several of his letters are quoted in Bartholomeusz, and others may be found in *The Letters of David Garrick*.)

Garrick can, however, be more wholeheartedly appreciated as an actor than as a reshaper of the text. As actor-manager he controlled the entire production, and the character of Macbeth ruled. Francis Gentleman dismissed as beneath his notice all the thanes, the witches, Macduff and Lady Macduff, and even Lady Macbeth. The play for him was Macbeth as performed by Garrick. He described the actor in the *Dramatic Critic* of 1770:

> Through all the soliloquies of anxious reflections in the first act; amidst the pangs of guilty apprehensions, and pungent remorse, in the second; through all the distracted terror of the third; all the impetuous curiosity of the fourth, and all the desperation of the fifth, Mr. *Garrick* shews uniform, unabating excellence; scarce a look, motion or tone, but takes possession of our faculties, and leads them to a just sensibility. (*TQ*, p. 19)

The introduction to a 1773 text (the year of a revival by Macklin, some time after Garrick had ceased to act the role) included this remark, apparently by Gentleman, about Garrick:

> He sustains the importance, marks the strong feelings, and illustrates the author's powerful ideas, with such natural, animated, forcible propriety, that the dullest heart must receive impressions from him, which the clearest head cannot adequately express. (Shattuck, *Macbeth* 8; also quoted in Burnim, *Garrick*, p. 107)

This last disclaimer explains why, in spite of intense admiration and many general descriptions of Garrick's acting style, Gentleman offers no moment-by-moment description of Garrick's Macbeth. Ideas about his performance must be gleaned from many sources (Berkowitz's *Guide* is a great help).

Garrick's main idea, according to Donohue, was to 'exploit the basic Shakespearian dramatic contrast between Macbeth's hesitancy and vacillation and Lady Macbeth's stern inveteracy' ('Macbeth', p. 22). His Macbeth was a noble man, capable of high ambitions but not innately evil, urged to act by his wife. 'He brought together', says Bartholomeusz, 'the sensitive and the satanic elements in the character' (p. 81). 'The spine of the character', Donohue notes, 'is the courageousness that supports him to the last' ('Macbeth', p. 23). Donohue sums up Garrick's verbal achievement: 'controlled variety, graceful rapidity, and syntax-breaking pauses' (see 'Macbeth', p. 23). Although in his promptbook Garrick smoothed the abrupt rhythms of the Folio – influenced, as it appears, by the editors of his time (Pope and others) – in practice on stage he avoided regularities of verse that could not possibly reflect the perturbations of Macbeth's mind. His great gift was to convey, even in as narrow a compass as a single line, multi-layered contradictory or harmonious emotions. Bartholomeusz, who offers a full comparison of the promptbook and the Folio and Garrick's achievement in variations on the iambic line (pp. 41ff), maintains that Garrick's appeal as an actor rested not only on the naturalness of his speech and manner but also on his dancer's ability to move his body (Bartholomeusz, p. 38) – a skill Betterton did not possess, at least towards the end of his long career (Aston, II, 300). Some of Garrick's flexibility and bodily expressiveness can be seen in drawings and paintings by Fuseli and others.

Garrick's best acting reflected his Macbeth's sensibility and remorse, his intense suffering for succumbing to temptations that run counter to his essential nature, an interpretation that was successful when it was complemented by the fierce Lady Macbeth of Mrs (Hannah) Pritchard. These qualities, perhaps, are present in almost every attractive Macbeth and explain, in part, the fascination that audiences feel for him in spite of his brutality. But Garrick raised these aspects to supremacy, aided by Mrs Pritchard's strikingly powerful Lady. In fact, his Macbeth was fully appreciated only after Mrs Pritchard joined him, and he seemed to understand this, because, except for performances of set speeches (see *Letters*, no. 730), he stopped playing the role when she retired, in spite of many promises to mount a new production (no. 726).

Like Betterton, Garrick remained in character throughout the performance – something of an exception to the rule in the eighteenth century and especially difficult in view of the audience's exuberant response to everything it liked (or disliked), much as audiences today respond to moments in opera or dance. Audiences, it seems, were more interested in the delivery of each line than in overall effect. Their constant outbursts must have had the effect of interrupting the flow of the drama as a whole for themselves, and Garrick complained at times that their excessive talking interrupted his feelings. A concept of dramatic character as a series of unconnected peaks is a residue from the days of Beaumont and Fletcher and can be found throughout the eighteenth century (see Donohue, *Dramatic Character*, pp. 28, 222–3). Disconnectedness appears also in the period's continued lack of concern about scenery changed in full view of the audience. No worry about interrupting the continuity of the drama inhibited this practice; indeed, the scene changes were interesting in themselves, a momentary marvel forgotten after the acting recommenced. Scene changes afforded opportunities for the audience to chat about the beauties of the moments they had just seen and to recover from the emotional wringer they had gone through with the actor.

And Garrick, who through his face, his body and his voice could reveal his thought processes and minute changes in thought, carried his audience away. He was able to whisper so that the sound could be heard in the farthest gallery, 'without losing the appearance of a whisper' (*Theatrical Review … 1757*, p. 4). He used this whisper to terrific effect in the daggers scene, when Macbeth returns from murdering Duncan, yet his voice could be so colloquial as to fool a pick-up actor playing the first murderer into thinking that Garrick, and not Macbeth, was telling him there was blood on his face (Burnim, *Garrick*, p. 117).

Thomas Wilkes's 1759 account is worth quoting in full because it shows what this author was looking for – among other things, acting that could elicit a reflection of the character's emotional response in the audience:

> There is not any character in Tragedy so seldom hit off by the Actor as Macbeth, perhaps there are few more difficult; and in the hands of Garrick it acquires an inconceivable ease. It is curious to observe in him the progress of guilt from the intention to the act. How his ambition kindles at the distant prospect of a crown, when the witches prophecy! and with what reluctance he yields, upon the diabolical persuasions of his wife, to the perpetration of the murder! How finely does he shew his resolution staggered, upon the supposed view of the air-drawn dagger, until he is rouzed to action by the signal, viz. the ringing of the closet bell!
>
> It is impossible for description to convey an adequate idea of the horror of his looks, when he returns from having murdered Duncan with the bloody daggers, and hands stained in gore. How does his voice chill the blood when he tells you, 'I've done the deed!' and then looking on his hands, 'this is a sorry sight!' How expressive is his manner and countenance during Lenox's knocking at the door, of the anguish and confusion that possess him; and his answer,

''twas a rough night', shews as much self-condemnation as much fear of discovery, as much endeavor to conquer inquietude and assume ease, as ever was infused into, or intended for, the character. What force, what uncontrollable spirit does he discover in his distresses, when he cries out,

> They have tied me to a stake – I cannot fly;
> But bear-like I must fight my course.

In short, he alone, methinks, performs the character. (pp. 248–9)

Wilkes valued above all the psychological credibility of Garrick's portrayal. 'If [Garrick] has faults', he says, 'they are like spots in the sun, hid beneath a blaze of majesty; an effulgence of beauty that astonishes, while it dims all things liable to censure, so that they become imperceptible' (p. 263).

The pictorial evidence suggests that Garrick's costumes were variable. A painting by Dawes shows him in the cauldron scene with no wig, puffed bloomers, tights and a short cape (see '"Macbeth" on the Stage', *English Illustrated Magazine*, 1888, p. 235); but the frontispiece in a promptbook reflects a different practice (Shattuck, *Macbeth* 8). It has a picture of Garrick near the cauldron in Grecian dress with feathered hat. Still other pictures show him in more formal attire, in a knee-length cutaway coat, an elaborate hip-length vest, breeches, stockings and shoes, with a small, curly wig (Zoffany print, *TQ*, p. 23; also Carr and Knapp, p. 840). Garrick's most commented-upon costume was that of an eighteenth-century military man, with a scarlet and gold suit and a wig. A painting that shows him so dressed is discussed at length by Stephen Leo Carr and Peggy A. Knapp. Since in the eighteenth century a move towards authentic costumes began, expressed by the innovations of Charles Macklin and others and conceivably inspired by a 1757 Edinburgh production (Nicoll, p. 171), Mrs Inchbald and others faulted Garrick for his costume, which she considered no costume at all. In spite of Garrick's contemporary dress, however, he was evidently as able to inspire belief as can current productions in modern dress.

Garrick's aim, it appears, was realism, and for that purpose, he subdued the Davenant-introduced exuberance of the witches' entrances and exits (Bartholomeusz, p. 40). His mid-eighteenth-century impersonation, considered the best since Betterton's, was that of the noble Macbeth, worthy of an audience's pity through all the murders of the second, third and fourth acts. Above all, especially when supported by Mrs Pritchard's Lady, he was the main reason for seeing the play, the focus of everyone's interest.

Sarah Siddons

Mrs Siddons, who found an almost hidden core of vulnerability in the character, nevertheless continued the line of development brought to maturity by Mrs Pritchard – the powerful lady to complement the noble Macbeth. The difference is that with Pritchard Garrick dominated, while Mrs Siddons towered above the Macbeth of her brother John Philip Kemble. Weak and poetic, Kemble's Macbeth was not as interesting as her Lady; yet their conceptions suited each other well. Hers was created in 1785, with a Mr William Smith, as nondescript as his name, as Macbeth (see Hogan, II, 387–9). Kemble was willing, it seems, to submerge his Macbeth, allowing her to take the lead in a role that she had constructed before he was given the opportunity to perform in *Macbeth* with her. Her effect on her audiences may be inferred from the fact that so many artists sought to capture her mesmerising grace and beauty (Highfill, Burnim and Langhans, XIV, 37–67, list 367 examples, a few of them caricatures, to be sure). Her performances are worthy of close study, because she may be the best actor who has ever played the role of Lady Macbeth and because actors have emulated her in many individual choices – if not in the entire characterisation. We can pay her that attention because she is one of the first actors who received the kind of minute descriptions of voice, gesture, movement, thought and feeling that later spectators applied to the work of Edwin Booth and Laurence Olivier. Only a few actors at any period excite this sort of observation. She herself wrote about her intentions and about the character of Lady Macbeth, though many critics think she surpassed her own analyses. Detailed reports of her performances show that hers was a nuanced, rich performance and that she developed facets of her character to meet the demands for variety that Shakespeare built into the role.

One of the most illuminating of her revelations is that, when she first played the role for a performance in the provinces around 1779, she did not begin until the night before the performance to read her part, thinking she could con it easily since it was short. The images so frightened her that she was unable to continue her lonely study and was not letter perfect the next day

(Siddons, quoted by Campbell, pp. 184–5; *TQ*, p. 25). It appears, then, she did not know the whole play. (Mrs Pritchard, Dr Johnson later told Siddons (Siddons, p. 14), never did read the whole play.) The anecdote also proclaims her capacity to enter into the life of her character. From the beginning, she responded fully and emotionally to the power of the role, and as she cultivated her formidable ability to concentrate she learned to force an audience to share in the terror. She did not rehearse with a troupe; no manager (the person most likely to take on the role of director at the time) told her what to do. Some years later, when she made a London debut in the role (1785), she worked on her part more thoroughly, but the construction of the part was still, apparently, up to her. Though Garrick, to be sure, had referred to preparing an individual to go on to replace an ailing Banquo (*Letters*, no. 484), the Renaissance custom (as I surmise) of few rehearsals by a complete cast continued, partly because the production as a whole was not the main focus. Two or three rehearsals with the whole cast were the most an actor could expect at any time; study on one's own was the rule (Siddons, pp. 8, 10). Her independence demonstrates again that the play had then two separate centres of interest – first, the protagonists; second, the spectacle. These were not necessarily fused into a coherent whole.

Siddons's well-known anecdote about Richard Sheridan, the dramatist who was the Drury Lane Theatre manager, further illustrates the actor's interpretive judgement and independence. At the last minute before a performance he insisted on speaking to her to urge her not to deviate from Mrs Pritchard's practice of holding the taper throughout the sleepwalking scene. The age apparently prized conventional acting business unless a new piece of business could clear the old away. Siddons had decided to set down the taper because she saw the handwashing gestures as vehement, not dainty. Though she would have, she wrote, deferred to his judgement, it was too late. She was already committed to the business and could not work out another at that late moment. Afterwards he praised her for her innovation, which electrified the audience (Siddons, quoted by Campbell, pp. 186–7). A key inference to be drawn from her narration is that she worked out the business by herself, using the gesture to express the character's state of mind as she interpreted it; further, sitting in her dressing room before the performance, she was so intent on becoming the character that only reluctantly could she allow Sheridan to enter.

[29]

That fervent concentration relates to the actor's embodiment of the character and to the 'reality' of that possession.

Siddons dominated the stage partly because the production as a whole did not equal her intensity – however rich may have been the costumes, however beautiful the scenery. Kemble, when he was manager (at first under Sheridan), emphasised the banquet through the lavishness of the display, following, as Donohue says, the precedent of Garrick (*Dramatic Character*, p. 261). Still, it should be pointed out that overall Kemble's setting was decorative rather than realistic, and the company's use of backdrops and flats did not necessarily reflect the story line. Throughout his study, Southern argues for the lateness of the change from decorative to integrated scenery (later in the nineteenth century). After 1794, with the building of the new Drury Lane Theatre, the stage was too large for the old sets, making the discrepancy between action and setting more obvious. No one involved in these productions appeared to have the urgent passions about the design or the overall concept that Siddons had for her role. The Renaissance practice of single performances of a play in repertory with many others continued the rule, and this practice did not encourage extensive, elaborate set building.

Like Laurence Olivier, Siddons could, through the animation of her features, suggest that she was more handsome than she was (see *The Beauties*, p. 13). *Blackwood's*, in 1834, long after her retirement, described her as 'sternly beautiful', with a

> brow capacious of a wide world of thought, overshadowed by the still gloom of coal-black hair – that low, clear, measured, deep voice, audible in whispers – so portentously expressive of strength of will, and a will to evil – the stately tread ... – all these distinguished the Thane's wife from other women, to our senses, our soul, and our imaginations, as if nature had made Siddons for Shakespeare's sake, that she might impersonate to the height his sublimest and most dreadful conception (Rosenberg, *The Masks of Macbeth*, p. 207).

Her voice was her most distinctive feature; Thomas Campbell, her biographer, speaks of her solemn, magisterial tones, which could frighten anyone and which seemed to frighten her Macbeth (p. 377). Above all, her mental capacity, her power to concentrate and her strong opinions once she had studied her role made her a force on stage. She was not content simply to continue the conventions of the past. An innovator in matters of costume, she

2   Mrs Siddons as Lady Macbeth in Act V

turned away from contemporary elegance to simpler, more classical and less encumbering styles of dress (a contrast to a contemporary who played the role in an enormous farthingale). John Taylor in his review of her official debut faults her for wearing white satin during the sleepwalking scene, a mode reserved for the mad – which she was not (*TQ*, p. 26). She thus broke through a rigid symbolism.

Her great gifts were not immediately recognised by all. Surprisingly, Garrick fired her after her first season at Drury Lane, the last year of his management (1775–76), and she did not return until 1782 (Siddons, pp. 4–9). If at first her genius was unappreciated, in later years her range of emotions seems to have been forgotten by some, and she became in memory merely fiendish, a dominant feature of her passionate enactment. Ellen Terry, for example, refers to Mrs Siddons's Lady as a 'remorseless, terrible woman, who knew no tenderness, and who was already "unsex't" by the enormity of her desires' (Rosenberg, *The Masks of Macbeth*, p. 158). But George Henry Harlow's picture of her in the sleepwalking scene softened her in a romantic haze (as Rosenberg notes, p. 161). The epithet of 'fallen angel' given to her by a contemporary spectator belies the later opinion that Siddons was merely a virago (in Speaight, p. 41).

Many contemporaries described her full gifts. In a commentary that George Joseph Bell, a professor of Scottish law, wrote around 1809 in his copy of Mrs Inchbald's edition, possibly during a performance or performances, we may gather how Siddons affected a perceptive and alert member of her audience (Jenkin reproduces the Bell commentary along with the text as Bell marked it). He was interested in her alone and barely noted Kemble or the production. The spine of the Siddons performance was Lady Macbeth's powerful will; only disillusionment broke her.[3] Remarkable expressiveness of feature, voice and gesture served to impress the Siddons Lady on the audience.

She had an infallible ability to make the audience sense the offstage life of her character and to grasp and appreciate the working of her mind. In her first appearance, in I.v, Siddons showed that she had read enough of Macbeth's letter to understand it and now she eagerly reread it to enjoy its implications fully. Her excitement built as she read it aloud, creating more of an effect of the supernatural, said one commentator, than either Macbeth or Banquo did in the presence of the witches. Bell noted that her startlingly firm declaration 'and shalt be' seemed to come from an 'exalted prophetic' vision, as much as from determination of will. With 'a slight tincture of contempt throughout', she considered Macbeth's compunctions that could prevent him from realising his ambitions – reservations and ambitions familiar to her from previous discussions of the matter. Then, with 'Hie thee hither, That I may pour *my* [italics indicate Bell's emphasis] spirits in thine ear' she 'starts into higher animation'. Her '*Thou'rt mad to say it*' to Seyton, who announced the arrival of the king under her battlements, almost revealed too much. Alarmed that she had exposed her thoughts, she softly, reasonably, added her question about Macbeth, revealing to Bell how quick was her mind, how able she was to supply a rationalisation for her outburst. (Most modern Lady Macbeths follow her lead in these lines.) During the pause allowing Seyton to exit, she conveyed to Bell the solidifying of her intention. As she moved from 'Come to my woman's breasts', through the crescendo of this speech to 'Hold, hold', her 'Voice [was] quite supernatural, as in a horrible dream'. Bell described himself as 'Chilled with horror by the slow hollow whisper of this wonderful creature'.

This scene also established the relation between the thane and his wife. When Macbeth arrived, her first words were 'Loud, triumphant, and wild'. Siddons believed that 'not one kind word of greeting or congratulation does she offer' because she is 'so entirely swallowed up by the horrible design', so full of her triumph (Siddons, quoted by Campbell, p. 173). When she said 'And when goes hence?', Bell noticed 'High purpose working in her mind'. She paused before 'O never (never) / Shall sun that morrow see' (quoted from Jenkin, I.v.60–1); then she

> turned from him, her eye steadfast. Strong dwelling emphasis on 'never', with deep downward inflection, 'never (never) shall sun that morrow see!' Low, very slow sustained voice, her eye and her mind occupied steadfastly in the contemplation of her horrible purpose, pronunciation almost syllabic, note unvaried. Her self-collected solemn energy, her fixed posture, her determined eye and full deep voice of fixed resolve never should be forgot, cannot be conceived nor described.

Finally she turned to look at him. From 'Your face' to 'like the time', she examined him searchingly. In her next lines, she varied from the 'slow, severe and cruel expression' of '*be the serpent under't'*, to the 'assurance and gratulation' of 'solely sovereign sway and masterdom', to the cajolery of her last lines. Bell and others thought it vulgar (masculine) that she should, at these final lines of the scene, clap Macbeth on the shoulder and lead him out. 'Macbeth', he said,

> in Kemble's hand is only a co-operating part ... Her turbulent and inhuman strength of spirit does all. She turns Macbeth to her purpose, makes him her mere instrument, guides, directs, and inspires the whole plot. Like Macbeth's evil genius she hurries him on in the mad career of ambition and cruelty from which his nature would have shrunk. (Bell, quoted by Jenkin, I, p. 50)

In her next scene (I.vi), Siddons revealed something of her full range by speaking, Bell wrote, in tones that soothed and satisfied his ear. Even in her first scene, if we read his comments rightly, there was much more than fiend, but in her second scene she showed herself able to charm, with the sweetness and gracious-ness that must, in Siddons's view, have captivated her lord. The greeting of Duncan is the one chance of the actor playing her role to represent the flower for an audience, which has already seen the serpent (see I.v.64–6). Bell described her speech to Duncan as 'dignified and simple. Beautifully spoken.'

Siddons also was a master of reaction, both in ability to communicate her thoughts and to vary them meaningfully. In the persuasion scene (I.vii), except for the lines asserting that he 'dare do all that may become a man', Bell faulted Kemble for non-acting, unbelievability and failure to convey, as Siddons did, the workings of the character's mind. Siddons, in her acting, in her reaction to him, played *his* role as well as her own. Her Lady Macbeth's will to power was not to be impeded by Macbeth's reluctance to murder Duncan, but she did not so much trample over him as manipulate him – by her reaction to his reluctance as well as by her words. Her first line was a question expressed with an 'eager whisper of anger and surprise'. As Macbeth spoke of the honours he had won, Bell said that 'the sudden change from animated hope and surprise to disappointment, depression, contempt, and rekindling resentment, is beyond any powers but hers'. Siddons saw Macbeth as returning to his former benevolence and goodness unless she could bring him around again through withdrawing from him her respect and regard, through deter-mination and 'a tone of cold contemptuous reasoning', and finally through the force of her earnest declaration 'I have given suck'. For this speech, Bell noticed, Siddons, who 'has been at a distant part of the stage ... now comes close to him – an entire change of manner, looks for some time in his face, then speaks'. Siddons saw the image of the nursing child as evidence that Lady Macbeth *had* felt feminine tenderness. She was willing to put it and everything else aside for ambition; so too should he:

> Horrific as she is, she shows herself made by ambition, but not by nature, a perfectly savage creature. The very use of such a tender allusion in the midst of her dreadful language, persuades one unequivocally that she has really felt the maternal yearnings of a mother toward her babe, and that she considered this action the most enormous that ever required the strength of human nerves for its perpetration. (Siddons, quoted by Campbell, p. 175)

Similarly, as Lady Macbeth awaited Macbeth she showed a moment of warmheartedness when thinking of her father (II.ii.12–13). Siddons herself thought that 'we behold for the first time striking indications of sensibility, nay, tenderness and sympathy' when she tries to comfort Macbeth after they are king and queen (Siddons, quoted by Campbell, pp. 177–8).

Splendid as Siddons was, her Lady Macbeth was not frozen but a flexible, developing work of art. Like Burbage, Betterton, Garrick and Pritchard, Siddons had a long period to develop her part, playing the character only a few times each year over the span of her career. During the long pauses between performances of the play, she tried to develop truer, more interesting interpretations. Siddons went through three ways of saying 'We fail' in response to Macbeth's question, 'If we should fail?': first, a question, then an emphasis on *we* and finally the simple declarative (Muir, I.vii.60n). Her way was different from Pritchard's scornful exclamation. Some criticised Siddons for her final choice, but it demonstrated in Lady Macbeth a mind fearless enough to hazard defeat (Rosenberg, *The Masks of Macbeth*, pp. 277–9) and has been the chosen intonation in recent productions – though not necessarily with her understanding. Bell described her persuasion: 'With contempt, affection, reason, the conviction of her well concerted plan, the assurance of success which her wonderful tones inspire, she turns him to her purpose.' On 'Who *dares* receive it other', she expressed 'great and imperial dignity', as if she and he had every right to the supremacy they seek (quoted in Jenkin).

Most of all, the audience was captured by their sense of her nerve, her terrific will. Everyone and everything had to give way before that power. A backstage spectator who viewed the 1816 'return' performance from the opposite prompt door was close enough to see her face, 'with all its terrible workings ... that terrible mixture of hope, apprehension, and resolution' as she awaited Macbeth's return from Duncan's chamber (Furness scrapbook I, 9–10, clipping dated 3 October 1868, with journal title missing). Apprehensive at first that the deed was not done, she was contemptuous when she saw Macbeth had the knives. Siddons in her notes spoke of fierceness continuing when her husband declared his fears. But Bell cited 'her inhuman strength of spirit overcome by the contagion of his remorse and terror'. The spectator behind the scenes said that though he was privy to the workings of the illusions of the drama, seeing the maid daub Siddons's hands with paint before the actor's re-entrance, he nevertheless was filled with terror when she re-entered with the knives. Before their exit, Bell notes, 'she at first directs him with an assured and confident air. Then alarm steals on her, increasing to agony lest his reason be quite gone and discovery be inevitable.'

Since she did appreciate her character's vulnerability, Siddons might have managed the faint in the discovery scene (II.iii.116), but the Garrick–Pritchard promptbook she used cut Lady Macbeth from the scene. Mrs Pritchard was unsuccessful in her try at the faint (Bartholomeusz, p. 65), and Lady Macbeth was not reinstated in the scene until later productions introduced less powerful Lady Macbeths. In not entering for the first court scene (III.i), Siddons was again following Pritchard – a brilliant choice, for if Lady Macbeth's first appearance as queen is private and worried rather than public and grand, there is an immediate ironic contrast between her splendid queenly garb and the emptiness she feels. Bell detected 'great dignity and solemnity of voice' when she spoke to the servant (III.ii.1), though 'nothing of the joy of gratified ambition'. And he saw 'the flagging of her spirit, the melancholy and dismal blank beginning to steal upon her' when she tried to comfort Macbeth (quoted by Jenkin, I, p. 50).

The banquet scene and its aftermath are the last opportunity an actor has to portray Lady Macbeth as herself, before we see the unconsciousness of the sleepwalking scene. Siddons showed her at first as recovered from the despair of the last scene, strong enough to dominate the scene, yet quivering with nervous, arid remorse within. At 'The table's full' Bell considered 'her secret uneasiness very fine, suppressed', so that the onstage audience could not detect her apprehension, 'but agitating her whole frame'. Her 'O, proper stuff!' was 'peevish and scornful', but she tried, by mentioning the stool, 'to bring [Macbeth] back to objects of common life. Her anxiety', Bell said, 'makes you creep with apprehension: [she seems] uncertain how to act. Her emotion keeps you breathless.' At Macbeth's 'Avaunt!' announcing the ghost's second appearance, Bell notes her agitation, which can be ascribed to Siddons's attempt to suggest faintly that she saw the ghost then (Siddons, quoted by Campbell, p. 182). Though Bell says that she 'rises and speaks sweetly to the company', Siddons saw her behaviour differently. She wrote that she queried Macbeth 'with smothered terror, yet domineering indignation'; when she returned to the table, she attempted to behave normally, but with 'over-acted attention' and 'terrifying glances' at her husband, she threw 'the whole table into amazement' (Siddons, quoted by Campbell, p. 180). The extent of the amazement may be inferred from George Steevens's satirical review of her excessive warmth toward her guests to divert their attention from her husband (Boaden, *Kemble*, I, 245). More appreciatively, the 1816 backstage spectator discussed her astonishing expressive range:

> The 'aside' rebukes to her scared liege lord contrasted singularly in their subdued but deep tones with the exquisite grace and softness, obviously controlling anxiety, of the addresses to the assembled guests ... the last injunction [to them] being uttered with a striking admixture of impatient command and gentle entreaty. (Furness scrapbook I, 10)

In response to Rosse's question, 'What sights, my Lord' (line 115), Siddons rushed down from the table, her 'voice almost choked with anxiety to prevent their questioning' and his disclosures. By the close of the scene, Bell saw her as 'sorrowful' and 'exhausted'. At the last, she *followed* him out, a meaningful counterpoint to their exit in the persuasion and murder scenes, I.vii and II.ii. Though the onset of her blankness began almost immediately upon her achieving her goals (III.ii.4–7), she seemed at the start of the banquet almost convinced that their plans could work after all. Thus for Siddons, the character remained strong if agitated until almost the end of the banquet scene, when she and Macbeth reversed positions.

One of the reasons, Siddons asserted, that Lady Macbeth collapsed (as indicated by her offstage illness and her sleep-walking) while Macbeth did not is that he had a chance to relieve *his* feelings by talking to her before and after the banquet but she had no opportunity to unburden her own charged heart (Siddons, quoted by Campbell, pp. 183–4). She had also, Siddons maintained, 'a naturally higher-toned mind, than that of Macbeth' in spite of his noble nature. 'Her frailer frame, and keener feelings, have now sunk under the struggle.' Still, 'their grandeur of character', she said, 'sustains them both above recrimination ... in adversity'. Lady Macbeth had no petty vices, such as anger or revenge, Siddons said, but was all ambition and intellect. She saw no evidence of contrition; rather, despair and desolation were Lady Macbeth's governing emotions in the latter half of the play.

Finally, in the sleepwalking scene, actors playing Lady Macbeth have their last great opportunity. The Siddons production cut Acts IV and V of the text drastically to emphasise her closing scene. Isolated on stage, with the gentlewoman's and doctor's fixed attention on her, Siddons created an impression of frailty as Lady Macbeth relived the scene of the murder. She walked and spoke so as to awaken unwonted pity for her sufferings, which the quivering of her body suggested. She spoke of the death of Lady Macduff with profound sadness, showing that her own suffering made her alive to pity. Siddons was not afraid to make herself look ugly, twisting her face when Lady Macbeth smells the blood. Motionless for much of the scene, except for the washing of the hands, she entered and exited hurriedly, with sudden flurries of motion. Bell would have liked her to enter more slowly, with interrupted steps, but Siddons chose a less stereotypical depiction of sleepwalking, one that she felt was more natural. She employed her powerful whisper throughout the scene (Furness scrapbook I, 10), but what the doctor described as a sigh was, to Bell, 'a convulsive shudder – very horrible. A tone of imbecility audible.' The contrast between this sorrowful creature and the grand, demonic soul of her first scene moved her audience to terror and compassion.

In sum, every great Lady Macbeth, every *Macbeth*, has to be measured against her performances. Her achievement can be judged by responses to her stage persona. It was not unusual for members of the audience to start out of their seats, as some did when she said 'Give *me* the daggers' (Boaden, *Siddons*, p. 310). Or for Sheridan Knowles to swear that he could smell the blood in the sleepwalking scene (Sprague, p. 67). Or to say, as Hazlitt did, that to see her was the event of a lifetime (see Bate, pp. 155–6). In spite of dancing witches, Mrs. Siddons made her character not merely believable but compelling, terrifying, mesmerising. She developed her interpretation from what had gone before – the noble Macbeth of Garrick and the termagant of Pritchard – but she brought to it every ounce of her considerable genius.

Macready and Forrest

While Garrick in the mid eighteenth century and Siddons soon after stood high above any competitors, British actor-manager William Charles Macready (1793–1873) in the mid nineteenth century had a mighty opposite in the American actor Edwin Forrest (1806–72). Probably the best-remembered event of their careers is the New York Astor Place riot in 1849, which occurred while each was performing in *Macbeth*, Macready at the elegant Astor Opera House, Forrest a few blocks away to a full house at the Broadway Theatre (*Account*, p. 19). Forrest's working-class fans had disrupted a performance of *Macbeth* starring Macready on 7 May 1849: chairs thrown from the balcony on to the stage and into the orchestra pit abruptly ended the performance. Aristocratic Americans persuaded Macready to perform again on 10 May, and he did so without violence within the Opera House because police, alerted to potential trouble by the events of the earlier engagement, fairly quickly moved noisy people in the audience to a basement (*Account*, p. 19). Outside, however, the overreactions of men with guns to noisy rioters with stones picked up from the street were fatal to several innocent bystanders. Astor Place rioters broke some windows; militiamen shot and killed. Bridget Fagan, walking with her husband two blocks away, was shot in the leg; she died in her husband's arms after the leg was amputated (*Account*, p. 29). Macready had to be spirited away in disguise (*Account*, p. 21). The anonymous author of *Account* deplores the excessive use of force:

> Humanity has its claims as well as law; and it may not be necessary to the maintenance of public order, that ignorant and misguided men, laboring under a temporary madness, should be shot down like dogs, if they can be controlled by means more gentle. (p. 31)

The rioters were inflamed by chauvinism and class hatred rather than by questions about whose Macbeth was more effective. Forrest, by all accounts a boor and a bully but one of the first national idols of the American stage, had been well received by Macready when he first visited England (1836) – despite Macready's worries about newcomers diverting paying customers from his performances and thus affecting his ability to support his family. But when, on a subsequent visit, some rude men in the audience jeered Forrest's Macbeth (1845), he blamed Macready, and his hatred from then on was implacable. He stood and hissed Macready's performance in Edinburgh a short while later, turning the British against him. Though not implicated in fomenting the Astor Place riot, Forrest unquestionably inspired his fans to act upon his hatred for Macready, by articulating it in newspaper pieces. In 1990, Richard Nelson published the lively play *Two Shakespearean Actors*, based on the events surrounding the riots, which played on Broadway among other venues, and Lawrence W. Levine, in 1988, writes about the riot as part of his study of American culture (pp. 63–9).

Both men seem to have been difficult characters. Macready, in his diary, regretted his native irascibility and was ashamed of himself when rage and jealousy overtook him. Forrest, it appears, felt no such compunction over his behaviour. Macready was an actor out of necessity and would have much preferred to be a gentleman. He retired without a single look backward in 1851, just a few years after the riot. Forrest was a committed actor, who performed up to the year of his death and whose estate went to found a home for aged actors.

Lawrence Barrett speaks of Forrest as morose, preemptory, large and muscular (pp. 134–5). He quotes James E. Murdoch in 'The Stage':

> The acting of Forrest was natural, impulsive, and ardent, because he was not so well trained as his English rivals in what may be termed a false refinement. Forrest was not considered as polished an actor as Macready, and was often charged with rudeness and violence in his impersonations, and even ridiculed for muscularity of manner ... It must be remembered that Mr. Forrest was a strong man, and when excited his passions appeared more extreme than those of one more delicately organized; and unqualified condemnation was only heard from those who were either unable or unwilling to perceive that the traits which distinguished our then

young actor were really more natural than the elaborate presentations and precise mannerisms of Macready ... Although Forrest in his youth had only received what was then called a good school training, he furnished in his manhood an example of what might have been profitably imitated by the young men of his time who, with all of the advantages of collegiate education, failed to exhibit the progressive intellectual improvement which steadily marked his course from year to year. Many who did not admire his earlier dramatic performances were greatly impressed with his manner in the later parts of his career

– especially his Lear.

Nationalism vies with taste in the comments of another author quoted by Barrett; Charles T. Congdon, in 'Reminiscences of a Journalist' (1880), writes:

As an American, I am under constitutional obligations to declare Mr. Forrest the finest tragic actor of this or of any age; but as a man and a critic, I resolutely refuse to say anything of the sort. 'If this be treason', as Patrick Henry said, 'make the most of it!' Fanny Kemble, somewhere about 1832, during her first theatrical triumphs in the United States, went down to the Bowery Theatre to see the young tragedian about whom there was so much talk; and I think her sole criticism upon him in her diary is, 'What a mountain of a man!' Well, he was tall and he was muscular. Such calves as his I have seldom seen. It was with admirable instinct that Dr. Bird wrote for this large person the play of 'The Gladiator.' He was born for single combat. The *Macduff* with whom he contended had a hard time of it, nor did he easily succumb to the most valiant Richmond. Supernumeraries did not like to be handled by him when the business required pulling about and mauling ... Of course, all this mastodonian muscularity was a disadvantage in characters of predominating intellect, like *Hamlet*, with which our actor never meddled without reminding us of a bull in a china-shop ... Whatever he played he was the same man. One remembers him, nor as *Macbeth*, nor even *Spartacus* or *Metamora*, but as the Great American Tragedian ... He was rather worse when he attempted to be quiet than when he o'erdid Termagant and out-Heroded Herod. Any attempt to utter anything *sotto voce* instantly suggested suffocation. Nor could Mr. Forrest move his ponderous limbs with ease, except in garment of the loosest description ... He had some original business, but it was not good; even if it had been better, he would have spoiled it by over-consciousness and by thrusting it upon the attention of the house. (Barrett, pp. 135–7)

[41]

Though reviewers often wrote detailed descriptions of their acting in one or two scenes, Forrest and Macready did not rouse in anyone a wish to write a detailed analysis of their acting from beginning to end. In his unpublished manuscript, written in the 1890s and now at the Folger Shakespeare Library in Washington, D.C., George Becks wrote voluminously about the interpretations of many Macbeths, including Macready and Forrest, but without a sustained narrative of any actor's interpretation. His purpose seems to have been to write a workbook for actors and directors by describing what actors had done at particular moments and what critics and reviewers had said about them; it might be termed an incipient Shakespeare in Production (a current Cambridge series). Becks mentions for instance that Macready, Phelps and Irving said the first line from Act I, scene vii, with a stop after 'well': 'If it were done when 'tis done, then 'twere well. It were done quickly if the assassination &c.' C. Kean, Forrest and Edwin Booth said it as in their texts, without a stop after 'well', but Booth also stressed the word 'done'. Becks envisions actors choosing whom to follow. The folio has a comma after *well*, but, as Furness shows, the full stop was available as a conjecture from Samuel Johnson's edition in 1765.

Becks quotes the *Morning Herald*, which described Macready's response to the ghost of Banquo:

> Instead of intimidating the Ghost into a retreat, he fell back, sank into a chair, covered his face with his hands, then looked again, perceived the Ghost had disappeared, and upon being relieved from the fearful vision recovered once more the spring of his soul and body.

Becks, from an unspecified source, describes Forrest's approach:

> Mr. F raises his robe as if to shield him from the sight, advances sideways, wafting the Ghost off, rises to great passion of fear and horror as he repeats 'hence' at each step – four or five times: then, as ghost vanishes, he [speaks] the next line in a low exhausted breath – as of great relief.

Line by line, as Becks shows, each actor gave nuanced readings, but overall their interpretations were much alike: the noble Macbeth, undone by his Lady, his ambition and the Fates, but nevertheless an object of admiration through the power of his suffering and sensibility and through the grandeur of his ambition. He was larger than life.

The nineteenth-century *Macbeth* that best captures the multiplicity of *Macbeth* could well be Verdi's opera, the subject of the next chapter. Although no complete record exists for stage versions from Garrick to Forrest with their singing witches, Verdi's work continues to be performed; contemporary productions can suggest how his *Macbeth* might have looked in the nineteenth century. Some of its interpretative moves anticipate the innovative perspectives of Kurosawa's *Throne of Blood* and Polanski's *Macbeth*.

CHAPTER II

Operatic Macbeths: what we could still learn from Verdi

GRAHAM BRADSHAW

Conical hats and broomsticks

The idea or ideal of music drama – 'dramma per musica', or drama through music – has inspired many composer dramatists, from Monteverdi and Gluck through Verdi and Wagner to Janácek and Britten, and it has always been radical and reformist. Verdi's *Macbeth* was his tenth opera, and his first music drama. It was composed in late 1846 and early 1847, after a kind of breakdown or period of enforced rest, when the thirty-three-year-old composer spent six months doing sweet nothing (*dolce far niente*) – or so he said. His chosen companion during much of this period was 'St Andrea' – that is, Andrei Maffei – another passionate Shakespeare enthusiast, who would later help Verdi with the witches' chorus and sleepwalking scene. Verdi's 1847 *Macbeth*, revolutionary in several ways, was also *the* first Shakespearean opera – that is, the first opera that genuinely engaged with a Shakespearean poetic drama, instead of merely raiding Shakespeare plays for bits of their plots, like Rossini's *Otello* or (to descend, sharply) the Italian operatic *Hamlet* in which the Prince of Denmark became a soprano. Rather than transform Shakespeare into an Italian *bel canto* opera, Verdi set about transforming Italian opera until it could accommodate his Romantic, and Italian, 'Shakespeare'. His attempt to recover 'Shakespeare' was in some ways more impressive than what was happening on the English stage, which was and had been for a long time, and continued to be, 'operatic' in a far more pejorative sense (see Bradshaw, 'A Shakespearean Perspective').

In the first performances at the Globe music served, as usual, to make some *dramatic* points: for example, the First Folio records two brass 'Flourishes' for Duncan, three for Malcolm and none for Macbeth. However, since the Folio text also includes brief quotations from Middleton songs that were written between 1610 and 1614, it probably brings us closer to whatever happened in later stagings at the indoor Blackfriars Theatre – but without telling us just what happened. Do Folio stage directions such as '*Musicke & a Song. Blacke Spirits &c.*' or '*Come away, come away &c.*' show that later stagings included brief snatches from Middleton's songs, suitably edited so that they no longer referred to characters and creatures otherwise entirely absent from Shakespeare's play? Or must we suppose, with Stephen Orgel (p. 143) and Nicholas Brooke, the editor of the new Oxford *Macbeth* (2000, pp. 54–5), that these stage directions, and especially the '*&c.*', were incipits for *full* performances of lengthy non-Shakespearean songs and dances? In that case, *Macbeth* was becoming 'operatic' shortly before or after Shakespeare's death, and the extended interpolations would be striking examples of the more general change that Ben Jonson's 'Prologue' complained about in *The Staple of News* (1626): 'For your owne sakes, not his, he [the Poet] bad me say, / Would you were come to heare, not see a Play.' Hamlet and other Elizabethans usually spoke of going to *hear* a play. We don't do that, because the change that Jonson deplored was irreversible. Hence the casually revealing title of Dennis Kennedy's *Looking at Shakespeare*, and the way in which Kennedy and the modern directors he most admires are preoccupied with the visual aspects of performance.

The history of *Macbeth* in performance shows how Shakespeare's sisters became less frightening when they become less equivocal. In Davenant's and Garrick's versions they were unequivocally 'witches' but then became conventional caricatures of witches, played by comedians with conical hats and broomsticks; Hecate's part was often sung by a bass. This inevitably altered the play's inner dynamics for Garrick and later actor-managers who wanted to present 'noble' Macbeths. If their unequivocal but also unmenacing witches were no longer a force, and if a 'noble' Macbeth had to be somebody's victim, Lady Macbeth had better be or become more than ever 'fiend-like', as did Mrs Pritchard or Sarah Siddons. Later nineteenth-century attempts to recover a 'feminine' Lady Macbeth, like that of the fascinating Helen Faucit, seemed correspondingly startling or new. But do the spirits come, when Lady Macbeth calls them? Here too Shakespeare's play equivocates.

Macbeth had been presented at the Globe by a cast that probably numbered no more than fifteen actors, but by the 1770s John Philip Kemble was offering more than fifty witches, and a century later the 1864 Drury Lane production with Samuel Phelps and Helen Faucit boasted a 'hundred or more pretty singing witches', according to one happily bewitched reviewer (Rosenberg, *The Masks of* Macbeth, p. 8). When Edmund Kean played Macbeth in 1814 there were still conical hats and broomsticks, and more of them; forty years later Charles Kean had his Hecate enter with a small army of 'Black and White imps', 'Red and white imps', 'Ladies of the Ballet' and 'Singing Witches' (Rosenberg, *The Masks of* Macbeth, p. 501). After seeing *Macbeth* during his 1825 visit to London, the astonished Tieck (Schlegel's collaborator in the great Schlegel–Tieck German translations) observed, in a wonderfully wry letter:

> One never finds out why enormously many witches of all ages and sizes appear on stage where they celebrate the triumph of their sabbath [after Duncan's murder] with multi-voiced singing, from soprano, alto, tenor to bass. One should at least expect the scene, in the manner of Reichard's witches' choirs, to be a wild, screaming, malicious, horrifying jubilation. But no, these fifty characters (at least that many and among them some rather good-looking, charming ones) present a noble, artfully fashioned musical piece … And the Englishman … hears … without protest these wicked and mean creatures sing a long-winded concert, interrupting the tragedy for a long time with choral fugue, and church-like music, turning the theatre into a concert-hall. (Rosenberg, *The Masks of* Macbeth, pp. 8–9)

My purpose in beginning with non-operatic operatic Macbeths is not to look back in anger but to confront the likely responses of a modern spectator who knows Shakespeare's play but not its performance history, and is watching Verdi's opera for the first time. His or her first shock would come when the curtain rises to show not three bearded witches but a large and probably beefy operatic chorus, divided into three covens. When each coven starts singing in the first person singular about what it has been doing that day it may be difficult to suspend disbelief – or derision. A historical defence is available, if we remember what the English did with the witches from the Restoration to the late nineteenth century; but that would be a very mean defence. If we watch and listen, what young Verdi is doing seems remarkably intelligent.

Verdi recognised and then built upon the *ambivalence* of Shakespeare's wayward sisters, making that the basis of the musical structures and contrasts in his *'Introduzione'*. When Verdi told Léon Escudier that in 'both their singing and acting' the witches should be 'brutal and coarse' with each other, but 'sublime and prophetic' when they confront Macbeth (letter of 8 February 1865), he was echoing the great critic who was his chief critical guide in *Macbeth* and, forty years later, *Otello*. In his *Course of Lectures on Dramatic Art and Literature* Schlegel observed:

> With one another the witches discourse like women of the very lowest class; for this was the class to which witches were ordinarily supposed to belong: when, however, they address Macbeth they assume a loftier tone: their predictions, which they either themselves pronounce, or allow their apparitions to deliver, have all the obscure brevity, the majestic solemnity of oracles, such as have ever spread terror among mortals. (p. 408)

Schlegel's great and massively influential Vienna lectures were delivered in 1808 and published ('with additions') in 1811; Giovanni Gherardini's Italian translation appeared in 1817, and the relevant passages were then often included in Italian Shakespeare translations such as those by Carlo Rusconi and Verdi's close friends Giulio Carcano and Andrea Maffei. So, in Verdi's 1847 *Macbeth*, the 'brutal and coarse' witches are first presented in a musically vivacious, earthy way that makes much of the threefold repetitions; but, when Macbeth and Banquo arrive, the witches' music is transformed into something 'sublime and prophetic'. This transformation is achieved through Verdi's brilliant use of two musical *topoi* that were employed by many composers and are discussed in different chapters of Frits Noske's masterly *The Signifier and the Signified*. Immediately before Macbeth tells the witches to speak, we hear the anapaestic motif that Noske calls the 'Musical Figure of Death' (pp. 171–214) that subsequently 'permeates the whole score' (p. 186), just as it permeates the *Todesverkundigung* (Annunciation of Death) scene in Wagner's *Die Walküre*. The prophecies are then delivered in a tripartite sequence of eerily linking thirds, which Noske discusses in his chapter on 'Ritual scenes' (pp. 241–70). By keeping faith with the ambivalence of the witches Verdi could make something very powerful of Macbeth's idea of 'supernaturall soliciting'.

My argument so far can be summarised by this passage from a remarkable essay by Jonas Barish, whom nobody could accuse of anti-theatrical prejudice:

> In short, in the years before Verdi's opera there was no tradition, either in England or on the Continent, of authenticity of performance to which an audience could have appealed or by which it could have judged a new version; and on the other hand, there was a long tradition of *in*authenticity, of deliberate playing-up of the sensational features of the text, which had routinely turned the play into something sometimes actually spoken of as an opera. Verdi's version, then, far from being bizarrely or outrageously theatrical, seems in many respects a heroic effort to *recover* in music something of the spirit of Shakespeare's tragedy. (p.149)

I want next to consider some ways in which Verdi's 'heroic effort' might still challenge us to think about *Macbeth*.

Thinking about *Macbeth*

In 1846 Verdi wrote to Francesco Maria Piave, his nominal librettist: 'In this *Macbeth* [of ours], the more one thinks about it, the more one finds ways to improve it.' Verdi's idealistic concern was not to 'improve' in Davenant's or Garrick's sense, but to be as faithful as he could. To his rage and disappointment, the much and justly abused Piave wouldn't think very hard, but Verdi went on thinking about *Macbeth* long after the 1847 première. In June 1848, when he visited London to supervise performances of his next opera, *I masnadieri*, he could at last see a performance of Shakespeare's play. Given the dates, he must have seen one of William Macready's Drury Lane performances on 7 or 14 June. Macready was an intelligent, unusually self-critical actor whose performance probably impressed Verdi. As an actor-manager Macready had also been successful in restoring more of Shakespeare's text in *King Lear* – but not in the case of *Macbeth*: the army of witches remained, Macbeth still had a dying speech and of course there was no Porter or onstage murder of Macduff's wean. If only Verdi had been in London in October he could have seen Phelps's unprecedented but short-lived attempt at an authentic staging, which reduced the army of witches, eliminated the dying speech, and even reinstated the Porter and the Macduff family. After being admonished by critics and audiences, Phelps went back to giving his public what it wanted or paid for. Nothing in Verdi's correspondence suggests that he knew of this Phelpsian ripple in the spectacular stream, but by the 1860s – when the Théâtre Lyrique agreed to give Verdi's *Macbeth* its Paris première, and Verdi agreed to the predictably Parisian demand for a ballet as well as a final chorus – Verdi had discovered that the Shakespearean Macbeth didn't have a dying speech and was already wanting to remove his Macbeth's brief but powerful final aria. In the event Verdi went much further, rethinking and revising about a third of the 1847 opera and producing what was in effect a new though more mosaic-like work. The 1865 *Macbeth* shows Verdi once again engaging with – or rethinking – Shakespeare, as well as his own 1847 version. Indeed, I suspect that he acceded to the Parisian demand for a ballet in order to make the other changes, although the ballet music is very impressive in its own right.

This 1865 *Macbeth* is what is usually performed today, without the ballet. But although the intensity of Verdi's engagement with Shakespeare in his two last operas, *Otello* (1887) and *Falstaff* (1893), is now almost never questioned, there is less agreement about the importance of Verdi's first Shakespearean opera. And yet, as I have suggested, Verdi's 1847 *Macbeth* was not only his but *the* first Shakespearean opera, and was also, in several ways, Verdi's most revolutionary opera.

One aspect of the 1847 *Macbeth* revolution is still obscured by the way in which vocal and orchestral scores persist in listing Verdi as the composer and Piave as the librettist. At a time when opera posters would often print a composer's name in smaller type than the librettist's, Piave's chief responsibility was to be no more (and regrettably less) than a competent versifier. As Verdi himself recalled, years later: 'I wrote out the whole drama in prose, with divisions into acts, scenes, numbers, etc., etc. then I gave it to Piave to put into verse' (letter of 11 April 1857). The truth of that account is abundantly clear from the copious material assembled in David Rosen and Andrew Porter's magnificent and indispensable *Verdi's Macbeth: A Sourcebook*. And when Verdi set about revising the opera, Piave's responsibility was no less forcefully limited: 'Turn the pages,' Verdi wrote to Piave on 28 January 1865, 'and you'll find everything laid out in full. The lines need polishing, and you'll do it, but do it quickly.' This concern for polished verses

[49]

might seem strange now, but was historically important in the 1840s. The *scena* (main aria or duet, etc.) was just one part of the more extended musical 'number'; the versification was important because the *scena* would be written in loose, normally unrhymed and enjambed verse (*versi sciolti*), whereas the rest of the musical number would be written in lyric verse (*versi lyrici*), and the ensuing structure would build a contrast between kinetic, or confrontational, and static, or reflective, musical-dramatic sections. In this sense the music would articulate the drama, but the music would be articulated through contrasts between different kinds of verse, which in turn depended on different dramatic situations. A highly dramatic situation or confrontation would then prompt a more static reflection on whatever had changed or developed in musical-dramatic terms. Translating Shakespeare's numerous scenes into musical numbers or *schizzi* was in this sense a major part of Verdi's (not Piave's) creative effort.

Another revolutionary development was that young Verdi concerned himself closely with many aspects of production, including lighting, costumes and *mise-en-scène*. Italian librettists such as the hapless Piave or, more impressively, Salvadore Cammarano would often do this, but not composers. Many years later, Casa Ricordi took to publishing a *scena disposizione* for each of Verdi's last eight operas, and every detail in these production books had to be approved by the composer dramatist.[4] The young Verdi could not demand that degree of deference, but some of his many letters about the 1847 *Macbeth* give very precise directions about costumes and staging. Letters such as that of 24 January 1847, in which Verdi reminds Lanari that there are no 'silks and velvets' in eleventh-century costumes, echo or anticipate the 'archeological' (and decidedly 'nineteenth-century') approach of actor-managers such as Macready. In other, more important letters Verdi instructed his actor singers, and of course he rehearsed and conducted the first performances – insisting on more than 150 rehearsals of the great Act I duet. In general, the letters show Verdi fired by the sense that he was introducing *Macbeth* to Italy. And so he was: Shakespeare's play was first performed in 1848, a year after Verdi's opera. Even in the 1870s, when the famous Italian actor Ernesto Rossi played Macbeth – a breakthrough in the history of Shakespeare in Italy – the translation included phrases from the operatic libretto (Weaver, p. 148).

What happened in performance after the 1847 Florence

première was a different matter. Other performances in less liberal Italian cities and towns followed with remarkable rapidity, but with constant interference from the different powers that occupied and ruled what was not yet 'Italy'. In one sense the authorities were right: another aspect of the *Macbeth* revolution was that the opera was revolutionary in obviously political ways. Verdi was passionately committed to the *Risorgimento* goal of national liberation and unification, *'Va pensiero'* had already become an insurrectionist anthem, and the extraordinary wave of revolutions that swept through Europe in 1848 had begun in Italy and France. In Milan, where Austrian forces had savagely suppressed the Milanese revolution just months before the first La Scala staging of *Macbeth*, there was no question of allowing the Milanese audience to hear yet another Verdian chorus grieving over their oppressed country (*'Patria oppressa'*): as the occupying forces and the La Scala audience knew, Verdi's Scotland was Italy. In papal Rome, the opera had to begin with gypsies telling fortunes from cards, since there could be no suggestion of witches with supernatural powers; even the lines about the 'pilot's thumb' had to go, because the papal censors guessed that 'the public will probably find in them an allusion to the vessel of St. Peter' (Rosen and Porter, p. 358). Elsewhere, references to regicide had to be expunged: in regal Naples and in the Kingdom of the Two Sicilies Macbeth murdered not Duncan but Count Walford, 'a very rich Scottish nobleman' (Rosen and Porter, p. 356).

Fortunately there was a world elsewhere, but it was a world in which Shakespeare's own compatriots remained remarkably impervious or indifferent to Verdi's Shakespeare. By 1860 *Macbeth* had been performed in more than twenty countries, and in that year it was at last performed in England, but only in what the English disdainfully call the 'provinces': a production with the renowned Pauline Viardot as Lady Macbeth travelled from Dublin to Liverpool (a historically familiar and often tragic route for the destitute) and then to Manchester. But there was no performance in London, and there were no further English performances throughout the nineteenth century. Later, Verdi's 1865 *Macbeth* would be staged in various cities throughout the world, including Sydney and Auckland (1871), but there was no English performance until the 1938 and 1939 Glyndebourne stagings. The next British production took place in Edinburgh in 1947, but *Macbeth* was not performed at Covent Garden until 1960.

This seems extraordinary; and if we are trying to understand this century of almost uninterrupted English indifference, consider the idea of Duncan as a holy king. Verdi's presentation of Duncan could hardly be more secular and is as forcefully demystified as Polanski's. So, the next shock awaiting a modern spectator who knows Shakespeare's play but is watching Verdi's *Macbeth* for the first time is that Duncan doesn't appear until he is in the Macbeths' castle, and, even then, doesn't say or sing a word. Instead, he and his retinue progress cheerfully but silently from one side of the stage to the other, as a small band under the stage plays a 'rustic' march. Even critics who know the opera well divide sharply over this little *siciliano*-like march. Some critics, from Abramo Basevi to Julian Budden, find it as trivial as the rum-ti-tum stuff for servants and messengers, and think it more appropriate for a small-town Italian mayor than a (putatively) sacred king; but Gabriele Baldini greatly admired it as 'one of those light-hearted, carefree passages of early Verdi which Donizetti always tried in vain to achieve' (p. 113). Certainly, we never hear music like this again, and that, I think, is the musical-dramatic point: this is the only moment when the opera can be light-hearted and carefree.

Yet this *scena muta* is also curiously charged in a political way, since the band or *banda* was not usually, in 1847, part of the opera house orchestra. It was often provided by the occupying powers, who also frequently demanded several rows in the front stalls. Like other *primo ottocento* opera composers, Verdi was obliged to provide some music for the *banda*, which he usually refused to score. Sometimes, as in the first acts of *La traviata* and *Rigoletto*, the *banda* music is deliberately superficial. It is possible that Verdi's decision to make Duncan's role mutely ceremonial followed from a wish *not* to belittle the character by giving his dramatically important but unavoidably small role to a minor singer or *comprimario*. It is also possible, and more likely, that Verdi's decision was primarily formal, following from his – not Piave's – decision to translate the whole Shakespearean sequence from I.v to II.iii into a continuous Aria–Duet–Finale 'number', beginning with Lady Macbeth's *cavatina*, and then progressing through the Macbeths' *recitativo* and duet to the momentous Act I finale. Still, however we sift these various considerations, the march itself, the king's silence and Verdi's decidedly secular approach will be jolting to those who *want* the frail, holy figure in white robes, wearing a large cross. Yet that jolt seems to me critically salutary, since this 'foreign' view could challenge us to think again about what Shakespeare's play is or is not doing, and what 'we' may be blocking out.

The myth that *Macbeth* was a royalist play written to flatter or please the new Scottish king is all the more ludicrous because James would have found it so displeasing. Despite the myth, there is no record whatever of *any* court performance. That needs to be emphasised, since it is so often forgotten. Indeed, there are surprisingly (alarmingly?) few references to any performances of *Macbeth* in Shakespeare's lifetime: 'only three, all before 1611', Stephen Orgel notes, as against 'fifty-eight to *Hamlet*, thirty-six to *Romeo and Juliet*', and so on (p. 148). Yet Orgel also argues that the Folio 'version of *Macbeth*' was 'devised for a single occasion, a performance at court' (p. 144), and he takes for granted that King James would have enjoyed the play. The royalist reading, or myth, is still alive, in spite of the films of Kurosawa and Polanski.

But not in Verdi's opera. Verdi not only cuts out the early scenes involving Duncan, he cuts the so-called English scene as well – but not altogether. His final act – which is even more taut and powerful in the 1865 version – begins with the incandescent chorus, '*Patria oppressa*', the obviously revolutionary or *Risorgimentale* successor to '*Va pensiero*'. This, as Verdi told Piave (letter of 10 December 1846), describes 'Scotland's wretched state under Macbeth's rule' and should be 'a genre scene, a sublime, affecting picture of Scotland's misery' (*una pittura caratteristica sublime patetica della Scozia*). The chorus is all the more moving in performance, when one sees the unhappy Scottish refugees crossing the stage during the otherwise long orchestral introduction. But Verdi isn't kidnapping Shakespeare's play at this point: as he says in the same letter to Piave, the chorus is based on 'the dialogue between Ross and Macduff'. The chorus is then followed by Macduff's tenor aria, in which we learn of the deaths of his family. According to Orgel, the 'perennial problem' in Shakespeare's play is Malcolm's question about Macduff that 'never gets answered': 'where are your real loyalties; why is coming to England to join my army more important than the lives of your wife and children?' (p. 152). Verdi would have thought the answer to Orgel's question or questions painfully obvious, not least because Macduff's anguished conflict of loyalties is so quintessentially Verdian: 'For his country, and its people!' Of course one couldn't expect Verdi to have answered, like so many modern critics, 'For his God, and for his King!', since he was not only republican but almost certainly an atheist (Walker, pp. 280–1). Yet another effect of the royalist myth has been to block out what was so startling, and no less revolutionary, in the Shakespearean answer: 'For his country – but not for a king who is unfit to govern, or live.' Malcolm explains his test, but it is too late to soften or change this astonishing moment, and the rest of the play then follows the swerve, from disgusted rage to grief, in Macduff's response: 'Fit to govern? No, not to live. – O nation miserable!' Shakespeare's Macbeth is an anointed king, whose election was unopposed and who is now defending his country from a largely English invasion. None the less, he must be hunted down and killed: but why? Because this anointed king is also a *tyrant* who oppresses his *country*. In 1649 an English court (and a judge named Bradshaw, friend to Marvell and Milton) would make the same decision. When Malcolm tests Macduff the play is testing the audience: we too must choose between what Orgel's royalist myth blocks out and what Verdi's romantic and revolutionary opera recovers. If we then want to rethink these critical, Shakespearean issues, the best starting point is still Harry Berger's brilliant 1980 essay, 'The Early Scenes of *Macbeth*'. A good next step would be to locate a copy of Sigurd Burckhardt's shockingly neglected and out-of-print *Shakespearean Meanings*, which was the first book to argue that Shakespeare had already given up on the theory of the divine right of kings when he wrote *King John*: 'He saw that the picture was false and embodied the discovery in his play's "argument": in its plot and style as well as in its dialectic' (p. 117).

Performance as representation: metaphor *versus* mimesis

When *Macbeth* was to be performed at Naples in 1848, Verdi was disturbed to hear that Eugenia Tadolini (his Elvira, in *Ernani*) was to take the part of Lady Macbeth:

> Tadolini sings to perfection and I would rather that Lady [Macbeth] didn't sing at all. Tadolini has a marvellous voice, clear, limpid and strong; and I would rather that Lady's voice were rough, hollow, stifled. Tadolini's voice has something angelic in it. Lady's should have something devilish ... The chief pieces of the opera are two: the duet between Lady and her husband and the sleepwalking scene; and these pieces must not be sung at all. (23 November 1848)

Two years earlier Verdi had similarly, and no less anxiously, insisted that his first Macbeth must be Felicio Varesi because 'other artists, even those better than he, couldn't do that part for me as I'd like – not to detract from the merits of Ferri, who is better looking, has a more beautiful voice, and, if you like, is even a better singer, but in that role certainly couldn't give me the effect that Varesi would' (letter of 19 August 1846). When Laurence Olivier bravely insisted on singing in Peter Brook's film of *The Beggar's Opera* he showed how much could be achieved by a marvellously intelligent actor with an unbeautiful voice, but was *that* the 'effect' that Verdi was wanting?

No: Verdi didn't want actor singers whose acting would compensate for poor singing, he wanted singers who could act in or through their voices, while meeting the extraordinary demands he was making on his Macbeths (and Macduff) as singers. In one modern production of *La traviata* Jonathan Miller encouraged his dying Violetta to cough in her final aria, but Verdi certainly didn't want, and would have deplored, this kind of realistic effect. We know that from the fascinating letter in which Verdi describes, and recommends as a model, the great Italian stage actress Adelaide Ristori's way of playing Shakespeare's sleepwalking Lady – with one important exception:

> Ristori employed a rattle in her throat – the death rattle. In music, that must not and cannot be done; just as one shouldn't cough in the last act of *La traviata*; or laugh in the '*scherzo od è folia*' of *Ballo in maschera*. Here there is an English-horn lament that takes the place of the death-rattle perfectly well, and more poetically. The piece should be sung with the utmost simplicity and in *voce cupa* [a hollow voice] (she is a dying woman) but without ever letting the voice become ventriloquial. There are some moments when the voice can open up, but they must be brief flashes, as indicated in the score. (Rosen and Porter, p. 110)

This might still seem puzzling, for example to Miller. In what sense could a cor anglais 'lament' on the minor second *take the place of* Ristori's 'death rattle' (which another great Italian stage actress, Eleanora Duse, took to be snoring)? Lady Macbeth, not the instrumentalist, was 'dying'. Verdi's explanation of the *voce cupa* – 'she is a dying woman' – might sound like a realistic explanation, and Verdi's first Lady Macbeth, Barbieri-Nini, recalled how he made her spend three months trying 'to imitate those who talk in their sleep, uttering words (as Verdi would say to me) while hardly moving the lips, leaving the rest of the face immobile, including the eyes. It was enough to drive one crazy' (Rosen and Porter, p. 51). Yet there is no real puzzle. Verdi isn't asking for, or wanting, a *realistic imitation* of a dying woman, he is explaining how the *voce cupa* figures in his *musical-dramatic representation* of a dying woman. In what we like to call real life, dying women don't sing, and Verdi would doubtless have been annoyed with all those singers (from Callas down) who cut the second stanza of Violetta's final aria in *La traviata* because it seemed unrealistic for her to last so long. Barbieri-Nini's wonderful and funny account of her ordeal confirms that Verdi was indeed expecting her to act, but in ways that would support or intensify – not distract from, or stand in for – the musical-dramatic representation. As for Verdi's remark about what the cor anglais lament 'takes the place of', this shows how Verdi doesn't suppose that his representation of Lady Macbeth is confined to her vocal line. In Verdi as in Shakespeare, or in music drama as in poetic drama, some things belong to the representation but not to the character: I shall return to this point, but first we need to see how Barbieri-Nini's toughest trials were vocal, not histrionic.

Marilyn Feller Somville's essay on 'Vocal Gesture in Verdi's *Macbeth*' admirably explains what Verdi was demanding of his Macbeths in technical and physical terms, while also showing how these demanding 'vocal gestures' articulate an intensely nuanced psychological drama. After Lady Macbeth's first entry, reading the letter, she launches into the electrifying *'Vieni! t'affretta'*. And here, as Somville observes,

> Verdi has written tight little turns with added trills which are not so much ornamental or pretty as a strong gesturing of the lust for power that drives the Lady. These figures require the pithy, harsh quality of pure chest register even up to A flat. The challenge for the singer is that Verdi makes the voice soar up and out of this figuration for even more florid singing in the upper register. Few sopranos, even today, can grab with pure chest register, and leave gracefully, any note in the middle range. However, failure to produce these raucous and vicious gestures in the *cavatina* will destroy the character Verdi wished for. (p. 241)

Certainly Verdi's Macbeths (and Macduff) needed extraordinary power in the upper range. But, as Somville also emphasises and

explains, what was required was not 'some special natural endowment' (*can belto*?) but 'an *acquired technique*': the singer must be
capable of 'carrying a large component of chest-register quality
(maintaining chest-register, vocal-cord action) into the acute
range with concomitant tensing of extra-laryngeal muscles to
hold the larynx in place against enormous breath pressures' (p.
240; my emphasis). Verdi's doubts about whether Tadolini ('who
sings to perfection') could take on the part of Lady Macbeth, and
his reasons for wanting Varesi as his first Macbeth (not Ferri,
with his 'more beautiful voice'), were in this sense technical –
musical and dramatic, not histrionic. In this respect, Gary
Schmidgall's suggestion that *Macbeth* 'forced' Verdi to 'become a
verismo composer' (p. 183) is seriously misleading.

Macbeth doesn't ask for sustained, beautiful singing in the *bel
canto* tradition. Verdi's repeated, and often ironic or dramatically
exaggerated, remarks about what must not be sung 'beautifully' –
or 'must not be sung at all'! – are always warnings against singing
in a traditional but inappropriate style. Rodolfo Celletti's 'On
Verdi's Vocal Writing' (first published in Italian in 1974) provides
an excellent account of Verdi's revolutionary departures from the
earlier *bel canto* tradition of Rossini, Bellini and Donizetti. As
Celletti explains, one problem hadn't so much to do with high
notes as with registration, or how to sing them: Donizetti and
particularly Bellini 'had given the tenor even higher notes than
Verdi, but in the years of Donizetti and Bellini the very highest
notes were sung in falsetto, whereas, in Verdi's day, they were
produced with full or "chest" voice' (Celletti, p. 219). Somville
similarly observes that Verdi required 'tense, cutting, and violent
sounds in the upper register with as much insistence as Rossini
had exploited limpid and smooth agility throughout the upper
range' (p. 240). For dramatic and expressive reasons Verdi was
raising the *tessitura*, or basic vocal range, of all the different
registers, so that a baritone, who had previously been 'considered
a subspecies of bass and was even called *basso cantante*' (singing
bass) became a kind of 'mezzo-tenor': 'in France even today the
term *baryton Verdi* designates a baritone with an extended and
tenorlike high register' (Celletti, p. 226). Verdi repeatedly required
his singers to sing in full or 'chest' voice in their highest registers,
and even required them to articulate (instead of 'vocalising')
syllables when in the higher or acute register. Hence Rossini's
famous jibe at Verdi tenors whose 'yelling' resembled the scream

of a slaughtered capon (*l'urli d'un cappone sgozzato'*) or Bernard Shaw's repeated criticisms of Verdi's 'sins against the human voice'. Both Somville's and Celletti's essays resort to the same adjectives, such as 'cutting', 'tense' or 'violent'. Verdi didn't want his Macbeths to be golden-voiced, like Rossini's Otello. But – despite unforgettable shock moments such as that in the Act I finale, when Lady Macbeth hurls a high C over the whole orchestra and a full chorus – much of the singing must be quiet and intensely introspective. The score is full of directions such as *voce cupa, soffocata, voce velata* or *voce muta*, and, as Somville explains, these terms 'refer to various techniques of covering or damping vocal tone, accomplished by tensing and shaping the pharyngeal wall and/or coupling small amounts of nasal resonance', while *cupo* and *soffocato* also 'refer to shaping the mouth, jaw and tongue to achieve articulations that are imploded rather than exploded' (p. 242). Of course the point of such precise signals is always dramatic, and often intensely nuanced in a psychologically intimate or subtle way: Verdi was asking his singers to respond, from moment to moment, to suggestions of tension, inner conflict or hidden motivation, instead of offering 'beautiful' but sustained or static 'singing'. Like Shakespeare in the 1590s, Verdi was thinking from, and if necessary against, the representational conventions of his own time, and his own dramatic art.

Once again, I am suggesting how we might learn from Verdi. Most contemporary Shakespeare critics discuss Shakespeare's poetic dramas as though they were or might as well have been written in prose. Most contemporary actors and directors make their livings from television or film, and favour a 'realistic', 'from-the-inside-out' or 'feel-for-it' acting style: Stanislavsky filtered through some version of the 'Method', and then drained or sluiced though Hollywood and television. George T. Wright, whose *Shakespeare's Metrical Art* (1988) is the best study of Shakespeare's verse, suggested in a 1994 essay that 'most American listeners to plays are deaf to metrical verse: they have not grown up with it, it is foreign to them, and ... most of the strongest American poets of our time have found it uncongenial – of our language but not of our speech' (p. 65). Whatever the cause, one contemporary Shakespearean equivalent for what Verdi thought 'must not and cannot be done' in music drama is what I have elsewhere described as the 'Eureka! effect': 'fouling the Shakespearean line with many curious hesitations or barks, the actor casts about for the appropriate word or metaphor, and then delivers it as the character's own excited discovery, or choice' ('*Othello* in the World of Cognitive Science', p. 33). When Macbeth says that his hand will rather 'The multitudinous seas incarnadine / Making the green one red' we should not suppose, and the actor should not suggest, that this character is a secret reader with a tremendous vocabulary who is thoughtful enough to provide a monosyllabic gloss for the less well educated. Shakespeare, like Verdi, often represents his characters in ways that belong to the representation but not to the character.

If we could ask Verdian characters such as Lady Macbeth, or Alfredo in *La traviata*, or Jago in *Otello*, what they were doing when they sang their drinking songs, they would all answer, 'Singing'. But if we could ask Lady Macbeth what she was doing in '*Vieni! t'affretta!*', or ask Jago what he was doing in his '*Credo*', they would say, 'Talking', or maybe just 'Thinking'. These representational issues were first broached in Edward T. Cone's *The Composer's Voice* (1974); since then they have been explored very searchingly by critics such as Carolyn Abbate, Jean-Jacques Nattiez and Cone himself in his later book *Music: A View from Delft*. Cone's earlier book considers that the 'composer's voice' is an 'intelligence in the act of thinking through the musical work' (p. 35), whereas Abbate considers this conception too close to the idea of a virtual author, too 'monologic (in the Bakhtinian sense) and monophonic' (*Unsung Voices*, p. 11). But these critics are all concerned with the representational implications of a curious paradox. Operatic characters are usually deaf: they don't know that they and the other characters are singing, and they can't hear the orchestra.

This paradox has a significant Shakespearean parallel: Shakespeare's characters never choose to speak prose, because they never know that they are or were speaking verse. Othello doesn't *choose* to speak prose throughout the eavesdropping scene: he is confined to prose in a representation that measures his distress, derangement and degradation. Similarly, Lear's harrowing descent into prose when he speaks of 'unaccommodated man' belongs not to the character but to the representation. It then measures his descent, and also the truth and value of his belated discovery, which may be more spasmodic or intermittent than talk about Lear's 'progress' implies. I doubt that the shift to prose will be heard, unless spectators share or can reconstruct the relevant poetic-dramatic convention, or expectation: kings are expected to speak verse, unless they are simply giving instructions to servants. Later, Lear's 'Pray you, undo this button' is no less electrifying because it is a wrenchingly naturalistic, and in that sense prosaic, detail: the king is an 'old man' (like Lady Macbeth's Duncan) who is fumbling and asking for help. But we are not used to hearing this old man request anything, let alone say 'Pray you'. The seemingly prosaic and humble detail is once again embedded in blank verse: this king is speaking poetry again, but of course he is not choosing to do so. Rather, this representational mixing of the formal and the naturalistic suggests how this king has in a sense recovered while becoming more human and ever more helpless.

Of course real kings speak prose, and no real father discovering his dead daughter would speak blank verse, like Lear, or sing an aria, like Verdi's Rigoletto. If he did, we'd think him mad. But that would run counter to another convention in Shakepearean poetic drama: when Shakespeare's characters go mad, they stop speaking verse and speak prose, like Lear or Ophelia. In a non-realistic way, that marks one difference between Ophelia's helplessly real madness and Hamlet's feigned madness. Some representational conventions seem to have been shared between poetic drama and music drama: for example, not singing, or speaking verse, when reading a letter. Verdi's audience would still have been surprised by Lady Macbeth's entry, because Verdi was using one convention against another: in the 1840s the prima donna's first entry was expected to lead to a grand slow aria, followed by an exit to tumultuous applause, and one or more encores. In her final, sleep-walking scene, Shakespeare's Lady Macbeth speaks fragmented prose, and in this case Verdi could have followed Shakespeare rather easily by following the similar Italian operatic convention developed by Bellini and Donizetti in their various 'mad' scenes. But Verdi (not Lady Macbeth) chose not to do that: his Lady Macbeth sings three lucid, intricately rhymed double quatrains of *versi ottonari*. Since Italian audiences in the 1840s had metrically, as well as musically, educated ears, such deliberate departures from convention, or audience expectation, functioned as a constituent of dramatic meaning. But, as Jonas Barish so brilliantly shows, although Verdi's sleepwalking scene 'makes no attempt to equate somnambulism with madness' and 'shuns the devices of musical discontinuity that correspond to the discontinuities of Shakespeare's prose', Verdi's musical-dramatic translation of

Macbeth's dagger soliloquy 'not only adopts all the conventions for rendering madness, but extends and intensifies them' (pp. 151, 153). Barish's searching essay concludes that, in Macbeth's case, 'hallucination is treated musically as a species of madness, while in Act IV the sleepwalking is treated more as a kind of meditation, in which the serenity and splendor of the vocal line work in some degree against the disruptions indicated in the words' (p. 153).

What Somville calls Verdi's 'vocal gestures' are – *like* the shifts between different registers of verse and prose in Shakespearean poetic drama – metaphorical representations, not realistic imitations. In Shakespeare's case, contemporary critics too often insist that the text is a script, while forgetting that the text of a poetic drama is also a score.

CHAPTER III

Protagonists: chiasmus interpretations on stage

Laurence Olivier and Vivien Leigh
directed by Glen Byam Shaw

Though Garrick's production highlighted Macbeth and Siddons's Lady Macbeth, later in stage-history a crossing over of the ascendancy of Lady Macbeth and Macbeth within one production – what I have called 'a chiasmus' – allowed each of the protagonists to shine. The play's chiasmic language – for instance, 'Fair is foul, and foul is fair' in the first scene – invites directors to tease out the play's chiasmic structure. An impressive example is the 1955 production starring Laurence Olivier and Vivien Leigh, directed by Glen Byam Shaw at the Memorial Theatre, Stratford-upon-Avon. A chiasmus compensates for the problem that Orson Welles saw in the play and expressed with typical flamboyance in a 1974 interview with Richard Marienstras:

> no actor in the history of theater has ever been a great Macbeth. Why? Because there has never been an actor who could perform the first and second part of the play. For this play has a great defect ...: the Macbeth who is the victim of Lady Macbeth is not the one who then becomes king ... The actor must be brutally simple and completely natural to play the first part, and extremely cerebral to play the second part. In other words Laurence Olivier would have to play in the first part, and John Gielgud in the second. (Estrin, p. 151)

By focusing attention on the Lady and then the thane the production avoids the defect Welles describes – which is a defect only if one interprets *Macbeth* as he does.

The failure of Olivier to finance a filmed version of this *Macbeth* creates an unfortunate gap in the performance history of the play. This towering director-actor of Shakespeare on film, whose

Henry V, Hamlet, Richard III, Othello, and finally King Lear (on video) mark him as one of the outstanding interpreters of the twentieth century, was prevented by failing to secure financial backing from leaving to posterity what might have been the apotheosis of his Shakespearean characterisations. Olivier's stage production, like the early productions already discussed, must be reclaimed solely from memory and from aids to memory: from promptbooks and notes, from photographs, newspaper reviews and scholarly analyses.

Many people consider Olivier's to be the finest Macbeth of the twentieth century: among others, Dennis Bartholmeusz, Richard David, Gareth Lloyd Evans ('Macbeth in the Twentieth Century') and Michael Mullin, who edited one of the most important artefacts for recovery of the production, the director's prompt-book and notes (Macbeth Onstage). Marvin Rosenberg, in his exhaustive survey of Macbeths, believes Olivier to be one of the few polyphonic interpreters of the thane. Nevertheless, considering immediate responses to the performance is instructive. Some contemporary reviewers were less enthusiastic about the perform-ance and the production. In fact, one critic's praise for any aspect can be balanced by another's disapprobation, a point that should be kept in mind as the details of the production are presented here. Several critics who attended the opening night, 7 June 1955, blasted it for Macbeth's quiet, unheroic beginning, for the weak-ness of the minor characters and even of Vivien Leigh, and for the ordinariness of the director's concepts, including his idea of the supernatural.

By the time Olivier played Macbeth, many reviewers expected something more than a bravura performance with several lightning-flash scenes. Although the eighteenth century looked for 'Nature' connected to the psychological states of the moment, in 1955 plot and integrated spectacle had become as important as character, and character was more valued as a whole than for isolated moments of brilliance. Doubtless this development has much to do with the rise of realism, the demand by audiences and critics for everything to fit together, emanating from the now somewhat tarnished assurance that a coherent motivation can be inferred from a character's moods and actions. In 1955 ambiguity was less prized, it seems, than now. Similarly, the reviewers did not conceive the theatre as a place for reflection: they wanted the actors and the action to sweep them away.

However different their audiences, Garrick and Olivier are connected in their use of mimicry coupled with mimesis, that is, a combination of outward show in grease-paint and gesture connected with an inner feeling, which the outward show either precedes or follows. Donohue (*Dramatic Character*, pp. 217–18) speaks of the debate over the connection between form and expression in the eighteenth century, and Olivier addresses this point directly, in *On Acting*, discussing the 1937 Old Vic production directed by Michel St Denis: 'I "made up" to play Macbeth, instead of letting Macbeth play through me. I had everything outwardly and not enough inwardly' (p. 72). Comparing the 1955 to the 1937 production, he says:

> The first time I had aged through pure imagination; now I could bring knowledge to bear. I was also happy with the make-up and the costumes. I found it was genuinely possible to make every second of Macbeth human, despite all that murdering of children. By luck, that second time I found a complete experience which belonged to the part, and I was able to get the right mixture of style and down-to-earth reality. I found the right ingredients in the right proportion ...
>
> I don't know why my second Macbeth came together then, but like everything in this extraordinary work of theatre, it happened and it did. It was my moment ... somehow I had grown into [the role]. (pp. 75–6)

Olivier does not attribute the greater success in 1955 to a change in interpretation but rather to his greater ability to balance mimicry and mimesis, his ability to inhabit the role.

The differences between Garrick and Olivier are, of course, great, probably greater than one can comprehend, but there is similarity in excellence. Both men were able to reconcile the discordant elements of Macbeth's character – along with his evil, they could integrate the man of sensibility, whose suffering engenders pity, and the man of courage, whose intrepidity earns admiration. Above all, they exploited the richness of Shakespeare's verse. They both made the audience see that Macbeth is a villain in spite of his natural humanity. Through the solicitings of the supernatural and of his fierce wife in Garrick's version, through sheer force of will coupled with his wife's persuasion in Olivier's, each overcomes his better nature. The inevitable dissimilarity of Garrick and Olivier can be understood through the distinction between the two productions and between their two Ladies, the impressively obdurate, physically dominant Mrs Pritchard so unlike the visually frail, delicately beautiful, snake-like Vivien Leigh: Garrick's Macbeth was the more noble, more uxorious, Olivier's the stronger, more self-motivated.

Though directors by 1955 generally had a great amount of control over a production, Shaw was less responsible for Olivier's interpretation and Leigh's than he was for the other aspects of the production, since Olivier, like Garrick, shaped his own character-isation. Olivier had already played in *Macbeth* – cast as Lenox as early as 1924, as Malcolm in Barry Jackson's modern-dress production in 1928 and then as Macbeth in 1937 at the Old Vic with Judith Anderson. He had already directed and produced outstanding stage productions and films. Not an easy person to influence at any time as a mature artist – Tynan lumps him with Polanski among the artists who impose their will on others (*Sound*, pp. 89–90) – he was not likely to take very much direction from Shaw, then producing his first *Macbeth*. In *On Acting*, Olivier barely mentions Shaw but speaks, in general, of his own discoveries for the role (pp. 68, 75–6). He was anxious for Leigh to succeed in her role and undertook the job of coaching her, shap-ing his portrayal to enhance hers and hers to enhance his.

Shaw did, however, have many ideas about specific points in the play and a sense of the play's meaning. He wrote interesting, reflective notes on each scene, recorded by Mullin in Macbeth *Onstage*. Though it was 'Macbeth's play', in Richard David's opin-ion 'Sir Laurence's success was fed by the brilliant direction' (p. 127). The weight of evidence suggests, though, that 'competent' is a more appropriate term than 'brilliant'. Since Shaw's main concern was the overall design, he consulted with the designer before working on the promptbook and developed the blocking before rehearsals began. Prescriptive rather than creative rehearsals follow from such plans.

The eight sets by Roger Furse, who had worked at the Old Vic and with Olivier on films but who had not before done a stage production at Stratford, were expressionistic, intimating by their tilted angles something awry in the kingdom, contributing to the miasma of doom that hung over the action. 'Stark', 'teutonic', 'jagged and barbaric', 'harsh and charmless', 'grim' are adjectives the reviewers used. Unlike the insignificant sets in the Garrick–Siddons eras, these sets were meant to contribute to interpretation. In between had come excessively illusionistic sets like those of Henry Irving in the late nineteenth century, sets that necessitated sharp cuts in the text to accommodate scene changes. But in the early twentieth century modern prophets had begun to preach new theories of the relation of set to action. Furse seems to have followed the ideas of Gordon Craig (Odell, II, 461–2), with a spare use of architectural features and with lighting that suggested emotional states. Lighting also effectively focused and magnified attention, as when the full light of the setting sun shone on Macbeth's face for his first entrance. One reviewer found particularly memorable 'the moment when Vivien Leigh appears, against the blue, midnight sky, up among the arches of Inverness castle' (James Courtenay, *Stratford-on-Avon Herald*, 10 June). Furse's best set was for the sleepwalking scene, where in darkness, through a nest of arches, the faint taper was seen in the far distance, and where no stairway impeded Lady Macbeth's swift entrance. Echoes of asymmetry showed in the Macduff castle and even in the English scene to suggest similarity between Macbeth's world and the world of Macduff and Malcolm – as opposed to productions that present their scenes as sharp and bright contrasts to Macbeth's. Similarly, Lady Macduff, acted by Maxine Audley, instead of contrasting with Lady Macbeth was another strong-willed character. Though his design and casting evoked these correspondences between Malcolm and Macbeth and between Lady Macduff and Lady Macbeth, the production was not consistent in this regard, for Shaw directed his Rosse, Macduff and Lady Macduff to be simple, good-hearted folk. Such conflicting interpretive elements can lead to incoherence and audience confusion and may explain some of the reviewers' disapprobation.

Compared with the weirdly asymmetrical sets with arches askew, Furse's rugged woollens for the men's costumes, in rough-textured greys and browns, richly coloured mustards, reds, black plaids and tweeds, greens and blues, were realistic and authentic looking. His body-encasing, silken costumes for the women (snake-green for Lady Macbeth), with breasts and navels shadowed with paint to suggest the naked body beneath, were sensuous. Thus settings, men's costumes and women's costumes illustrate three different aspects of the play – for a kind of production polyphony, to paraphrase Rosenberg's highest accolade. The expressionistic settings reflect tormented mental states; the men's costumes brute force and violence; the women's, sensuality and the body. Props, too, were used effectively: a red cushion directed attention toward the coronet for Malcolm (I.iv). And the too-large crowns on

Macbeth and his lady signalled that royalty is beyond them. Though some reviewers criticised the excess of sound effects (both toad and cat sounded in the first scene), the knocking at the gate was quietly insistent without interfering with the flow of the scene (David, p. 129), background silence held throughout the sleepwalking scene, and the last 'Victorious flourish' was 'quite short' at the end, according to the Music Plot. Thus, for the most part, the production elements suited the interpretation.

Because that interpretation was dominated by the two protagonists, the witches were part of a subordinate structure. But since nothing contributes so much to the atmosphere of the play as the witches, a director walks a razor bridge in determining their power. In the twentieth century the witches are even more of a problem than they had been for earlier producers, when comedic witches were the norm and little effort was made for supernatural sublimity. As Richard Payne Knight, writing in 1895, says, 'Every person, who, after having been a reader, has become a spectator of the witches in *Macbeth*, has felt how totally they lose their grandeur by being exhibited on the stage in distinct forms' (quoted by Donohue, *Dramatic Character*, p. 265n). But grandeur, as we have seen, is perhaps not what the text intends: if a reader's concept cannot be acted without textual cuts or expansions, it could be wrong. Though Shaw downplayed their effect on Macbeth, he generated interest in the witches theatrically. He dressed them in the colour of the background in pink body suits and grey gossamer rags so that they seemed not of the earth though on it. For their first appearance, he had them float down from the air, as if by magic. Next they were on the heath (I.iii), finally beneath the earth – 'as though ... in hell', said Shaw in his notes (Mullin, *Onstage*, p. 159). But in spite of the space they control they are not, he said, the Fates; they do not exert a power over Macbeth impossible for him to resist, and, in fact, they are themselves 'condemned souls out of hell' (p. 30). Shaw wanted them to have tragic stature, to be 'terrible & yet strangely wonderful' (p. 30). Adjectives used to describe them, such as 'prettified' and 'nondescript', suggest that though Shaw tried to dress and block them to increase their mystery he did not succeed for most spectators. In the first scene, they remained almost motionless, a choice that can go far towards intensifying their presence (as Orson Welles discovered in his 1948 film). Greeting Macbeth, the voice of each was softer than that of the one before, so that 'that shalt be King' was like the whisper of his own mind. As Macbeth spoke urgently to the second Sister, the first slipped away; as he spoke to the third, the second disappeared; as Banquo and Macbeth looked at each other in amazement, the third disappeared. Reviewers found this theatrical sleight of hand satisfying.

The witches were less successful in the cauldron scene, which did tip towards the ludicrous, full of smoke and screeches, according to some reviewers. The first apparition was Macbeth's own head, pierced with a dagger, facing forward with Macbeth behind it where he could not see the face, and he himself in a trance spoke its words. Later in the run, according to David, 'all three oracles appeared to come from the apparitions themselves – a safer, if tamer solution' (p. 130n). David wanted the women to be more commanding than they were: 'Their performance had not quite the concentration required to persuade us that evil was here personified'. To say, as he does, that 'at least they never broke the mystery or fell out into the full daylight of ridicule' (p. 125) is to damn them with faint praise. In the opinion of many reviewers they were downright bad. But if the witches and their show were less than compelling, that vacuum gave Olivier more scope to dominate the closing scenes and to deepen the irony of Macbeth's confidence in the apparitions – confidence that even he knew was misplaced.

Other production choices made for fullness and complexity, even among the minor characters, who very definitely remained in the background. Their main function, to Shaw, was to concentrate attention on the principals. He urged them to intensify their reactions. 'An actor', writes Shaw, 'who has no imagination cannot even walk on in this play without doing harm' (Mullin, p. 17). David praises the director, not so much for an overall concept as for the multitude of small decisions:

> Scene after scene was lit by touches of genius: sometimes the merest details in aid of continuity and plausibility, as when the attendant, who is later to usher in Banquo's murderers, at Macbeth's state entry takes a step forward but checks at the look in the King's eye warning him not to broach the business at so public a moment. (p. 127)

The move not only gave an anonymous supernumerary a moment of presence; it also motivated the king's early dismissal of the court. Like many directors whose career trajectory has largely been fuelled by acting, Shaw paid careful attention to the problems that actors in minor roles have in generating enough stage presence to avoid becoming black holes on stage. It was important, he said, that the thanes should exhibit the qualities of nobility which can make them arresting figures on stage and that the attendants should have some sort of inner life they could call on. He also pleased his actors by giving them more to do than the script calls for. His Seyton was not only the ubiquitous servant, as in so many productions since Davenant; he was also the completely trusted attendant, on whom both Lady Macbeth and Macbeth relied and who could be seen observing in many scenes that did not call for him, as in the interview with the murderers. Menteth, Cathness and Angus appeared in every scene that had thanes. Yet, paradoxically, many reviewers commented on the weaknesses of the minor characters. In spite of concern for their characterisations, then, Shaw it appears kept them subordinate to the point of making them nonentities. It is possible, also, that he did not spend enough time with the actors playing the minor characters. Only a few weeks were allotted to rehearsals (from the end of April to the first week in June), and perforce much of Shaw's time had to be spent with the principals to go over the fully developed blocking that he had mapped out in advance in about one month of work on the script (Mullin, *Onstage*, p. 10). Trader Faulkner, who played Malcolm, refers to the small amount of time Shaw spent on him and also mentions that Shaw, Olivier and Leigh rehearsed in sessions closed to the others (Mullin, *Onstage*, pp. 251–2). Thus the minor actors could not absorb what the principals' interpretation would require of them. It is a telling point, for example, that in speaking to Michael Mullin about the production, Faulkner says, 'Olivier grew and grew in strength in the play and she waned. This was *I think* [emphasis mine] deliberate policy of direction' (p. 251).

Some reviewers said that no one but the principals was even worth mentioning. David spoke to their almost universal objections:

It was idle of [them] to object that the lesser parts at Stratford were weakly played, since it was a condition of the production that they should be played down. This Banquo was never … [a] formidable antagonist. but a forthright, bustling, unimaginative soldier with no inkling of the powers into whose orbit he had ventured. Malcolm was a mere boy, and unsure of himself; but this indeed was a virtue, for he attracted pity and sympathy without ever directly competing with Macbeth for the audience's favour.

[69]

Macbeth had no *need* to fear such opposites. The killing of Banquo, the frantic fortifying of Dunsinane, were superfluous acts of savagery. Macbeth brings his end upon himself. Only the Macduff of Keith Michell, the fated instrument of heaven and by his birth himself outside normality, showed something of Macbeth's super-human stature. (p. 126)

Lady Macbeth, in the scheme of the production, also had to take a secondary role, but only after Macbeth slowly began to catch fire. The one or two reviewers who found her more inter-esting than her husband, especially in Shakespeare's first and second acts (comprising Act I of the production's three), correctly noted the production design without recognising it as a con-sidered choice for portraying the pair: they couch their praise of Vivien Leigh's decisive Lady Macbeth in terms of blaming Laurence Olivier's passionless Macbeth. Her power, more self-willed than innate, extended only far enough to prod him into action. Still, the crossover did not rupture their relationship. In the first court scene, she exited at the same time as Banquo, without necessarily having heard Macbeth question Banquo (because of the distance between them indicated in the blocking), before Olivier dismissed the rest of the court. In the next scene, though she was no longer his partner and confidante – her fragility made that change understandable – he was still affection-ate, and they exited together, his arm about her. Thus, Macbeth could sincerely mourn her death.

The production exploited her petite figure to make the chiasmus more believable. Some reviewers who liked her overall were disappointed by her small size, which made it impossible for her, they felt, to create the truly horrendous Lady. But her delicate frame, so unlike Mrs Pritchard's massive one, authenticated her sinking into passivity and impotence and made her terrible passion and determination in the early scenes a frightening exertion of her will. Many reviewers did not seem to understand that she was not going to be Pritchard or Siddons, nor was she intended to be; in the twentieth century a Lady Macbeth can be splendid in many ways besides indominability. Indeed an actor can be magnificent by meaningfully exposing Lady Macbeth's vulnerability as well as by expressing her strength. Patrick Gibbs, not grasping her complexity, said Leigh came 'far short of the splendid domination of will and personality required. A display of physical attraction is no help in this part' (*Daily Telegraph*,

London, 8 June). Desmond Pratt even more obviously wanted his Lady Macbeth to be the one Hazlitt described, and Hazlitt's Lady Macbeth was, of course, Siddons (*Yorkshire Post*, 8 June). On the other hand, Leigh was a fiend-like queen who hazarded all, 'a brilliant barbarian, full of flint and sensuality'. She earned respect for her steely will, with her voice lowered almost an octave, a half-octave lower than his tenor tones. 'Bitch', 'adder', 'viper', and 'snake' were the terms used to describe her. Yet, greeting Duncan and the thanes, she was all charm.

Against some critics' objections to Leigh's performance, David and others defended her interpretation, especially when she was in the ascendant phase of the chiasmus:

> Lady Macbeth, too, was a force to be reckoned with, and the scenes between husband and wife were always exciting in their give and take, in the dramatic modification of one character by another ... Vivien Leigh has superb attack: such an opening as 'Come, you spirits That tend on mortal thoughts, unsex me here' was tremendous; but she lacks the gift of phrasing in verse necessary to carry her through a long speech ... This disability, however, hardly affected any but her first scene, and for the rest her force and drive whipped up the play and saved it from the courted risk of dragging. (pp. 126–7)

The 'courted risk' refers to the choice of hoarding Macbeth's reserves for the last act. In the scene following the murder of Duncan, according to David, 'Vivien Leigh was at her searing best' (p. 129). She thundered her command, 'Infirm of purpose! / Give *me* the daggers' (II.ii.51–2), chilling the audience with the 'glinting cruelty [that] is pointed by her beauty and her grace' (*Birmingham Weekly Post*, 10 June). Yet 'her scenes with Sir Laurence [had] all the harmony and understanding of a husband-and-wife relationship, so that even in their verbal clashes they act in perfect accord' (Peter Rodford, *Western Daily Press*, Bristol, 9 June). Thus, in the next scene she was all wifely solicitude when she softly begged her lord to 'sleek o'er [his] rugged looks'.

By the banquet scene, her strength was subsiding, in harmony with the chiasmus design, for here Olivier's Macbeth was gathering power. Few reviewers mentioned her in this scene, and any who did faulted her lack of command and presence. Shaw in his notes expressed his admiration for Lady Macbeth here: her courage and loyalty are 'magnificent' and 'beyond praise'; but it is uncertain whether his idea about her character came through in the violent action. The scene was designed to be the most exciting one in the performance, not only because Olivier took command of the stage but because Shaw's production choices – particularly the way the ghost appeared, then walked off between Macbeth and Lady Macbeth, and finally disappeared through a trap – gave the scene a terrible power.

Though a mere blip on the curve of Macbeth's decided dominance of the last act of the play, Vivien Leigh's last scene was for many critics, even those generally critical of her performance, her best. Some noted and deplored the change in wigs for the sleepwalking scene that turned her hair into a mousy brown from the deep red of the beginning. But most admired her actions and expressiveness. 'Her sleepwalking subtly conveyed the entranced horror of a woman whose conscience is awakened only in dreams', said one reviewer (Stephen Williams, *Evening News*, 8 June). Her voice effectively 'alternates senile and childish tones', said another (Gibbs, *Daily Telegraph*, London, 8 June). 'She delivered her lines with a staccato urgency which brought new life and new meaning to them. The audience was made to share [her] terrible nightmare' (*Wolverhampton Express*, 10 June). The chiasmus did not prevent her from achieving a memorable effect at the last.

Similarly, the design enabled Olivier as Macbeth to develop Macbeth's softer qualities at the beginning. While reviewers such as Marion Rathbone expressed disappointment with Olivier's opening scenes – that is, his failure to express the 'rugged, hardy, Scottish chieftain' (*South Wales Argus*, Newport, 9 June) – Gibbs understood the beginning: 'This Macbeth was slow-spoken, reflective, kindly and noble. By a consistent return to this manner between the later wild passages of fear and passion, Sir Laurence kept recalling the essential character, making a wonderfully moving contrast between the man of honour and the man burdened by guilt.' Similarly, another reviewer valued the pace of the opening scenes. The production

> thundered and flashed ... in our imaginations, though the storm did not begin at once. That is as it should be. The idea must grow in Macbeth's mind, and it was exciting to watch and to hear Sir Laurence Olivier as he screwed his courage to the sticking place, and in that ominous setting of night-blue and dark red (the hue of congealed blood) moved, with Tarquin's ravishing strides towards his design ... We have never pierced more deeply into Macbeth's mind. (*Birmingham Post*, 9 June)

[72]

Kenneth Tynan in his review was even clearer about the design (*Sunday Obsever*, 12 June). He faulted the play itself, blaming Shakespeare for the paucity of excellent productions: 'As the play proceeds, the hero shrinks; complex and many-levelled to begin with, he ends up a cornered thug, lacking even a death-scene with

3 Laurence Olivier and Vivien Leigh, 1955

which to regain lost stature.' Olivier, who 'shook hands with greatness', turned the play inside out and made it mount with excitement instead of wane:

> He begins in a perilously low key ... This Macbeth is paralyzed with guilt before the curtain rises ... Far from recoiling and popping his eyes, he greets the air-drawn dagger with sad familiarity; it is a fixture in the crooked furniture of his brain. Uxoriousness leads him to the act, which unexpectedly purges him of remorse ... There was true agony in 'Else I had been perfect'; Banquo's ghost was received with horrific torment ... I have been cheated! [Olivier's Macbeth has] the anguish of the *de facto* ruler who dares not admit that he lacks the essential qualities of kingship.

J. C. Trewin, disagreeing with Tynan about Shakespeare's Act V Macbeth, asserted that the thane must always be, especially at the end, the fallen angel, 'Lucifer lost'; the pity of it gives the ending its power. He thought Olivier had achieved Shakespeare's intention (*Birmingham Post*, 15 June).

The overall contours of the role are clear: Olivier began standing astride a rock, looking down at the witches below him, expressing through his stance the quiet confidence of the successful soldier in a community that values soldiering. When he entered to Duncan, a ceremony was in progress, for, already mindful of Macbeth's ambition, Duncan, a physically frail king who had needed support on either side, purposely named Malcolm as his successor moments after he rewarded Macbeth. With his wife's encouragement, Macbeth committed a murder that he understood was wrong, but the crime did not much exercise his imagination: if it had, he could not have maintained the low-keyed approach. Thus, in his deliberation before the murder he is 'merely petulant' (David, p. 128). Olivier initiated the moment of change after the murder, when conscience began its work. Harold Hobson recognised the intent: with 'Sleep no more' Olivier 'comes upon what he evidently regards as the heart of "Macbeth", namely, not Macbeth's imagination of Duncan's murder, but his conscience after it' (*The Sunday Times*, 12 June). In this decision, Olivier followed Henry Irving (Furness, *Macbeth*, p. 497). His behaviour thereafter was a reaction against his conscience. Though Olivier was thought by some reviewers to be too passive even after the murder, several noted his soliloquy. 'I shall long remember', says David, 'the despairing, fumbling abhorrence with which Olivier sought to ward off the multitudinous seas of blood that seemed to be swirling about his very knees' (p. 129). Hobson called it 'tremendous; it is greasy and slippery with an immense revulsion. As distress and agony enter into him, the actor multiplies in stature before our eyes until he dominates the play.' Hazlitt's comment on Edmund Kean can apply as well to Olivier: Macbeth 'banishes remorse for the past, by meditating future mischief' (Donohue, *Dramatic Character*, p. 340). Though conscience and fear threaten to overcome him at times, he perseveres, saying as does Milton's Satan, 'Evil be thou my Good'. While it is not possible to set aside Macbeth's crimes as mere infirmities, Olivier managed to keep before the audience the image of Macbeth the noble soldier. At the last, this aspect came forth most decidedly.

The curve of Macbeth's development did not alone account for Olivier's success in the role: rather, it was his ability to inhabit the characterisation, then to express it from the inside through 'his flexibility of voice, and his ability to match every motion and movement with his mood' (Rodford). His voice ranged from a whisper that, like Garrick's, could be heard throughout the theatre, to screams and shouts; his facial expression from stalwart heroism to Satanic fury; his mood from defeat to triumphant victory. Gareth Lloyd Evans refers to 'the ghost of a Scots accent which he used with superb judgement of tone and effect' (p. 98). Olivier, he goes on, 'seems to seek out, and invariably succeed in finding, phrases, half-lines, apparent debris on the great tide of Shakespeare's iambics, and to collect it into a form that gives its existence a relevance'. As an example, he cites the way Olivier said to the murderers, 'Well, then, now' (III.i.74), giving each of the three words distinct and harrowing meaning. The effect of 'Olivier's way with a text' is 'to synthesise all the elements in it – high and low verbal tension, poetry and prose, plain and decorated – to the end of intensifying the dramatic impact of character' (p. 99). His great gift is variety of expression connected to every nuance of every thought; the audience knows what he is thinking. Olivier established that his Macbeth was hearing from the Sisters what he has thought many times before. Soon after, Olivier deepened the audience's perception of his ambitions by staring hungrily at Duncan's symbols of office, there for the ceremonial crowning of Malcolm (I.iv). His Macbeth moved with the fluid and sinuous grace of a tiger, and he risked gestures that no one else could have pulled off, like the pushing movement he made when speaking of being pushed from his stool (III.iv.81).

In keeping with his low profile in the beginning, Olivier allowed Leigh's Lady to dominate the persuasion scene (I.vii). For the dramatic moment of her horrifying declaration about killing her baby, Olivier turned his back to the audience and toward her so as to focus full attention on Leigh, while the stance of his body, with his hand on her arm, expressed Macbeth's love and sympathy. Shaw thought that there *were* babies, specifically a son (notes for I.vii), but even so, it is not her declaration that convinced Macbeth. For it seemed that Macbeth neither believed his own arguments against killing Duncan nor was persuaded by her. Rather, he reflected for a time and in the pause before 'Will it not be received ...?' persuaded *himself.* The Macbeths of Jon Finch, Ian McKellen and Eric Porter followed Olivier's in convincing themselves rather than being convinced by their Ladies.

David speaks in praise of Olivier's handling of the discovery scene (II.iii), especially the sense of inevitability that the acting generated:

> Olivier, in a black monkish cassock, paced the stage uneasily, by fits and starts, during the conversation with Lenox, his guilty hands closely folded in his long sleeves except when, with a gesture at once furtive and half-automatic, he withdrew them for a moment and hurriedly inspected them front and back. The flurry of the alarm was well done ... In the hurly-burly 'What, in our house?' was no more than faintly off-key, but Lady Macbeth, anxiously aware of her slip, was fain to feel her way to the support of the proscenium arch. Macbeth re-entered from Duncan's room at the opposite side and at the back, and began his act, glancing uneasily for support to his wife, now divided from him by the whole diagonal of the stage. She instinctively took a step forward to assist him and, as Macbeth's web of deception grew more and more tangled, slowly, inexorably, the two were drawn together by the compulsion of their common guilt to the centre of the stage. Just before she reached her husband Lady Macbeth fainted. Genuine? Feigned? No need even to ask the question, Her collapse was as inevitable a result of the dramatic process as is the spark when two charged wires are brought together. Here was first-rate theatre. (p. 129)

David's description suggests that the crossover in power began here, marked by the blocking.

Shaw's notes, however, show that he considered the first court scene – rather than the discovery scene – to be a point marking the crossover for Macbeth and his Lady: 'Where before Lady Macbeth was active, Macbeth slow to move, they have now changed.' Macbeth spoke with easy charm to Banquo, giving not a hint of the scorpions in his mind. After overhearing the princes' plans to flee the country at the end of II.ii (as in the 1954 Schaefer production for television), Macbeth and Banquo met, Macbeth descended to him and walked off with Banquo following him. Shaw thus hinted at Banquo's tacit acceptance of the crime; his silence about the prophecy was based on his ambition, 'in which case', Shaw believed, 'he is a guilty man & to some extent gets what he deserves' (notes for III.i). Many critics praised the scene with the murderers of Banquo, presented in full:

> Contempt for the miscreants he sets on to murder Banquo and Fleance is powerfully shot across by overtones of self contempt, and when he bids his wife take comfort from the hint that Banquo and his son are doomed a note of resentment against crime's awful necessities creeps into his ironic 'Then be thou jocund'. (*The Times*, 8 June)

At the banquet scene, 'he could whisper: "If I stand here I saw him" with all the agony of a scream when the gaping ghost of Banquo drifts in and out' (*Daily Mail*, 8 June). Yet he also shouted and screamed his rage and defiance. Though he let the cup nervelessly fall out of his hand, he had the temerity to leap on to the banquet table, enlarging his presence by swirling the folds of his crimson robe as he confronted the ghost, just as earlier he so swirled them when he paced around the murderers.

The most amazing scenes came at the end, when the audience was utterly convinced of his evil, yet almost against their will forced to sympathise with him and almost made to agree that the penalties exceeded the crimes. Gibbs said that Olivier spoke the 'sere, the yellow'd leaf' soliloquy 'with furrowed brow and breaking voice ... nobility bewildered'. Later, 'the restrained, almost resigned manner in which the news of Lady Macbeth's death is received was no less moving'. The soliloquy that follows was so full of 'poetic weariness, pity could hardly be withheld' (*Daily Telegraph*, London, 8 June). Hobson said, 'There are tones here like the notes of some divine music: echoes of years of departed happiness' (*The Sunday Times*, 12 June). Earlier, speaking to the doctor, Macbeth, 'with a tender flexibility of phrasing, not only showed us the bond of affection between husband and wife but also (the hands gesturing dumbly and half-consciously towards his own breast) included himself in the plea for mercy' (David, p. 125). By the end of the 'tomorrow' monologue, 'and with the mazed head-shake of the final "nothing" – [he] perfectly conveyed the hurt bewilderment of Fate's victim. Almost one said "a man more sinned against than sinning"' (David, p. 126). But he also 'lurches through his murders in a conscience-stricken nightmare, his face white with the loss of other men's blood, his eyes staring with lack of sleep, and his voice mounting to a desperate tenor as guilt envelops him' (*Daily Mail*, 8 June).

In spite of deep sorrow, this Macbeth roused himself to fight the last battles with Olivier's characteristic energy – in spite of a twisted ankle on the first night that had him stepping where he might have leapt. Macbeth did not fight alone but was assisted by his faithful followers, and he killed several English soldiers before Macduff accosted him. All Macbeth's sorrow became fuel for his valiant fury, his sense that Fate had cheated him. As the *Times* critic put it: 'The smouldering anger with the universe that had betrayed him to his own damnation flashes into flame and throws over the end of the bloody tyrant a sense of the tragic sublimity of his trespass against nature' (8 June). Here were lightning flashes, as rage stirred him almost to madness. The last battle was designed to insist on the riskiness of the struggle, with Macduff forcing Macbeth to retreat backward up winding castle steps, until at the top they disappeared. Many critics felt cheated when the severed head of Macbeth was not brought on at the end. Instead, Macduff pointed to it aloft and offstage. Since Macbeth's head had been one of the apparitions in the apparitions scene, it would have been, as David says, a 'fine irony' had it reappeared (p. 130). Nevertheless, the first night ended with thunderous applause and countless curtain calls, and the production continued through the run to please the audience, whatever some reviewers had to say.

It gives one pause when even such a fine actor as Olivier cannot find a way to satisfy all the reviewers. Their remarks are valuable for the specific moments they describe but their overall judgement must be weighed carefully. Later writers who describe the 1955 production tend to ignore the negative responses, so that one might think that Olivier's Macbeth profoundly moved every spectator. Some detractors did not understand the chiasmus design, with first Lady Macbeth and then Macbeth primary in the audience's attention. Some understood but did not assent to that design. Some did not understand why the minor characters had to serve the principals rather than flare up on their own. In retrospect, it seems that the other actors were, as Alan Dent wittily says, a mere semi-precious setting, 'small cairngorm for two such large and lustrous first-water diamonds' as Olivier and Leigh (*News Chronicle*, London, 8 June). The chiasmus is a logical and satisfying way to set off such diamonds.

CHAPTER IV

The protagonists: chiasmus interpretations on television

Television is a curious hybrid form, partaking of attributes of both stage and screen. It uses the editing technology of film – that is, it cuts freely from character to character and from space to space, from long shot to closeups, from one-shot (one person in the frame) to group shots. These editing choices would seem to give the director a great deal of control, but with television's natural affinity for closeups (especially in the 1950s when screens were small), and with those closeups ordinarily focused on the protagonists or on reactions to them, it also favours stars. The small screen, then, should conform comfortably to the play's concentration on Macbeth and Lady Macbeth. The one-shots and two-shots of television work well for the chiasmus interpretation adopted by productions that focus evenly on Macbeth's and Lady Macbeth's equivalent strength, hers in the earlier half, his in the latter half of the play. But television is unlike film in that realistic settings are not essential for excellence. With its shallow depth of field from the 1950s to the 1980s, it was technically unable to capture the expansive feel of large spaces. Therefore, even for realistic settings, it did better with interiors than with open landscapes; even now, an actor cannot enter into the frame and dominate a large space as an actor can on stage or film. Though early television was too small and flat and grainy to have either stage's or film's overpowering here-and-nowness, it could be more intimate than stage in its potential for bringing the audience into the actor's mind through closeups (see Kliman, 'Setting').

The three television versions that are the concerns of this chapter are interesting for their solutions to the constraints of television and for their connections to the stage productions that preceded them: all have stage antecedents. The first production is actually two. George Schaefer, an American, first directed *Macbeth* for the Hallmark Hall of Fame television series in 1954 as a live broadcast (preserved by kinescope) and then again in 1960 as a made-for-television film. These two productions may be considered one, in a double manifestation, because they feature the same principal actors and essentially the same interpretation. BBC TV is responsible for the second and third productions under consideration here: in 1970 John Gorrie directed a production starring Eric Porter and Janet Suzman; in 1982, as part of 'The Shakespeare Plays' series, Jack Gold directed a production starring Nicol Williamson and Jane Lapotaire. Of the three directors, only Schaefer attempted filmic realism. Gorrie and Gold used lights, cycloramic backgrounds, platforms, rough or obscure shapes, and other features of theatrical ambience to create an artificial Scotland suitable as a background for the tragedy on television. The actors playing Macbeth in all three versions had created the character on stage in a major production at least once before. For this reason, the directors, while shaping the production as a whole, appear to have had little effect on the main characterisations.

Maurice Evans and Judith Anderson
directed by George Schaefer

Though the 1960 production directed by George Schaefer was released as a feature film in Britain and in the United States, it was made primarily for American television and broadcast there on 20 November 1960 and again on 20 October 1961. Not only do many of its details correspond almost exactly to those in the live 1954 production; the production's genesis goes back even further, to 1941, when Evans and Anderson starred in a Broadway version of *Macbeth* under the direction of Margaret Webster. Some of the strategies for Evans's later productions derive from the earliest one, from the main interpretation to details such as Macduff's throwing Macbeth over the battlements at the end. (See Maurice Evans, p. 151, and the Webster promptbook in the Billy Rose Theatre Collection at the New York Public Library at Lincoln Center.) The 'GI' *Macbeth*, produced for American soldiers in the Pacific Theatre during the Second World War, was the direct offshoot of the first production. The GI *Macbeth* was also the beginning of a long collaboration between Evans and Schaefer, then a young sergeant – the most famous instance being the GI *Hamlet* which in 1946 reached Broadway and in 1953 resurfaced on Hallmark television with Schaefer as an assistant director. At this early stage in his career, Schaefer seems to have deferred to his mentor – and thus the Macbeths may properly be called Evans's.

Both the Hallmark television Macbeths are sensible rather than passionate productions; though much has been thought out, they do not catch fire. Evans, whose interpretation drives the productions, returned to the play as to a familiar friend; he was not gripped by the need that sometimes moves actors or directors to produce a play again and again – the desire to re-explore a plenteous text (as, for example, Joseph Papp or Andrzej Wajda probed Hamlet every few years). Yet these and all of Evans's Macbeth productions could please audiences. The 1941 Macbeth ran for 225 performances, including ninety-four days of touring (Evans, pp. 152, 155). The GI version was successful enough to convince the army that other Shakespeare productions were in order. The 1954 adaptation launched Schaefer's highly successful career as a television and film director, and the 1960 version won five Emmy awards for the director, the stars and the film itself. At the same time, in part for her performance as Lady Macbeth, Anderson was made Dame of the Order of the British Empire. All of this acclaim betokens, at least partly, that these Macbeths soothe and affirm rather than unsettle and dismay.

A comparison of the videotapes of the 1954 and 1960 productions shows their similarities in setting, characterisation and overall interpretation. The opening shots of the three witches' reflections, as if inside a cauldron, and their encounter with Macbeth in a grotto are all but the same in both productions. In both, an unseen chorus echoes the greetings of the witches. King Duncan's war tent for the bleeding sergeant scene – a suggestion that this old king Duncan is at least near the scene of battle – is found in both, but in the film the camera can enter the tent while on live television the actors remain outside it. In both, Lady Macbeth moves to a balcony to call forth the malignant powers. In both, there is only one castle. And so on. The changes from a television studio production to a film production are in scale rather than in interpretation, with the studio sets somewhat more spacious for the film. Still, both are very much television productions, with concentration on close and medium shots. In keeping with the new format, the film adds location settings in Scotland to good effect (only some ten minutes of film time), with spirited rides by the bleeding sergeant across a lush landscape, a funeral procession for Duncan and a sizeable army converging on Dunsinane (Hermitage Castle in Scotland). The film also uses a matte (a special effect to give the impression of a deep setting) for a coronation sequence for Macbeth and Lady Macbeth (Hutton, pp. 35–6). However, the film's interiors, modelled on architectural features of a crusader castle on the Isle of Rhodes (Maurice Evans, p. 265), and even the 'exteriors' that were studio-shot in Elstree Studios in England are equivalent to those in the earlier production. Both productions have similar additions, such as the banquet setting for Duncan's visit to Inverness.

The *mise-en-scène* of both television production and film is appropriate, with medieval-looking stone stairways, arches and chambers. In the film, a tapestry in the Macbeth bedchamber showing Jesus holding the orb of the world is an effective reminder that God oversees events in Scotland – though it is doubtful that Macbeth would have chosen this decoration over his bed. A bed figures again when Macbeth goes to his Lady to see her dead body, and he speaks his 'tomorrow and tomorrow' speech directly to her, closing the bed curtains decisively on her without giving her a further glance after the message comes about Birnam Wood. Obviousness is sometimes a lapse, as when Macbeth stands in a shaft of sun when he says 'I 'gin to be aweary of the sun' (V.v.49). Colours, on the other hand, cannot be faulted; costumes, as they were in the Webster stage production, are rich and elegant – with deep royal blues, golds, and reds. Plaids slung over shoulders and a Scottish accent among some of the minor characters evoke the Scottish milieu for a modern audience. Theatrical suggestion rather than historical accuracy is the point.

Even some of the transpositions are the same in the two television versions. At the banquet for Duncan, immediately after Macbeth hears that Malcolm is to be heir (I.iv.35–42), he leaves the banquet chamber responding to that news: 'That is a step, / On which I must fall down, or else o'releap' (I.iv.48–9), but as soon as the implications of what he is thinking strike him, doubts follow: 'If it were done, when 'tis done, then 'twere well / It were done quickly ... He's here in double trust' (from I.vii.1–28). The transposition allows Evans's Macbeth to declare his murderous thoughts after and not before the urgings of his wife in the letter scene (I.v), for Evans's is the story of a noble Macbeth moved to act out his pale ambitions by a strong-willed wife – the favourite interpretation of the eighteenth and nineteenth centuries.

[83]

The film solves problems in a workmanlike fashion. Duncan's chamber has a back door through which Macbeth can safely enter without disturbing the drunken grooms. Macbeth holds the daggers that have drawn Duncan's blood so that Lady Macbeth does not see them until she cries out: 'Why have you brought the daggers?' It is thus not hysteria on her part that prevents her from noticing them, for this production places the beginning of her decline somewhat later. Reading the text, one may wonder why Malcolm and Donalbain do not rush into Duncan's chamber to see their murdered father. Here Rosse prevents them, as if to spare them. The actor playing Rosse also takes much of Lenox's role, a not-uncommon doubling in many promptbooks; this choice give the audience fewer unremarkable thanes to keep in mind. Macbeth, the eavesdropper, listens while his Lady greets Duncan (I.vi), his expression suggesting how difficult it is for him to encounter Duncan. When Macbeth sees Malcolm and Donalbain run off (II.iii.135–44), it dawns on him – and Evans's face telegraphs his thinking – that he can use their flight for his own purpose. The scene of the disaffection of the two lords (III.vi) interrupts the banquet scene (inserted into III.iv after line 120); it begins with the dispersal of the guests after the two appearances of the ghost and is followed by the conclusion of the banquet scene, which Schaefer places in the bedchamber (III.iv.121–43). The production thus justifies Macbeth's shift in demeanour from terrified at the banquet to determined afterwards; alcohol both heartens him and leads to his drunken dream of the witches, the substitute for the cauldron scene. The dream idea may derive from Wyntoun's *Chronicle* (cited in Aitchison, p. 114). Seyton, not Lenox, comes to Macbeth at the end of the dream to tell him Macduff has fled, avoiding the issue of Lenox's pretended loyalty to Macbeth. And in the last scene, Seyton, along with others, fights for Macbeth, so that Macduff's line about not wishing to fight against 'wretched Kernes' (V.vii.17) makes some sense (though of course Seyton is not a mercenary).

But at times the production creates new problems of its own. Banquo, played in 1960 by the superior Michael Hordern, seems suspicious of Macbeth, or at least deeply concerned, as soon as he sees Macbeth brooding about the prophecies (I.iii.127–42). Why, then, does he not tell Duncan about the prophecy? Banquo could have told Duncan as they approach Macbeth's battlements (I.vi) because as the sequence is filmed Banquo has ample opportunity to do so. (Shakespeare does not give the audience opportunities to ask such questions; a director by expanding the space – and thus time – invites the question.) To ensure the unfolding of the prophecy for his sons, Banquo will await events. His suspicion is strengthened as Macbeth, before sounding him out, says improbably, 'I think not of them [the witches]', and Banquo's concern is still further heightened when Macbeth tells him, 'If you shall cleave to my consent, when 'tis, / It shall make honour for you' (II.i.25–6). Yet Banquo, it seems, supports Macbeth's election and offers his allegiance to the new king. Banquo is a problem in any production, but it is disingenuous to pretend that he can be wholly the good man *if* he suspects Macbeth; it is better to make him oblivious of Macbeth's evil if he is to be the noble foil to Macbeth, as Hordern, through his demeanour, suggests that Banquo is. Schaefer makes all the thanes suspicious of Macbeth. This decision may help the audience to understand what they are to feel about the protagonist but undercuts the director's interpretation of Macbeth as a noble man and makes Macbeth's election puzzling.

The production, mainly calm and deliberate, does have some chilling moments. The witches, who appear dirty and wild but knowing and evil (as in the Polanski film, one is young), contribute to the atmosphere, though after their initial prophecies (in I.iii) they appear only in Macbeth's dream, perhaps a hint taken from George Buchanan's Chronicle, the least credulous of several sources for the play (see Paul, pp. 212–13). When Lady Macbeth pulls Macbeth to their chamber after the murder, their hands are so bloody that his slips from hers – a fit emblem for the coming collapse of their relationship. In her sleepwalking scene, she will use this same tugging gesture to pull the Macbeth of her imagination to her room. The character of Seyton is well developed – as in many old promptbooks from Davenant on – and his presence here is thrillingly evil. Played by Trader Faulkner, who took the part of Malcolm in the Olivier stage production of 1955, he is the cool messenger who brings Lady Macbeth the news of the arrival of Duncan (I.v.31), who, in one of the rare changes in the film from the 1954 television production, watches out for eavesdroppers while Macbeth suborns the two murderers, and whose passing-by silences the two lords who speak satirically of Macbeth's reign (III.vi).

While the cinematography is acceptable for the most part, there are inept manoeuvres, such as two scenes in a row using the only examples in the film of double exposure: first, Macbeth dreaming of the witches for the first part of the cauldron scene (the film cuts the show of kings) superimposed over the sleeping Macbeth, and, right after, Macbeth's face as he declares that he will destroy Macduff's castle superimposed on a montage of scenes showing the devastation that Macbeth wreaks. Still, with this montage, which replaces IV.ii, Schaefer more successfully provides visual evidence for Macbeth's tyranny as described by Malcolm and Macduff (IV.iii.4–50) than he did for the live version where he kept the scene of the killing of Macduff's child. On the other hand, the television film makes no good use of the gentlewoman and the doctor (in 1960 the excellent Felix Aylmer) during the sleep-walking scene: we see Lady Macbeth over their shoulders or in close shots; the camera rarely focuses on their reactions, rarely has them move from their hiding place. And for some reason we see them first at Lady Macbeth's well-lit bedside, yet their lines 'How came she by that light?' and 'she has light about her continually' (V.i.20–2) are kept.

The production concept, inasmuch as there is an informing principle, is a chiasmus. Lady Macbeth is the stronger of the two at first, and, as she subsides, Macbeth's fortitude and perseverance against an overwhelmingly superior enemy earn him some respect. But Evans's Macbeth never reaches anything like her power. Both Evans and Anderson, in choosing to make Lady Macbeth the chief architect of the plot to kill Duncan and Macbeth the noble soldier who cannot resist her manipulations, borrowed well-worn ideas of the characters and thus did not grasp them with fervour. The insipidity of Evans's portrayal may stem from his conception of the play, and from the conflict between his idea and his enact-ment. As Evans says of their stage production, 'true to form for this particular play, Macbeth himself came in second best' (p. 152). Believing as he did, Evans could not give his portrayal the charge it needed. Before he found Margaret Webster to direct the Broad-way production – mainly to direct the other actors, he implies (p. 150) – he studied the part and came to the conclusion that '"Power corrupts, and absolute power corrupts absolutely". That, to my mind, was the nub of the play and was to be the basis for my interpretation' (pp. 148–9). But his performance suggests that this was not really the basis, for Evans does not show a Macbeth who desires power and then is absolutely corrupted by achieving it. By making Macbeth honourable, Evans made the tragic conflict turn

4   Judith Anderson and Maurice Evans in George Schaefer's *Macbeth* for the
Hallmark Hall of Fame series

around Macbeth's nobility of soul in conflict with his uxorious-
ness, his need to be approved by his wife. He selected Judith
Anderson to play his Lady having seen and liked her in the film
Lady Scarface; he knew also that she had played in a 1937 *Macbeth*
opposite Laurence Olivier (Evans, p. 146). He wanted a Lady whose
demonic force could bury his honourable scruples. His Macbeth,

though like Garrick's stirred by ambition, does not want to kill Duncan. Rather, his Lady's insinuations about his cowardice sting him as few Macbeths are stung. But to emphasise the noble – that is, the *moral* – Macbeth, Evans compromised by banking the fires of his ambition. For the stage production, he had worried that his five foot nine inch stature might keep him from playing the heroic soldier that he felt tradition demanded. Stature is not a problem on television, for the cameras are well able to obscure such liabilities – and indeed acting can overcome them. Garrick, after all, was only five foot four inches, shorter by far than his Lady. Rather, the problem was that Evans could not find a way to be both the warrior and the honourable man, as Garrick, Macready and Forrest evidently could.

In addition, Evans showed little sympathy for the responsiveness of audiences to Macbeth's high imagination and the images with which he expresses it. He confided in his autobiography that he found Macbeth's verse monotonous, with an overwritten lyricism, as in the 'incarnadine' speech (p. 153). While it is true that an actor is a professional who should be able to rise above his own judgement – Siddons overcame her antipathy for Lady Macbeth – Evans, apparently, could not inhabit the role convincingly. Only in his last scene, for the fight with Macduff, did Evans bring some high spirit into his performance (and some reviewers faulted him even here). His great strength was his clear speaking of the verse, so that his early audiences heard Shakespeare as never before. Richard Watts in *The New York Herald Tribune* in 1941 called him 'alive, vigorous and eloquent' (quoted in Evans, p. 154), and certainly the eloquence comes through in the film.

Anderson, to complement Evans's Macbeth, portrays the powerful woman, urging her weaker, softer husband to do what on his own he never would have done. The price Lady Macbeth pays for taking first place is his disgust both with himself and with her. As Anderson plays her, she is not completely the virago, however. When she returns from Duncan's chamber she is almost choking with terror (an interpretation she played also in the GI *Macbeth*), and she does faint, it seems, when she hears of the murder of the grooms. Her wretchedness after the banquet is convincing and pathetic (III.iv.126, 128, 140). Anderson suggests several layers of possibility for the character, including sexual magnetism, breathing her encouragement to Macbeth to murder Duncan as she presses her body against his (I.vii.61–73), standing near the very bed where the king will be killed. Moments later, she is cool enough (though inwardly agitated) to meet Duncan in the passage-way and bid him goodnight – an added segment. Even in her sleepwalking, she continues to be seductive as she re-enacts her persuasion. And though she has been a powerful woman, she brings genuine pathos into her cry, 'all the perfumes of Arabia will not sweeten this little hand' (V.i.47–8). Peter Morris in his excellent filmography (superseded now by Rothwell and Melzer) quotes the *Monthly Film Bulletin* on Anderson: 'though a little too theatrical and extravagant, [she] does get a touch of the demonic, a whiff of sulphur into her performance: a quality sadly lacking from the film as a whole' (p. 152).

Overall the production, particularly the film version, is pretty to look at and lucid in its interpretation, with a fairly even balance between the two leads exchanging places as active players in the tragedy.

Eric Porter and Janet Suzman directed by John Gorrie

Eric Porter, like Evans, first played his Macbeth on stage. Porter's co-star was Irene Worth in 1962 for the Royal Shakespeare Company, his director Donald McWhinnie, one of three associate directors of the company along with Peter Brook and Peter Wood. A review by Kenneth Tynan said what might be said about many a twentieth-century production: '"Macbeth" (Stratford-upon-Avon) once again repels an attempt to conquer it' (*The Sunday Observer*, 10 June). Many disagreed, certainly. Desmond Pratt called it the finest *Macbeth* he had seen, including the one with Olivier in 1955 (*Yorkshire Post*, 6 June), while J. C. Trewin placed it just after Olivier's (*Birmingham Post*, 6 June). Many praised John Bury's bleak setting and interpretative lighting. But the general opinion was that the production failed to achieve greatness – either because of acting or direction or both. A selected group of headlines from various reviews convey the general impression: 'Macbeth Sans Spark', 'Macbeth Drags its Feet at Stratford', 'Slow-Paced Macbeth is a Dull Miss'. They do not, however, fault the interpretation – a chiasmus, with Macbeth first led into evil by a strong Lady and then exceeding her in evil and leaving her behind him as she sinks from the weight of remorse.

Eight years later, Porter had another chance at Macbeth, this time for BBC television with a new production team and cast, including as Lady Macbeth Janet Suzman, who would in 1974 create a powerful Cleopatra for stage and television, and, as Macduff, John Woodvine, who subsequently played a complex Banquo in the Trevor Nunn production on stage and television. So many elements link stage and screen that generic distinctions can be counterproductive. The *Macbeth* directed for television by John Gorrie traced the same interpretative chiasmus as had Porter's earlier production and was similarly found wanting by critics, not because of the concept but, again, because of something missing. Kenneth S. Rothwell finds it 'a production that does not quite seem to have found its own vision of the play's "metaphysical core"' ('Shakespeare and the People', p. 4), and, in a generally favourable review, H. R. Coursen 'does not feel vividly enough Macbeth's early struggle between his corrupt will and his virtuous understanding' (Bulman and Coursen, pp. 247–8). In spite of such criticism, this version of the play is interesting because of its particular enactment of the chiasmus. The portrayal of Lady Macbeth, especially, rises above the limits of the production.

Like the productions with Evans and Anderson, this one sometimes pays careful attention to implicit stage directions and shows how satisfying such attention can be when word and image match where the language demands. Unlike them, however, the Gorrie production adopts a purely theatrical space, focusing attention on the language and the passions. The setting, with close contiguity among all parts (a unit set), invokes through dark architectural shapes a rough, abstract medieval time. A wild heath leads to the castle, where the hall features an L-shaped stairway with a platform landing. On the far side of the stair, as we first see it, is the banquet area; on the near side, close to the outside door, there is an entranceway under the stairs for Lady Macbeth and others. Often fires glow in sconces in the background, offering an unobtrusive but complementary background, especially when Macbeth and Lady Macbeth are involved in passionate debate. Lady Macbeth burns the letter from Macbeth in one of these wall sconces.

Blocking and camerawork have to be creative in the limited compass of this cramped setting. Orson Welles would have expanded the space with extreme angle shots, the camera at high or, more often, low angles, and with wide-angle lenses, but such choices lend themselves to an expressionistic interpretation and call attention to themselves. Since the aim in the Gorrie production is to make the drama unfold in as natural a way as possible, he unobtrusively applies blocking and camera strategies. After Duncan pointedly brushes by Macbeth and Banquo to shift attention abruptly from them to his elevation of Malcolm, Macbeth remains in near frame, in closeup, while Banquo moves to the middle distance, and Duncan, his hands on his son's shoulders, commands the far distance. Thus Duncan, a vigorous old man and stalwart king with a firm though genial demeanour, cannily undercuts Macbeth's ambitions by rushing into the announcement that Malcolm is his heir. On the triumphant conclusion of Duncan's announcement, 'Cumberland' (I.iv.39), Banquo turns to Macbeth who turns away from his gaze and towards ours, speaking his aside close to the camera (lines 48–53). The blocking in three planes extends the screen's depth. After murdering the grooms, Macbeth re-enters and comes down from Duncan's room at the top of the stairway, but Lenox stays at the top, giving three-dimensionality to the grouping. The camera, thus, makes the most of in-depth and vertical space.

As in the 1962 stage production, Macbeth shouts out his 'tale told by an idiot' to the idiot god he seems to find above him, but for television the camera impassively looks back down at him. Rothwell discusses the interpretive value of several high camera angles for Macbeth and Lady Macbeth:

> In outward beauty and inner degradation Eric Porter's Macbeth and Janet Suzman's Lady Macbeth suggest the fairness of the foul and the foulness of the fair. That equivocal condition, deeply embedded in the play's language, gets visual support from camera angles forcing the audience to look down, not up, at these two gorgeous but treacherous creatures. ('Shakespeare and the People', p. 4)

Through the high angle shots that serve the purpose of putting the camera in a position of judgement, the production also avoids at least partially the monotony of ever-recurring closeups and medium shots, a necessity on the small screens of the 1970s. In addition, straight angle shots varying from long to medium to closeup unobtrusively change the relation of subjects and objects. For example, long shots of Janet Suzman capture her moving with sensuous grace, and then, as the camera follows her, tracking her subtly in fluid long takes, it tightens gradually into medium shots and finally into closeups that show the play of emotions on her face. Closeups alone cannot show the actor's body in motion, but an excessive use of long shots distances an audience. Gorrie strikes a creative balance.

The camera often becomes the eye of characters rather than an outside eye: we do not see or hear Macbeth enter for the letter scene (I.v), but suddenly Lady Macbeth is aware that he is there – so acute is her connection to him – and then the camera turns to him, from her perspective. Several times, a character reacts to someone off frame and then the camera turns to that person: Malcolm sees the bleeding sergeant off-frame and runs to him (I.ii.3). Duncan notices Lady Macbeth off frame, and then the camera shows her to us (I.vi.10). Banquo turns after his soliloquy (III.i.11) to find Macbeth and Lady Macbeth with a small retinue standing above him, a position that puts him at a disadvantage. The effect is to place the audience within the action, to make them see both *with* the character and as one *of* the observers.

If setting and camerawork are artfully unobtrusive, costuming is outlandish and showy. The smooth-textured thanes' battledress is fancifully decorated with wing-like projections at the shoulders and with fantastic geometric designs in silver, grey and black, splendidly and differently marked for each. The thanes are distinguished from the soldiers, the latter wearing more modest black costumes but studded with silver all over. Lady Macbeth has a dramatically figured black and white close-fitting gown, layered with a full apron (or *houppelande*) in a soft gold for the first act, uncovered for the second. As king and queen Macbeth and his wife have gorgeous, brilliant red and gold robes, different from Duncan's soft grey-blue robe with silver and gold decorations. This Macbeth does not borrow robe, crown or throne. Duncan's silver winged crown was head-covering, as much helmet as crown; Macbeth's is lead, jagged toothed, not head covering; Duncan's field throne (for I.iv) is a colossus, Macbeth's in his castle a much smaller object, a red-cushioned chair. Symbolically, these differences mark Macbeth's inability to fill his predecessor's place.

The interpretation firmly places Macbeth and Lady Macbeth at the centre; no other character's viciousness obscures the meaning of their evil. Seyton is again the constant attendant, but in contrast to the Seytons in the other television productions, here he is a mild-mannered, discreet servant, who does not have any special pretensions or personality, even though he is the third murderer. As the vicious centre *outside* the society, the witches are, in spite of their rags, supernaturally frightening creatures; still, they do not control Macbeth. Almost always standing close together, they seem women (two old, one middle-aged) who have somehow tapped into dark powers. As a sign of their potency, they supernaturally vanish from view in I.iii, as called for in the stage direction at line 79. The camera effects their disappearance not by showing them vanish but by allowing us to see through Macbeth's eyes that they have: first the camera focuses on them, then cuts to Macbeth, and then quickly back to the spot where they had been. In their place is smoke and three stunted pillar-like protuberances. Bolstered by supernatural powers, the witches seem very certain of themselves. Their confidence makes chillingly poignant their fearful start back from Macbeth's threatened curse (IV.i.105); steeped in evil as they are, they recognise in him an even greater evil (Coursen, in Bulman and Coursen, pp. 247–8). The apparitions they call forth are visible, and each speaks with its own voice. Referring to the stage production – but noting what is true also for the television version – Rosenberg had 'the absolute sense that the Sisters spoke expecting to be believed – and were' (p. 115).

Still, by showing the witches with the titles, both at the beginning and at the end of the production, the camera makes them observers rather than principals, part of the peripheral rather than the central matter, much as the music accompanying them (horn and drum music in a minor key) is outside the narrative. They are a frozen grouping on the heath at the beginning beyond a steaming pool of unlovely black water, into which Macbeth at the end falls. Between these two views, we see the pool dried up and harmless when innocent men cross the heath but a foul cauldron and source of apparitions when Macbeth seeks out the witches. The last shot in the film shows the sombre thanes, who had been kept on their knees for Malcolm's last long speech, moving out of the frame so that the camera can reveal on the heath, just beyond the castle's open wooden door, the three Sisters, like three monoliths. The shot holds under the closing titles. The witches frame the action, and, with those titles fore and aft, the production invests the witches with its own artificiality; that is, the titles call attention to the fact that actors are acting, that cameras are rolling just outside the frame. The production thus expands Shakespeare's metatheatricality, explicit when Macbeth himself refers to life as a poor player. Harry Berger speaks of the effects of metathetricality:

By announcing that the world is imaginary, the poet, playwright, or painter [and, I might add, the director] simultaneously affirms his limits and asserts his power; he reminds his audience that it is all only play, but it turns out to be serious play. In separating imaginary space from the space of readers or spectators ..., the artists may suggest that the audience will see an image of itself as in a mirror, or an analysis of itself refracted through a prism, At the same time, he jealously isolates his own domain, proclaims its autonomy, and demands his audience to attend to the work for its own sake. (*Revisionary Play*, p. 55)

The metatheatrical (or metafilmic) ploy of the titles is a good one for the television production, for, though it may not encourage the audience to see images of themselves, it does force them to 'attend to the work for its own sake', to accept the supernatural on the director's terms, and to observe with some detachment the evil couple. In accord with the metatheatricality invoked by the titles displayed over the action, the director adds artificial sounds, sounds outside the narrative (or, as they are called, 'sounds under'), continually reminding the audience of artifice. Like transitions in radio productions (and in Welles's films, so often influenced by radio), fanfares and drum beats, sometimes for only a few seconds, link scenes. Sound within the narrative is used sparingly, low wind sounds for the witch scenes, for example, so that the external sounds – meant for the audience and unheard by the characters – dominate. Dissolves, the production's favoured transition between scenes, also call attention to artifice. Paradoxically, this artificiality has the effect of riveting attention on Macbeth and his Lady; while the production is artificial, their relationship is realistic and their concord in evil is fascinating.

Together the two actors provide the means for an audience to grasp the emotional reality beneath the words. They have spoken of Duncan and his crown before. Lady Macbeth shows this in her response to the word 'king' in Macbeth's letter; her hesitation and then the wonder in her features tell as much. This is the first time she has read the letter (unlike some other Lady Macbeths who have memorised it), and she gives it her initial, spontaneous response. Similarly, Macbeth's start in his response to the witches' prediction (I.iii.50) shows that he has thought of being king, just as Banquo's easy, unmoved attention to the various predictions testifies that he thinks nothing of such matters. Though he has already imagined murder, this Macbeth knows how wrong usurpation is.

His will drives him against his better nature. Porter incorporates these contradictory principles into his portrayal through the sorrowful expression of his large, brown eyes and through the quavering reluctance of his voice. He is awestruck that the supernatural has found him out, and he takes the witches' greeting to be 'solicitings': incitements to action, enticing temptations. When he responds to Duncan's praise, he can sound sincere and even *be* sincere because he is a moral man who has, like anyone, been visited by sinful thoughts. His reputation is attested to by the responses of those around him. Macduff, though uneasy, does not suspect Macbeth of murdering Duncan. Speaking to Rosse in II.iv, he tells him without a hint of irony that Malcolm and Donalbain appear to be the murderers. Rosse then follows Macduff in trusting Macbeth. Though like Iago in eliciting others' confidence, Porter's Macbeth is unlike him in being a moral man, one who well understands the nature of the sinful thoughts that visit him. Thus his fall into murder is tragic, and the responses of others to him help us to see the depth of the fall. Clearly, Macbeth's wife plays the key role in urging him to act on his sinful thoughts. After he kills the king the last shudders of his moral nature express his terror, regret and remorse. Once he kills the grooms he no longer allows 'compunctious visitings of Nature' to 'Shake [his] fell purpose' (I.v.45–6). This is a Macbeth whose moral commitments cease to haunt him.

From the beginning, he does not like the idea that Banquo will father kings; we hear it in the way he says 'Your children shall be kings' (I.iii.86). This thought rankles him and gives him pause early on; most Macbeths never think about this until it is too late. Though he and his wife are not old, they may be beyond childbearing, for this Macbeth is not especially moved by his wife's declaration that she would have dashed out the brains of her own child. In this production, they have no children, they had no children, and this is a moot point. Her declaration about the child she has nursed, his 'Bring forth men children only!' are purely metaphoric, not historically accurate, prophetic or hortatory. It is not, then, that he wants to preserve some dynasty of his own in preference to Banquo's; rather, his is the spleen of a man who sees another get for nothing something for which he has paid so dearly. Porter brings to life Macbeth's complaint:

For Banquo's issue have I fil'd my mind;
For them the gracious Duncan have I murther'd;

[95]

Put rancours in the vessel of my peace,
Only for them; and mine eternal jewel
Given to the common Enemy of man,
To make them kings, the seed of Banquo kings! (III.i.64–9)

All Macbeths say these lines, but for Porter especially they are another telling feature of his characterisation: the portrayal of the conscious man, who knows what he has done and what he is about to do. Rather than sinking in remorse, he suppresses all his sensibilities, all his morality. But in doing so, he cannot retain connections to others, particularly his wife. He does not even bother to dismiss her in the first court scene (III.i); he simply walks away from her, unthinkingly, and, her gaze following him (in long shot at rearframe, with his worried face in foreframe); then she turns and leaves him. When he speaks of the dreams that shake him nightly, she is all too familiar with this complaint, is tortured by the iteration of *his* torture (III.ii.16–26); like Siddons's Lady, she must suffer *her* tortures silently, stoically. Working together, Suzman and Porter show how often Macbeth and Lady Macbeth have gone over the same ground.

When we recall what he was and when we see what he is capable of in the statesmanlike *way* in which he speaks to the murderers (putting aside the content of his speech to them), taking both the higher-ranking and inferior murderer into his confidence, we are made aware of the depth of this Macbeth's tragedy. What a falling off is here! Once he embarks on this path, he does not look backward. He is still capable of painful reflections (as in the 'tomorrow' speech), but he takes full responsibility for his decisions and does not waste any effort in futile remorse and misgivings. Porter's Macbeth twice excuses his behaviour on the grounds of inexperience: By 'Things bad begun make strong themselves by ill' (III.ii.55) he means he is determined to become more adept at badness. By referring to the 'initiate fear, that wants hard use' and by saying 'We are yet but young in deed' (III.iv.142–3) he means that experience will make them both better evil-doers. With his intent stare at Lady Macbeth as he says these lines, he shows that the 'we' is not the royal pronoun but the 'we' of partnership. In the last act, as one would expect from this kind of Macbeth, he fights with spirit and loses to Macduff in the process of trying to brain him with a rock.

For Lady Macbeth, the end is different. Overcome with remorse, she cannot move forward to repentance. She understands her

husband very well, that mix of goodness – 'what thou wouldst
highly, / That wouldst thou holily' – and evil in him:

> wouldst not play false,
> And yet wouldst wrongly win; thou'dst have, great Glamis,
> That which cries, 'Thus thou must do', if thou have it;
> And that which rather thou dost fear to do,
> Than wishest should be undone. (I.v.20–5)

Like Macbeth, she assumes that the greeting of the witches bodes
'metaphysical aid', which she further invokes in her 'fell purpose'
speech. With a sibilant intake of breath when she says 'Come, you
spirits', she looks around, up, for them, her expressive hands
conjuring them. Her deep feeling for Macbeth goes well beyond
her ambition for herself and for him. She is warm, admiring,
affectionate. Her firm response, though, to his hesitant statement
that Duncan 'comes here to-night' frightens him. He had himself
said, 'let that be, / Which the eye fears, when it is done, to see'
(I.iv.52–3). However, he had said it neither reluctantly nor cruelly
but with full awareness of the implications. She speaks differently,
full of exultant amorality. She looks at him carefully. Troubled
because he knows his answer 'To-morrow as he purposes' is a lie
(as it is in this production), he visibly slumps at her reply: 'O!
never / Shall sun that morrow see!' (I.v.60–1). Yet he knew she
would respond so. This is a Macbeth who wrote his letter precisely
so that his Lady would persuade him, though he is not sure he
wants to be persuaded. He tries to break into her speech with
objections, but she will not let him; this is a pattern they follow in
their early discourse. Light-hearted, she is certain that she can
'chastise with the valour of [her] tongue / All that impedes [him]
from the golden round' (I.v.27). He says 'We will speak further'
(71) steadfastly, but without eagerness. He wants to defer the
decision rather than avoid it entirely. She kisses him at the end
and walks up the stairs, expecting him to follow. When he remains
behind, thoughtful, her hand reaches into the frame, takes his,
and she leads him away.

Their next scene (I.vii) amplifies the impressions of this last
one. Moved by 'When you durst do it, then you were a man', he
splutters out his final argument against her with real fervour and
fear: 'If we should fail?' He is frightened more of failure than of
doing wrong. By her 'We fail!' she means, 'So what, you baby; isn't
the chance worth taking?' She's angry and impatient. She pauses,

controls herself with an effort and walks away, deciding how to work on him. She returns, controls her tone of voice, puts her hands on him, embraces him and tells him how it can be done. It is this plan that convinces him. Up to this point, he had debated with himself about doing it without thought about how. His eagerness at the plan, his quick amplification of it ('Will it not be receiv'd ...') demonstrates that *how* had been the true stumbling block. With 'who *dares* receive it other' (*dares* drawn-out exultantly and thus pointedly echoic of his earlier 'I dare do all that may become a man; / Who dares do more, is none') she is conscious of the power they will wield, their ability to make falsehood into truth by sheer will. She thus speaks with unconscious recognition to his true and first reason for reluctance, his fear of discovery, judgement and human retribution. When he says he is settled, she closes her eyes for a second and lifts her head, then smiles, chuckles and off they go together. It would seem that Lady Macbeth is in control in this scene, that this marks the apogee of her ascendance. But the fact that she convinces him by echoing his concerns ('Who dares receive it other?') puts her in balance with him. She has simply allowed him to arrive where he wanted to go.

When she next enters waiting for him to murder Duncan, she is still full of notions of power. She feels aroused, saying 'He is about it' sensually. Calming herself by sheer will, she muses about her virtual accomplishment of the deed herself. From the text, we might infer from Lady Macbeth's declarations that she had fully intended to do the deed herself: 'my keen knife' she had said to herself (I.v.52), and 'Leave all the rest to me', she had said to Macbeth (I.v.73). Later, she implies they will carry out the murder together:

What cannot you and I perform upon
Th'unguarded Duncan? what not put upon
His spongy officers, who shall bear the guilt
Of our great quell. (I.vii.70–3)

Still, when we next see Macbeth, we understand that he is to wield the knife himself: 'Is this a dagger ... such an instrument I was to use' (II.i.33–43). Suzman interprets this point for her Lady Macbeth: she was to have been an accomplice only and never meant anything more than that she would prepare the way for Macbeth by daring to enter the room of the sleeping king with a drugged potion for the grooms and then ring the bell for Macbeth.

When Suzman says 'Had he not resembled / My Father as he slept, I had done't' (II.ii.12–13), she makes us understand that, if she *had* killed Duncan, she would have gone beyond her original intentions. She tightens her mouth and says it with quiet pride, as if a bit surprised at herself that she *could* have done it. At the very moment that she finds in herself a formerly hidden well of strength, however, we begin to perceive that her actual power over Macbeth, now that the murder has been committed, is diminishing. She is now subordinate to him in the sense that she can do little more than react to his starts and fears. Her response to Macbeth is maternal, supportive, and though she despises him for not being able to return the daggers to the grooms, she treats him still as an accomplice and is confidential and easy in her description of what she plans to do with the king's blood. When she returns, she sniffs at her hands, seemingly without abhorrence but for an aware audience foreshadowing 'Here's the smell of the blood still' (V.i.46); she then reaches her hands out to him for his approval. But he starts back in horror.

If she finds her ability to kill unexpected, if she is pleased with the blood on her hands, nevertheless her inability to dissemble appropriately when she responds to Macduff's shouts begins to undermine her confidence (II.iii.72). For here she is a poor player, obviously acting, asking false-sounding questions, casting uneasy glances up the stairs. Wrapped in a fur robe, she covers her mouth, which might give her away and which *does* give her away with the inane question: 'What! in our house?' (II.iii.86). The director does not allow us to see her faint in closeup, so he loses an opportunity to add another stroke to the character's portrait. If he had, it should have been a actual faint. While she did not faint at the sight of all that blood, blood sufficient to smear the sleepy grooms, she faints now when her inability to compose herself catches her unprepared. But her decisive moment of transition from confident ambition to wretched remorse begins when Macbeth ignores her in their first court scene (III.i.43–4). Then upon her re-entry in the next scene, rubbing her hands in another foreshadowing motion, she shows us the workings of her thinking between the scenes. Suzman illuminates Lady Macbeth's state of mind in her brief but telling soliloquy:

> Nought's had, all's spent,
> Where our desire is got without content:

'Tis safer, to be that which we destroy,
Than by destruction dwell in doubtful joy. (III.ii.4–7)

She is sunk in misery. Without knowing Macbeth's plans for Banquo and Fleance, she says 'But in them Nature's copy's not eterne' in full innocence. Having in their first scene led him out (I.v), then exited with him in their second (I.vii), she now follows Macbeth slowly.

From here on, she moves further and further from Macbeth. At the banquet, the camera keeps her mainly in long shot – except when she speaks privately to Macbeth – to emphasise her distance from him. After the others have left, when she warily, wearily, seats herself across from him, she reaches her hand out to him, not as a spontaneous but as a studied action. But there is no warmth in her gesture, and he as mechanically touches her hands with his for only a moment. He asks her to come with him, but she remains behind, staring at her hand and bringing it to her face with a look of wretched disgust. Their division is complete. The effect of the fadeout at the end of the scene, one of the few in the production, marks not only the break between them but also the turn in Macbeth to absolute and motiveless viciousness. The murder of Duncan is based on ambition, that of Banquo on fear and jealousy, but the murder of the Macduff family is gratuitously violent.

For her sleepwalking scene, Lady Macbeth speaks to Macbeth in tones she had never used to him – strident, harsh, bitter. As her mind takes her through former scenes with Macbeth to hateful knowledge of her present condition, her tones change to pitiful wretchedness. The director is too literal-minded here when he has Lady Macbeth dip her hands in an actual laver. This makes hash of the gentlewoman's words that 'It is an accustom'd action with her, to seem thus washing her hands' (V.i.27–8). Otherwise, however, Suzman realises the pathos of this beautiful woman caught in ineffectual remorse, unable to approach repentance, unable to use the water of purification and baptism to cleanse herself.

Though the production emphasises the two principals, other characterisations contribute to the overall effect. For example, the English scene is set very differently from the Scottish scenes, with soft gold draperies, gold pillars, a clean black and white tile floor, and the effect of clear, blue skies. The director thus points the differences between the two courts and signals the graciousness of the English one. Similarly, Malcolm grows from a boy with a few hairs on his face to a man with an established beard and moustache. Fully in control during the debate with Macduff, he shows a remarkable ability to play a part, able to lie about himself with tears of remorse for his wickedness. These tears elicit from Macduff an assurance that though Malcolm be immoral he can yet be a worthy king, 'With other graces weigh'd' (IV.iii.90). After he perfunctorily condemns Malcolm's supposed iniquities, John Woodvine's Macduff indicates that he will find them acceptable. Malcolm further plays a role when, in attempting to fortify Macduff, he withholds expressions of pity and fear for Macduff's tragedy, and yet, when Macduff leaves the frame with Rosse, Malcolm turns to the camera and allows his deeper feelings to show. He is not a completely known entity in this production, but he makes us sense that he does have the 'king-becoming graces' that augur well for Scotland's future. Thus, the production dramatises Janet Adelman's opinion that the scene with Malcolm and Macduff marks a decided turning point in the text as the forces of good begin to prevail (p. 11). But this turning point is far from inevitable, as we can see from the other productions that choose a more ambiguous ending or shed no light on the dark night of the soul. Such a one is the BBC production in their series 'The Shakespeare Plays'.

Nicol Williamson and Jane Lapotaire directed by Jack Gold

Nicol Williamson, the Macbeth for the 1982 BBC production directed by Jack Gold, recreated for television many aspects of his interpretation for two Trevor Nunn productions in 1974 and 1975, in which Helen Mirren played Lady Macbeth and Jane Lapotaire (Lady Macbeth in 1982) doubled as one of the witches and Lady Macduff. A major problem with the television production, about which some reviewers of the stage productions also complained, lies in Williamson's vocal technique. He is given to starts and fears that express themselves through rasping intakes of breath and hoarse, nasal declamation. While his voice ranges over a wide scale, the snorts become wearisome after a while. This irritation aside, Gold's interpretation effectively maps out, as does Gorrie's, the crossover of Macbeth from weakness to strength and Lady Macbeth from strength to weakness. But the nature of the chiasmus is different for Williamson's Macbeth and Jane Lapotaire's Lady. Their weakness results not from moral repugnance but rather from fear – for him, fear of failure and for her, fear of what he has become. Like Porter's Macbeth, Williamson's main question, like that of his Trevor Nunn Macbeths, is a fearful 'If we should fail?' Once Lady Macbeth shows him that they need not fail, he is very much 'settled', for nothing else has really stopped him – not all his other arguments about kinship, kingship and hospitality. If anything makes Williamson's Macbeth appear to be a heroic character it is his unbending will to follow to its bitter conclusion the path he has chosen, bouts of terror – as at the banquet – notwithstanding. At the end, bolstered by the predictions of the three Sisters, certain that he cannot be killed, he toys with Young Siward and outmatches Macduff. No other production considered in this study shows so explicitly that Macbeth could have beaten Macduff if not unmanned by the equivocal prophecy.

The exposure of this vein in Macbeth's character, the violent nature that is ready to spring into action once fear is removed, is precisely what causes Lady Macbeth's downfall. She pays for not having read him correctly. Thinking that he wanted to accomplish his ambitions 'holily', she thought she would have to be the one to do – or at least stage – the deed. She had been taken in – just as Duncan had been taken in – by the sincerity of his protestations. She thought that she knew the extent of his wickedness through a recognition of her own. But his far, far exceeds hers. Physically much smaller than he is, she seems vulnerable to his outbreaks of violence. Even early she has not much control over him, for she has to exert all of her little body's force to pull and then push him back to their chamber after the murder of Duncan (II.ii). Just as Judith Anderson's Lady in her sleepwalking returns to her gestures from II.ii, Lapotaire's returns in *her* sleepwalking scene to these pulling and pushing gestures. When Macbeth speaks to her before Banquo's murder, he unthinkingly almost throttles her; he is a dangerous man even with her, remembering her only when she quavers out 'What's to be done?' and he comes back to the present moment with a start. While he looks away from her, she is terrified, but, as his gaze locks with hers, she controls her demeanour, softening it to uneasiness: she is afraid to reveal how much she fears him. At the banquet, just feeling his hands on her shoulders as he says 'Fair remembrancer' makes her uneasy. Her moments of control over him had been few and had given her a deceptive illusion of power.

For the rest, the production, like Schaefer's, solves some

problems and creates others. Lady Macbeth is memorable for her orgasmic writings as she calls upon the 'Spirits / That tend on mortal thoughts'. When she says 'unsex me here', she most assuredly does not mean take away her sexuality. She means simply take away her woman's repugnance for violence. When she speaks of her baby (I.vii.54–9), Macbeth's reaction makes it apparent that there have indeed been such infants who were most precious to them both, whom both of them loved, and who are no more. The camera shoots him facing forward in mid-shot, his back to her. She is slightly behind him and also facing forward. We can thus watch them both. Her willingness to dash the brains out if she had so sworn is indeed a powerful willingness. The pain of this childlessness goes far to explain Macbeth's irrational hatred of everyone else's progeny – of Duncan's, of Banquo's, of Macduff's. Long before this production, Cleanth Brooks wrote of the importance of the 'naked babe' image and the other images of children that work with it. The BBC production, through Williamson's and Lapotaire's countenances, corroborates the effectiveness in performance of Brooks's analysis.

The mutuality of Macbeth and his wife is expressed through their language to and with each other. They are accustomed, evidently, to talking to each other in clichés, for after he is settled on murder, he recites the final couplet of the scene accompanied by her sotto voce echoes and her nods of the head in unison: 'Away, and mock the time with fairest show: / False face must hide what the false heart doth know' (I.vii.81–2). This happens again to a lesser degree just before they exit to attend the banquet: 'Things bad begun make strong themselves by ill' (III.ii.55). Their soliloquies, however, reveal the differences that separate them.

In his first soliloquies (or asides), he has no thought of her. His start at the witches' hailings uncovers the wicked thoughts he has already nurtured in his viper bosom. Though he has evidently managed until this moment to suppress them, only with difficulty does he restrain them now. In voiceover, he seems earnest, pleased at what is promised him: 'The greatest is behind' appears to mean that two of the three predictions have already come true – he is Glamis, he is Cawdor; he is two-thirds of the way to his goal. Just as plausibly, his joyful expression could mean happy anticipation that the greatest of the three predictions is still to come ('behind' could denote either idea). With these happy thoughts, he speaks to Banquo with ease and playfulness: 'Do you not hope

5   Nicol Williamson and Jane Lapotaire in Jack Gold's BBC
production of *Macbeth*, 1982, promotional photograph

your children shall be kings ...?' and responds to Banquo's more
serious rejoinder, 'That, trusted home, / Might yet enkindle you
unto the crown ...' with pretended modesty, with a negative shake
of the head; evidently Macbeth as king is not a far-fetched idea.
Banquo, however, continues with his warning that 'oftentimes, to
win us to our harm, / The instruments of Darkness tell us truths; /
... to betray's / In deepest consequence'. While appearing to listen
to Banquo's friendly warning, with Banquo looking deeply into
his eyes, Macbeth obviously does *not* hear him, for, moments
later, he questions how the supernatural soliciting can be ill, for

'why hath it given me earnest of success, / Commencing in a truth?' (I.iii.132–3). Williamson makes Macbeth's self-delusion complete and obvious, partly because of the attention he *seems* to pay to Banquo.

Williamson stresses the first three syllables of 'I am thane of Cawdor' exultantly. Then he continues to speak in deep tones, with decided pauses before 'horrible imaginings' and 'murther', reflecting psychological blocks to the goal he seeks:

> Present fears
> Are less than [hesitates] horrible imaginings.
> My thought, whose [hesitates] murther yet is but fantastical,
> Shakes so my single state of man,
> That function is smother'd in surmise,
> And nothing is, but what is not. (I.iii.137–42)

But Williamson's Macbeth reaches the summit of disquiet when he thinks of waiting for chance to crown him: 'If Chance will have me King, why, Chance may crown me'. Waiting is a way out of the dilemma to which his thoughts have carried him, but something about that possibility is unlikely; he recognises his thought, it seems, as self-deceptive, from the ironical tone in which he says the lines. Immediately after, his voice become harsh and bitter on 'Come what come may' – a line that could refer to waiting for chance or to taking action.

Michael Goldman, in *Acting and Action in Shakespearean Tragedy* (pp. 94–111), speaks helpfully of the smothering effect of Macbeth's images, not only in this soliloquy but throughout. Williamson captures the effect Goldman finds in the text, ready for an actor to exploit:

> Balances are set up which are quickly undermined by unassimi-lated residues of sound and sense, and this makes the movement from word A to word A' (and sometimes A") neither one of oppo-sition nor simple accumulation, but of a twisting and darkening, a thickening in which the speech thrusts forward into little thickets of sound and into reflections which don't allow the speculative movement to exist, ending literally in a smothering negation. (p. 95)

'Come what come may' is just such a twister, darkening and thickening with the effort to give the two *come*s their different meanings, to balance the proverb about waiting with the opposite intention, as exposed by tone of voice, of proceeding. Williamson finds the contradictions and 'entanglements' in Macbeth's speech without posing as a noble Macbeth seduced into evil. He is as Lady Macbeth describes him: he 'wouldst not play false, / And yet wouldst wrongly win' (I.v.21–2).

This Macbeth's magnetism – that is, his appeal to an audience in spite of his evil nature – is difficult to rationalise. His intelligence, the direct appeal of his speaking to us, that is, into the camera, the apparent respect others early on have for him, the charm he can call forth at will, as he does when he thanks Duncan for the new honours given him – all these strengthen our fascination. He knows and has often mimicked right behaviour: his relationship with Banquo shows that. A skin of civility covers the impostume beneath and might have covered it for ever, considering Macbeth's fear of action. His own wishes, coupled with the witches' prediction and his wife's urging, make him actively evil when otherwise he could have continued to seem outwardly good. In spite of his inherently corrupt nature, Williamson's Macbeth nevertheless plumbs the full depth of regret in 'Wake Duncan with thy knocking: I would thou couldst!' (II.ii.73–4) and in the 'sere, the yellow leaf' soliloquy (V.iii.22–8). Both aspects of his character – the selfishness of evil and the capacity for regret – well up in the 'tomorrow' soliloquy. He begins his response to Lady Macbeth's death with bitter impatience: why had she not died another time, when he was not so busy, when the outcome the three women have promised, as he thinks, the vanquishing of all his enemies, would have been accomplished – tomorrow. The word itself sets off his imagination: as Goldman says, Macbeth 'keeps acutely imagining the horror of what he is doing even while he keeps on doing it' (p. 110). In his 'Tomorrow' speech Williamson's Macbeth sneers his utter disdain for the life he has chosen, a life that has jumped the life to come, and thus a life that is meaningless, 'full of sound and fury, / Signifying nothing' (V.v.27–8). But he continues on with his choice, playing it out to the end. Williamson delineates a grandly diabolic Macbeth, somehow true to his own principles.

This Macbeth begins and ends without concern for his 'partner in greatness'. Though a sexual bond and the memory of the children they have lost joins them at the beginning, the murders and his rising rage sever those bonds absolutely. Her soliloquy after Macbeth has spoken to the murderers and then her colloquy with Macbeth show their separation. With a forced smile, she asks her gentlewoman if Banquo has left the court. Rubbing her hands just as she will when sleepwalking, she speaks her anguished lines of discontent – 'Nought's had, all's spent' (III.ii.4–7) – standing by the same narrow window where she had described her power over him: 'Hie thee hither ...' (I.v. 25–8). When he comes to her fresh from planning Banquo's murder, and when with a jerk of the head, coldly, he wants to know what she wants of him, she tries to smile, goes to him, and reaches her arms up to him. But he snatches them roughly and does not let her embrace him. He effectively cuts her out of his life. Her sleepwalking soliloquy depicts her as more concerned with herself than with him, though throughout he is certainly more in her thoughts than she is in his. He never mentions her or thinks of her in any soliloquy. When, sleepwalking, she can relive the earlier days, she regains her equanimity. She flashes a bright smile when she hears the bell and starts to walk through the arch leading to Duncan's room as if she will commit the murder herself. Then she stops, and with a most desperately frightened and miserable 'Hell is murky', turns away. Smelling her hands is a compulsion and a whip to her conscience. Lapotaire's portrayal is varied, believable and mesmer-ising. We pity the wretch.

The production designs are intelligent and effective without swamping the main characterisations. Gold employs the super-natural to create a mysterious atmosphere without detracting from Macbeth's culpability, beginning the first scene with a dreary, misty long view of a Stonehenge-like structure on which are three protuberances. Low thunder rumbles in the distance here and frequently in the performance. As the camera moves closer, the lumps unfold and rise to their knees – they are the rag-muffled figures of the three witches. Later, for the cauldron scene (IV.i), they will meet Macbeth under this structure, again beneath a dreary sky. For their first greeting of Macbeth (I.iii), they stand on the blasted heath in a triangle into which Macbeth and Banquo unconsciously enter. These hags, who might be, considering costume and skin texture, part mineral, do not control events supernaturally – though they do appear at moments throughout to observe (after II.iv, and between V.iv and V.v). Nothing much moves these phlegmatic figures, neither Macbeth's ranting threats in IV.i nor their own mischief. Similarly downplaying the supernatural, the director makes the dagger a dagger of the mind (as it is for all these television productions); the ghost does not appear, nor do any apparitions, nor does any show of kings. All, it seems, are in Macbeth's mind. Still, the witches through their quiet power are among the most enigmatic of any production.

Creative lighting and set design continue throughout the production, with, for example, a reddish haze, mist and a strange sky with a baleful red sun low on the horizon for the bloody sergeant scene. There is bright, clear but unsunny light for the castle – an abstract setting where outside and inside merge, with geometric shapes defining a window, a stairway to the thrones, the arch leading to inner chambers, the battlements, and a jagged-toothed portcullis. Deeper blue skies and brighter geometric shapes represent the English court. (The description by the set designer in the text published by the BBC is useful, pp. 20–2.)

The production also catches, through costume and gesture, the effect of rapidly unfolding events. Macbeth and Lady Macbeth, in sleeveless scarlet robes over the garments we have already seen, greet their court after the murder of Duncan. When Macbeth rudely dismisses her, we next see her just removing her robe and crown, as if her words with her gentlewoman (at the beginning of III.ii) are taking place while Macbeth is speaking with the murderers (III.i). When he enters to her soon after, he is still in his robe and crown, and at the end he replaces her crown on her head and leads her off to attend the banquet. Thus the murder of Banquo seems to be taking place at that very moment. Events take place concurrently instead of sequentially, speeding up the apparent pace.

The main visual flaw of the production is its static blocking. Information in the BBC text of the play reveals that a very large studio was used, allowing, it would seem, for ample movement and creative camera work. Sometimes this space works well, as when Lady Macbeth and Macbeth, starting from a far distance, zigzag between a long column of courtiers in their first court scene while Banquo in near frame speaks his soliloquy. They reach him in time for Macbeth's words with him, and Macbeth, his arm around his former friend's shoulder, walks with him while they speak. Aside from such moments, the aim seems to have been to render actions emblematic rather than realistic. After Duncan and his thanes enter the frame to find the bleeding sergeant, they all (except Malcolm) stand stiffly and implacably at a distance. Again, as the English and Scottish forces join in their march against Dunsinane, all the men stand stiffly in a row. Gold has not developed a stylised approach to the production that might motivate such static moments – as Nunn did for his production with Ian McKellen a few years before. Also, in group scenes, Gold's camera does not always allow us to see what we want to see. At the banquet, for example, for too long he withholds any evidence about how the thanes are taking Macbeth's outburst. (In contrast, Gorrie's camera allows us to see that the thanes do not overhear Macbeth speaking to Lady Macbeth until Macbeth raises his voice upon 'behold such sights', III.iv.113). Gold in effect denies us information about how much the thanes hear and understand. Near the end of the banquet, Gold has one-shots of first one, then another thane looking suspicious, and that must content us.

But there is an even more important interpretative problem. When Macbeth is essentially noble, as Porter's is, as Evans's is, Scotland can be seen as having regained its health once the tyrant is cut out of the body politic. But in the Gold version, Macbeth is so evil that it seems impossible to completely purify the country at the end. Gold heightens the ambiguity by reintroducing in the last scenes Fleance, whose halo of curly hair distinguishes him from the other thanes (though several reviewers, in fact, did not recognise him). He arrives with others in V.ii to join against Macbeth, and he is the one on whom the camera focuses at the end – Fleance at the steps to the throne, looking out at the camera with an enigmatic expression: beyond him, on the steps, lies the body of Macbeth. The camera then turns to Malcolm, then the thanes, but returns at the last to Fleance, holding the shot, which finally fades to blood red. Malcolm is king, but, the final shot asks, for how long? The look on the faces of the thanes is suspicious and apprehensive. Is Fleance as king, as new usurper, a good thing or a bad thing?

The doubtfulness about the ending is exacerbated by the characterisation of Seyton. As in the Schaefer film, he is the ever-present attendant but here even more chilling. While other men have longish hair or thick beards or both, Seyton is clean-shaven with a brush cut. The military costume and the haircut, as well as the look in his eye and about the mouth seem designed to make the audience think 'Nazi'. In the camera's last view of him he is silently standing at the foot of the stairs below the throne (the same stairs upon which Macbeth dies and where Fleance will stand) as Macbeth moves away to seek out his destiny (at the end of V.v). Seyton does not follow his master and in fact disappears from the production. When justice has not been dealt out fully, the play ends uneasily. For this Seyton is among the most vicious subordinates in any production – even more wicked than Polanski's Rosse, who at least has the motive of self-interest. Gold's Seyton appears to enjoy murder for its own sake, smiling as he wields the knife. He is not the messenger who comes to Lady Macbeth with news of Duncan's arrival; this Seyton is far too highly placed to be a mere messenger, and he has nothing to do with Lady Macbeth. He asserts the 'rightness' of masculine collaboration in murder. Macbeth chooses him over the Lady in the first court scene, dismissing everyone except him, decisively rejecting Lady Macbeth with a sarcastic 'While then, God be with you' (III.i.43). His tone to her contrasts sharply with the transposed, urgent and conspiratorial, 'Seyton [*sic*], a word with you' that precedes it (III.i.44). Seyton, ever the faithful attendant, watches carefully when Rosse and Macduff confer together after the murder (II.iv); he also stands with Macbeth when the two murderers are interviewed, looking on sardonically. He is the third murderer, of course, and as soon as Banquo is dead and Fleance has escaped, he stabs the two murderers, leaving all three bodies. Intent on watching his master, he tries to catch every nuance of his thoughts, even to anticipate him in evil. With three henchmen, he heads the attack on Macduff's castle, and leads the others in a game of tossing Macduff's son from man to man until a final toss impales the boy on his sword. A blurred view and a scream at the end of this scene suggests that Lady Macduff will similarly be played with before being killed. Productions that make others besides Macbeth as bad as this production makes Seyton introduce a problem; for, if Macbeth's chief trait is an overwhelming descent into his innate evil, and if there are others about him who have already, quietly, with no fuss, descended, a spectator is left questioning what the tragedy means. This questioning is not necessarily a bad thing.

But the society here does have some good in it. If Duncan and the thanes are mere stick figures (with Angus, Menteth, Cathness appearing throughout and thus, like other supernumeraries, not receiving any particular characterisation), Rosse does show feeling for Macduff after he brings the news of the deaths of his family. The effect may be due, in part, to the tight focus of the television camera, but Rosse keeps his hands on Macduff's upper arms, supporting him and palpably making his benevolent sympathy flow into the grieving man. With this characterisation, an audience is less likely to blame Rosse for underestimating the danger that Lady Macduff faced in being left alone – and thus less likely to blame Macduff. He, too, is a good man, who barely can stomach the thoughts of lechery and avarice in his monarch and who expresses, indeed, a deep repugnance when he says 'This avarice / Sticks deeper, grows with more pernicious root / Than summer-seeming lust' (IV.iii.84–6). We see that he is concerned less with losing his own possessions than with Malcolm's moral fiber. Gold sheds indirect light on Macduff's lines, creating what is conceivably the best interpretation of this thane – if what is wanted is a noble Macduff. Because other productions' Macduffs seem content with their future king's lechery and avarice, they lack rectitude.

Gold's Banquo, too, seems a good sort (Ian Hogg, who played the most vicious of the murderers in Polanski's Macbeth), warning Macbeth about the 'instruments of Darkness' as a worried friend, not one who fears Macbeth's integrity. Rosse, Macduff and Banquo preclude a nihilistic view of the society and make it impossible to see Macbeth simply as the product of his time. The BBC production offers a brilliant portrait of the thane that can be more appealing to modern sensibilities than that of the earlier television versions because it frankly confronts the mystery and power of demonic energy.

CHAPTER V

The production: visionary directors on stage and screen

Orson Welles's 1936 'Voodoo' *Macbeth* and its reincarnation on film

We Work Again, a film produced in 1937 by Pathé News and the Works Project Administration (the United States' government's answer to Depression unemployment), contains a few minutes of Orson Welles's 1936 staged *Macbeth*, frequently called the 'Voodoo' *Macbeth* because of its importation of African drummers and its foregrounding of the supernatural. Set in the Caribbean to provide an appropriate *mise-en-scène* for the all-black cast, the production evoked the bloody revolutions of nineteenth-century Haiti, adding an uneasy mixture of Christianity, Voodooism and witchcraft. In the filmed extract, a long shot of the full stage shows Lady Macbeth's body lying in state, with Macbeth in shirt-sleeves kneeling at her side and several bystanders looking on. The main impact of the shot, which is from the final moments of the play, derives from the setting, with painted tree shapes upstage behind architectural elements – stairs, a roofed tower and a bridge over a gateway arch, a setting that Welles said later he disliked (Estrin, p. 155). The promptbook calls for these tree shapes to press in as the messenger brings news of the moving grove, but these movements are not visible in the film. Macbeth – Maurice Ellis, who had by then taken the place of Jack Carter – the production's original Macbeth – is a man of action, one who chafes at inaction, who looks cheerful at last as he faces his enemies, who laughs with glee when he shoots Young Siward and then pushes the body off the bridge. Macbeth and Macduff start their battle with guns, turning to swords when the bullets fail to reach their marks, dashing up the stairs across the bridge. While they fight, soldiers (not obscured by the palms of this Birnam Wood, as called for in the script, but simply holding branches) enter the lower stage and fill the apron, shrieking and crying. On the bridge, Macbeth, caught off-guard after hearing that Macduff is not born of woman, is run through. As he teeters on the edge, the witches watch intently. Clutching his wound, he says before he falls from view: 'And be these juggling fiends no more believed'.

The promptbook describes the ending somewhat differently (and production photographs show both versions, indicating, possibly, that there was more than one version during the long run). Richard France, in *Orson Welles on Shakespeare*, not only supplies a copy of the promptbook but also helpfully indicates the textual origins of the lines, making it easy to trace Welles's complex weave. (The script is also available at the Billy Rose Theatre Collection and at the Library of Congress Federal Theater Project Collection in Washington, DC.) In the film, Macduff, on the bridge, raises the pole impaling Macbeth's head; in the promptbook, the three Witches shriek with laughter as

> Macduff kneels behind the battlements and rises to silence the laughter, holding in his hand Macbeth's bloody head. He throws the head into the mass of waving leaves below... At this, the army drops the branches and the jungle collapses, revealing a stage filled with people. Malcolm is on the throne, crowned. All but Hecate and the three Witches bow before him. They have caught Macbeth's head and stand above the body of Lady Macbeth ... [and] gleefully hold the head aloft. (pp. 96–7)

while Macduff says, 'The time is free. / Hail, King of Scotland!' The film clip cuts *of Scotland*, eliminating a name incongruous to the Caribbean setting.

Using the original promptbook, the Henry Street Settlement's New Federal Theatre revived the stage production in 1977, but changes were inevitable. The major one, of course, was the absence of Welles. In addition, casting a woman as Hecate (Louise Stubbs), instead of a man as in 1936, visually diminished the mass of this figure – though with high cork shoes and a full white afro hairstyle she compensated creditably. The orchestra and chorus were gone and along with them most of the special music, diminishing the power found in the original. The 1936 production featured few professionals among the large cast because black actors had then scant opportunities in legitimate theatre. Besides the principals, the only professionals were Eric Burroughs, a huge man who played Hecate with a twelve-foot bullwhip, and Canada Lee, who played Banquo (France, *Yale/Theatre*, p. 74). The presence of many more professional actors in the revival attests to the increased openness of the profession. The 1936 production, unlike the 1977 revival starring Lex Monson and television personality Esther Rolle, cast light-skinned African Americans as the two principals. The political situation, too, had changed by 1977, so the experience of the audience and actors cannot have been the same as it had been in 1936. The 1936 production was paternalistic, with white men in the positions of leadership – though years later the black staff members very readily affirm, in oral histories, that they had had full confidence in the talents of Houseman, the director of the WPA's Negro Theatre Project, and Welles. (Oral histories are in the George Mason University Library.) The 1977 production, on the other hand, with professional talent readily available, was an African American production in all respects. In 1936, though African Americans had suffered so much injustice and open prejudice, they were also, it seems, more hopeful about the future and what could be proved by actors excelling in this important production. It was indeed the point of entry not so much for black actors as for black stagehands, several of whom were enabled to join the unions formerly closed to them; and in its tour around the country, after its twelve-week engagement in New York, it gave African American audiences even in the American South opportunities to see black actors in classical drama. The revival was not expected to have an impact on race relations. The differences between the original version and the revival attest to the influence of social settings on meaning.

John Houseman invited Welles to direct this, Welles's first major production, and supported him without reservation. The twenty-year-old novice director, knowing he was launching a career that he and everyone else who knew him expected to be brilliant, risked all to actuate his vision. The cast was enormous, the total number of cast and crew 137, including thirty-seven 'main' actors. The spectacular effects made possible by the large cast suited Welles but also served the company's mission. The production was for the Classic Branch of the WPA's Negro Theater, whose function was at least twofold: not only to provide work for local (Harlem, New York) people, as did the Contemporary Branch, but also to enhance community pride through 'the performance of classical works ... without concession or reference to colour' (Houseman,

6   Orson Welles' 1936 production of a Voodoo *Macbeth*

p. 184). After its run at the Lafayette Theatre, *Macbeth* toured local high schools where admission could be had for as little as ten cents. To build up the sometimes insufficient voices of the novice actors for the larger theatres in which the production played, Welles invented the idea of amplifying the output of some speeches with wind machines and other sound effects created by a team of musicians backstage, under the distinguished Virgil Thomson's direction (France, *Yale/Theatre*, p. 76), and in his oral history Thomson vouches for the efficacy of the device. Not only was the cast enormous, but also there were spectacular scenery and costumes by Nat Karson; lighting by Feder; and music performed by The Negro Unit Orchestra, led by Joe Jordan, the project's musical director.

Designer Nat Karson's oral history of the 1936 production helps determine the intentions of the design. He attempted, he says, to start on a low key, with muddy reds and blues and with touches of yellows and greens in the principals' costumes. As the play proceeded, the colours became more intense and vibrant, up to the banquet scene, 'the mathematical centre of the play', framed as a coronation ball, with dozens of men and women dancing

[115]

Josef Lanner waltzes in brilliantly coloured and textured costumes, with butlers moving among them, serving them drinks from silver trays. Women were brilliant in jewel-like gowns; men splendid in coloured uniforms. The civilised decorum of the ball is gradually undermined by the insistent drums, as Macbeth, alone, invokes the powers of darkness (from IV.i). White reviewers' racism can be inferred from the comedy they discovered in the brilliantly clad ballroom dancers, served champagne by liveried footmen; it seems that they could not accept as serious the idea that Negroes should be waited upon by other Negroes. Welles, of course, meant the ballroom guests and servants to provide a visual and tonal contrast to the aloneness of the conspiring Macbeth.

From this gorgeous ball to the end, Karson recalls, the colour palate descends

> in key until we reach the sleepwalking scene. This is played in a misty haze of light. In the last act instead of climbing up again in colour, I intensified this misty haze. I felt that with the voodoo scenes so prominent in this version, the actual scenery should at times have an eerie luminescent quality.
>
> Lady Macbeth's nightgown in the murder scene is a white georgette that shades down to a deep red at the hem, obviously signifying the murderous instincts and lust for power, but not losing any traces of femininity. The same costume is used in the sleepwalk scene and manages to give the impression of a dreaming floating walk due to the fact that the red shadings in the gown blend into the background. As to the other costumes the men wear extremely exaggerated coats with flaring shoulders and tightly drawn waistlines ... The general colour scheme of the two opposing forces ... has been divided into green and its derivatives for Macbeth and his cohorts, and multihued reds for Macduff and his army and retainers.

Green is also Duncan's colour, to signify, when Macbeth wears it, the 'usurping of Duncan's position'. The nineteenth-century setting 'in Haiti or thereabouts' provides opportunities for 'an exuberant exaggeration' of the Empire style – a 'West Indian version'. The costumes of the principals are not, however, as exaggerated in shape as are those appearing in ensembles. The vibrancy of the designs contributed significantly to the spectacle, of course, but, even more, the grandeur of the court made audiences see the magnificence Macbeth and his Lady lusted after: for this they had killed Duncan, not for some abstract principle of rulership.

A collage with violent cuts and transpositions, the Voodoo *Macbeth* is Welles's vehicle to re-create his essential notion of the play's meaning – the drama of violent men manipulated and even controlled by supernatural forces. Welles crafted his collage of eight scenes into three acts, incorporating parts of the usually excised Hecate scene (III.v) into the play's first scene and sprinkling it through the production. The second scene illustrates his method of using Shakespeare's script as an open resource, to be exploited at will: Welles starts with the letter scene including Macbeth's entrance (I.v), continues with Duncan's brief greetings to Macbeth and Banquo followed immediately by his promotion of Malcolm (I.iv) combined with Duncan's arrival at the Palace (I.vi). Welles inserts a bit about Duncan healing the cripples inspired by the English king's powers (from IV.iii), then plunges into Lady Macbeth's persuasion (I.vii), immediately followed by the scenes before, during and after the murder (II.i, II.ii, II.iii), finally repeating part of the witches' sabbath (I.iii). For the most part, Welles keeps the basic chronology of Shakespeare's play but punctuates it with events out of sequence.

Posters at The Billy Rose Theatre Collection at the New York Public Library at Lincoln Center emphasise the Voodoo elements, promising mysterious spectacles. One poster for the Lafayette Theatre has, behind the writing, filling the page, a horned Voodoo head. Another poster that does not mention Welles shows three witches with a large cauldron. The promise was kept in performance: of eight scenes, Voodoo sorcerers appear in six. Welles's general method of amplifying the supernatural can be seen by the way he handles the aftermath of Duncan's murder. Cripples one by one enter and kneel humbly to Macbeth, looking now to him for their cure. The descriptive commentary is from the promptbook: 'Then, from above, come the hoarse voices of the three Witches, chanting quickly and sharply':

Weary sev'nights, nine times nine,
Shall he dwindle, peak, and pine. [I.iii.22–3]

(The three Witches are seen huddled on the wall. Under their chant has come the rapid throb of drums. This reaches a crescendo under a new voice that is Hecate's, loud and rasping. He is seen suddenly at the very top of the tower, leaning over the throned Macbeth below. The light of an angry dawn flames brighter behind him as he speaks. The courtyard is in shadows. The cripples are strange shapes in the gateway. Hecate and the three Witches are birds of prey.)

Hecate speaks the lines of the first witch from I.iii that refer to a sailor whose wife has insulted her. Here, though, they apply to Macbeth:

I'll drain him dry as hay.
Sleep shall neither night nor day
Hang upon his penthouse lid.
    (Drums stop.)
He shall live a man forbid.
    (A thump of the drum on the last syllable of 'forbid'.)
Blackout, end of act one. (France, *Orson Welles*, p. 62)

Though he cuts many of the witches' lines, Welles makes the powers of darkness dominant and powerful through repetition and through their constant presence. When the curtain falls after most scenes and after each act, the impression left with an audience is control by the supernatural elements. The first scene of Act II ends with Hecate in silhouette at the gateway, beckoning Macbeth into the jungle, to 'know ... the worst' (p. 76). Momentary darkness: then the act concludes in scene ii with a spectacular cauldron scene (IV.i), with Macbeth's resolution to kill Macduff and his family divided between him and Hecate. The second scene ends with another curse by Hecate (from III.v (p. 81)). In the third act, the last words of the play, from I.iii – 'Peace. The charm's wound up' – are Hecate's. Not only does Welles have the supernatural figures repeat their own lines, but also they take lines and roles given to other characters in Shakespeare: for the sleepwalking scene (V.i), Lady Macbeth is accompanied by witches – not a doctor and gentlewoman. Welles combines this scene with a mix from the scenes with the insurgents (V.ii and V.iv), with Hecate, not Malcolm, commanding the boughs of Birnam Wood to be hewn down (pp. 89–90).

To intensify the omnipresence of the supernatural elements further, the 1936 script often calls for a 'Voodoo effect', the sound of drums and at times chantings, distant rumblings of thunder, an aural underpinning of almost all the action (see France, *Yale/Theatre*, p. 68). Voodoo chants and dances were under the direction of Asadata Dafora Horton. An African witch doctor named Abdul, on stage as The Witch Doctor, led the team of drummers (and, according to Houseman, p. 203, practised some witch doctoring on an unfavourable critic). Welles also uses special visual effects to multiply the original play's supernatural elements: both the dagger that Macbeth sees before him and the ghost were crafted, it seems, from papier mâché, possibly enhanced by lighting effects (further information may be forthcoming if Feder's recollections of the production are ever released). The very fact that so much has to be done to magnify the supernatural underlines the relative weakness of those elements in the Folio text.

The powers of evil, in control from the beginning, never relinquish it for a moment. Welles's *Macbeth* is tragic only in the medieval sense: a king, descending with the wheel of fortune, falls from rule to death. Jack Carter, the actor who played Macbeth at the opening and who brought to his role the truculence of his own psyche, was a troubled person whose alcoholism finally forced him to leave the show. Six foot two, handsome and athletic, he had not known until adolescence of his African American heritage and embraced it belligerently (Houseman, pp. 194–5). Carter's Lady Macbeth, Edna Thomas, somewhat older than Carter, was a motherly person, and the sensuality of their onstage relationship was complicated by a faintly incestuous element (Houseman, p. 204). But the actors' personalities and the motives of their characters, while certainly adding interest to their portrayals, appear to have little to do with the ability of Hecate and the forces of darkness to control them, for, when those powers cannot manipulate men, they dispose of them. Though Welles's Duncan, for example, has the gracious, healing touch ascribed in the play to Edward the Confessor (IV.iii.141–59), Hecate and his cohorts, acting through Macbeth, murder him. At the end, because they dominate the scene visually and have the last words, Malcolm clearly will be subject to their manipulations also. Setting and lighting, use of supernumeraries, transposed speeches given new emphasis – all these combine to achieve Welles's purposes.

Welles moulds his interpretation in many ways other than by the transpositions and cuts of his collage. At times Welles gives the speeches of a non-supernatural character to another. Lady Macbeth, overhearing the announcement about Malcolm, says to Macbeth 'that is a step / On which you must fall down or else o'er-leap, / For in your way it lies' (p. 47); since her words are from Macbeth's aside in the text (I.iv.48–50), Welles magnifies her instigation, already implicit in the text as a whole. Characters often speak openly where the text has soliloquies. Further emphasising her culpability, Welles has Lady Macbeth, with the persuasion of I.vii merging into II.i and II.ii, taunt Macbeth with a challenge (from II.ii, where it is a soliloquy):

> The doors are open, and the surfeited grooms
> Do mock their charge with snores. I have drugged their possets,
> That death and nature do contend about them
> Whether they live or die. (p. 53)

When Macbeth appears to hesitate, 'she speaks sharply' to him, the prompt notes, saying 'Had he not resembled / My father as he slept, I had done't' (p. 53), which in Shakespeare is also part of her soliloquy. Her taunt persuades him and he goes. Lady Macbeth speaks her desolate lines beginning 'Naught's had, all's spent' (from III.ii.4–7) bitterly to Macbeth (rather than alone) as she stares at the throne, making the two seem more at one in their unease than do many productions (p. 68). Banquo, too, speaks his suspicions in Macbeth's first court scene openly to Macbeth, with 'menace and mockery in his tone' (p. 63), announcing himself as Macbeth's rival, inciting his own execution (this and many interpretative choices appear in Welles's filmed *Macbeth* also). By speaking, Banquo tempts Macbeth to act against him; he is surprised simply by Macbeth's speed. On the other hand, Welles also has soliloquies where the text has dialogue. After the murder, Macbeth speaks his 'Had I but died an hour before this chance' to himself; thus, instead of being the ironically true statement of a duplicitous Macbeth, it is the deeply felt remorse of a sincere Macbeth, as he descends the stairs (symbolically descending from grace) alone (France, *Orson Welles*, p. 61). Though Welles seldom allows us to see a good side to any of the characters, he shows a glimpse here of what Macbeth might have been.

With cuts of characters and lines, Welles worked to streamline an already streamlined play. Since Donalbain is cut, Malcolm and Macduff, after the discovery of Duncan's murder in II.iii, digest between them his few lines. Macduff runs off at the same time as Malcolm, in spite of his wife's entreaties to him to stay (her lines taken from IV.ii). Thus, instead of introducing a new character in a late scene as Shakespeare does, Welles has her enter here, making Macduff's betrayal of her consistent with the selfishness of those who will rule after Macbeth. There is to be no brighter day ahead. Welles also effectively constricts the characters' field of action, for instead of several castles, as in Shakespeare, there is but one palace, the focus of all political aspirations. Malcolm's testing of Macduff, since they agree about Macbeth, appears in the production to underscore the general air of suspicion that must prevail in a land so held in sway by evil powers. Accordingly, Welles cuts both the wish of the lords for better times (III.vi) and Macduff's sorrow for a bleeding land (IV.iii.31–3). Welles intensifies what is indeed implicit in the text, at least on one level, a possibility that can be ferreted out in production – a rottenness at the core of any society that can cheer at the unseaming of a man 'from the nave to th'chops' (I.ii.22). Summary justice, even when applied to a Cawdor, is no justice. Though Welles excises the bleeding sergeant entirely (from I.ii) and barely mentions Cawdor, he develops further than do those segments their ugliest implications.

Through such cuts, through reassigned speeches and new stage directions, Welles shapes his interpretation, but the strength of the supernatural forces, Lady Macbeth's guilt and her unity with her husband, Banquo's ambition, Macbeth's sensibility and society's violence – all of which Welles thus emphasises – are potentially available in the Folio text. True, Welles distorts the play to achieve his interpretation, but he simply follows the precept that once a director finds the essence of a play he must bring it out though he might sometimes violate the text to do so. His vision is no more one-sided than many a scholarly article. For him, the essence of the play is the controlling role of the supernatural in a militant society. In an interview, Welles insists that he 'didn't change the play's intentions, as I saw them ... I used Haiti, voodoo, etc., to foreground what I thought was represented in the play' (Estrin, p. 150). Welles denies vehemently that he changed the play in any way but when pressed by the interviewer's question: 'It was unabridged?' Welles responds, 'Unabridged? Never! I cut, cut, cut, oh yes.' He continues, 'Any director who directs a Shakespeare play or film can only realize a small part of it ... All we can do is grasp at or bite off a little bit, but what we grasp must be true and undistorted. I am entirely against distortion in a Shakespearean production.'

Though the play's production and reception were fraught with contemporary political realities, Welles vision is ahistorical, dependent more on eternal verities than on the situation of Negroes in 1936. Susan McCloskey, a sensitive critic of the production, thinks that it neglects the humanistic values she finds in Shakespeare's play, expressed in such characters as Macduff and

Malcolm (pp. 415–16). But others are not so sanguine about one or both of these characters (for example, Berger in 'Early Scenes', Horwich). The variety of scholarly opinion about Shakespeare's view of the human condition and human nature reinforces the notion of an ambiguous text, from which more than one valid performance can be crafted, even so extreme a reworking as Welles's.

The plan of Welles's script for the stage is not very different from that in his 1948 filmed Scottish *Macbeth* – except that a dank atmosphere replaces the riot of greenery of the Voodoo version. In fact, the film has, doubly, a stage genesis: Welles and his Mercury Productions (organised with Houseman right after the Voodoo *Macbeth*) gave the film its trial run in a production for stage, an ANTA (The American National Theatre and Academy) production in Salt Lake City at the Utah Centennial Festival in 1947. Welles's attitude towards the two genres shows how close he thought they were.

A full picture of Mercury's intentions is available through the Richard Alan Wilson Collection in the Special Collections Library at the University of California at Los Angeles, which includes Welles's filmscripts at many steps in its development, including those for the first film version (shot in 1947) and for the ultimately released production (1950). Welles's ideas are clearer in the 1947 version, which was restored in 1980 by Bob Gitt of UCLA (*Variety*, 18 April 1980) and has since become available on videotape. (See Kliman, 'Welles', for a discussion of the scripts.) Welles does not separate radically his concept of stage from his concept of film – as Andrea Nouryeh and others have shown. The first Mercury production for stage in New York City, a highly successful *Julius Caesar* in 1937, was as much a collage as the Voodoo or the filmed *Macbeth*. Nor is it a matter of Welles always having film in mind when staging productions (as Davies asserts, p. 84); just as certainly it can be said that he always has stage in mind when making films – more like an expressionistic Gordon Craig production than a drawing-room drama, to be sure, but still, a stage concept.

The main difference between the Voodoo *Macbeth* and the film (in which Welles also played the title role) is that the supernatural element in the film is confined to the three witches and a Friar. Even so, the supernatural pervades both productions. The film begins with the witches' boiling brew from which they, acting as midwives, pull a mass of clay that they shape into a likeness of a child-Macbeth, crowning it in derision as Macbeth and Banquo enter (a scene crafted from I.i and I.iii). If the witches, barely visible except in silhouette, are suitably evil-seeming, the Friar's bizarre appearance does not inspire confidence; indeed, in progressive scripts he evolves from 'Holy Father' to, simply, 'Friar'. He has a lantern jaw, grimy features, bangs, braids on the sides, and lank hair in back. (Welles, in a typewritten note on costumes and wigs, says he wanted him to look scruffy and poor.) In a late revision of the film, the Friar chases away the witches when they speak to Macbeth, establishing himself as their enemy. But Welles's narrated introduction asserts that the Christian religion which was attempting to supersede the older religion had gained little if anything of civilised mercifulness. In a ceremony presided over by the Friar, execution is done on Cawdor accompanied by a ceaseless tom-tomming by bare-chested drummers. Though he leads Duncan and his followers in a denunciation of the devil and all his powers (another late addition), the Friar seems a rather impotent and unsavoury figure. Since he takes many of Rosse's lines, as well as those of others, he is a persistent and disingenuous presence. In both the ANTA and film versions, he is the messenger who warns Lady Macduff but who is afraid to remain with her. In the film, he is an amanuensis to whom Macbeth dictates his letter to Lady Macbeth; yet after the murder, he does not speak of his suspicions about Macbeth. Macbeth's last accomplishment is to hurl from the battlements a multi-pronged stave into the heart of the Friar who stands far below with Malcolm and the army. Though the script says the thrust is meant for Fleance, who is with Malcolm and the Friar, Macbeth can be seen as successfully vanquishing the witches' enemy. As Macduff's sword swings (at the camera) to strike Macbeth, we see, in another late revision, a sword lop off the head of the clay doll the witches had made of Macbeth. The little crown then rolls to the feet of Fleance, who stoops to raise it. The last view Welles shows is a long shot of the three witches with their forked staves facing the castle. With the Friar gone, they will overcome the forces of goodness, Welles implies. Thus, not only are the powers of evil pervasive in both productions, but in both they are victorious. A difference is that the Celtic cross is adopted by Malcolm and Macduff, who, in contrast to their depiction in 1936, represent goodness, and Welles fills the screen with a forest of their army's cross-topped staves, backed by a dull sky. With a more sympathetic Macbeth, and with a Malcolm definitely if impotently on the side of good, the film, more than the stage production, invokes for the audience the emotion of the society's tragic loss in that victory of the supernatural powers.

The dark, papier mâché caverns, walls, arches, bridges and stalagmites of the film are, if anything, less insistently material than are the architectural structures of the stage production. (The film's caves were adapted from some leftovers Republic Pictures had on hand from an old serial.) Except for a few scenes with an immense empty space that emphasises Macbeth's moral dwarfishness, the film's settings seem more constricted than the stage setting. With its remarkable fluidity, the stage could become the jungle or the palace or the coast, the latter scenes played before backdrops that covered the palace (photographs are at Billy Rose Theatre Collection). In the film, weeping dark walls and a bleak heath confine the action but accord better with the text's Scotland. The choice of Haiti suited the African American actors and audiences – and even more suited Welles, giving him a reason (or an excuse) to adapt Shakespeare's play and carte blanche for embellishing the 'weyward' Sisters into dozens of witches and Voodoo practitioners. The choice of Scotland, however, fitted Welles's notion of Shakespeare's play for the mass American audience. By making his Scotland as primitive as he did, he was able to incorporate some of the supernatural force of the Voodoo version.

Frame by frame, with high angle and low angle shots, and with a wide-angle lens that exaggerates the distance between characters in near and far frame, the film creates a brooding atmosphere. For example, with the doctor and a gentlewoman in the foreground, we see in the far, far distance, in a very low angle shot, Lady Macbeth descending the stairs with her candle for the sleepwalking scene. The film's cinematic manipulation of space, of light and shade in the black and white medium, creates its own kind of realism. Welles's contrasts of light and shadow in the film are as brilliant and expressive as those in his *Othello*. While very many of Welles's techniques transfer easily from stage to film, he understood and could exploit the special qualities of each.

With all their differences, the Voodoo and film productions are remarkably similar in method and intention. Through lighting and the massing of crowds, both the staged and filmed *Macbeth*s create a similar atmosphere. The Caribbean accents in the stage production, however at odds with the Scottish placenames (as McCloskey points out, pp. 407–10), helped the actors in their impersonations as did the Scottish accent the film actors. The intention of the Scottish accent, as Richard Wilson explains, was not so much to recreate Scotland as to slow the actors' speech and allow them to sing the verse. It distanced them from the colloquial. The Jamaican accent did that for the 1936 players as well. Jeanette Nolan's unacceptable mid-Western twang deepened almost one octave when she took on the Scottish accent, giving her a persona she almost entirely lacked, Welles thought, in her own voice (letter in Wilson Collection). The film, like the stage production, has a unit setting, so that Macbeth can run directly from the banquet table to an exterior outcrop to invoke the witches. Since no conventional walls enclose this strange castle, Welles's camera can move freely from interior directly to the exterior in smooth pans. Film movement is usually accomplished by cuts from one space to another rather than by the smooth transitions more likely to be used on stage. Few location shots disturb the eerie effect of unenclosed space, more appropriate to stage than to film, though long shots (actually matte shots) of the castle and of marching armies more or less place the scene in a world – as expected of a film. While a special effect for the ghost scenes is sufficiently spectacular for the stage production, a filmic special effect – say, a transparent projection, all too easy on film – would not have been as compelling as the film's psychological approach. When the camera shows the table from the point of view of the thanes and Lady Macbeth, the table is full and there is no ghost. But from the point of view of Macbeth the table is empty except for Banquo, facing him from a chair at the far end. The wide-angle lens distorts the view, much as perspective settings can distort an audience's view of a stage.

Many of the film's shortcuts are the same as those for the stage. With no Donalbain, the film's Macduff again runs off with Malcolm. But there is no suspicious testing in the film. Instead, Malcolm struggles to persuade Macduff to return to Scotland and fight. Macduff says 'I am not treacherous' to comfort Malcolm rather than to protest his innocence; here, it is as if Macduff were saying, 'Don't worry, not everyone is evil'. The news of the death of his wife and children persuades Macduff to return. In both, Lady Macduff remains at the castle after urging her husband to stay with her, giving her an opportunity, in the film, to build a relationship with Lady Macbeth. For the scene of the killing of the Macduff family, Lady Macbeth takes some of Rosse's lines and some of Lady Macduff's lines. Macbeth himself is one of the murderers, and Lady Macbeth, who witnesses it all, is thus driven to madness. But the final version of the film omits what had been planned through many revisions: a view of Macbeth carrying one of the murdered children, then sitting on the throne in that vast, empty hall, holding the child and stroking his head. Even at the depth of Macbeth's depravity, when he kills the Macduff child, Welles wanted to suggest that hints of Macbeth's moral sensibility remain. With this sentimental notion excised, Welles strengthened Macbeth's decisive turn from potentially good to absolutely evil.

The same limitations make each production less than perfect. In both, the acting was inadequate in many of the ancillary and subsidiary roles, though with himself in the title role for the film, Welles at least nailed down that part to his own satisfaction (for a week he had played the role in the Voodoo *Macbeth* in blackface when Maurice Ellis, then the star, was ill (Houseman, p. 205)). Jeanette Nolan as Lady Macbeth garnered high praise too (and some brickbats). But in film, as on stage, not all the accents

7 Orson Welles and Jeanette Nolan, 1948

matched, and the cuts in each production sometimes made nonsense out of the dialogue that was left. Why, for example, is Macbeth surprised that Macduff will not come to him when he himself has seen him leave?

There are, of course, inevitable differences between the productions. Where on stage the dead Lady Macbeth is left in view, in the film she jumps to her death into a fathomless crevasse (neither her suicide nor that of their dwarf-servant Seyton was in the 1947 cutting continuity). Where on stage the soldiers with palm branches move into stage centre, in the film huge pines move eerily in distant mists. But overall, it seems that Welles's concept of the play, shaped, probably, in his school productions and then in his radio versions, grew and developed but did not in essence change. Welles's vision prevailed no matter who the actors or what the medium. Artists such as Welles and the many actors who move easily between stage and film – taking their concepts with them – prove that it is counterproductive to separate the performance genres.

Trevor Nunn's production with Ian McKellen and Judi Dench

Every performance uses parts to stand for a whole, a truth brought home to the audience of Trevor Nunn's 1976 *Macbeth* at The Other Place in Stratford-upon-Avon, where the bare-bones production allowed audiences to fill in the particulars of setting. The theatrical ideas of William Poel, who pioneered the return to bare thrust stages early in the twentieth century, might be the progenitors of this production, enacted within a stripped-down space. In a small barn-like theatre, the audience of no more than two hundred at each performance sat close up, three deep on three sides on stage level (with no raised platform) and two deep in galleries above. Actors (who frequently and sometimes tellingly doubled roles) variously remained on stage or exited and then returned, sitting around the black, chalk-demarcated, twenty-foot-diameter circle that was the playing space. Seated on upended packing crates, they observed the behaviour of those in the lit centre, heightening by their attention the audience's concentration, enhancing the ritual aspects of the production. Depending on the level of light, the audience could see the watching actors and each other as well as the players, or they could see only the players, captured in spotlights: the three witches, for example, observe as Macbeth and Lady Macbeth act and react in I.vii, the persuasion scene. Later Bob Peck, the actor playing Macduff, sees the murder of his child. (The videotape, to achieve a similar effect, since it does not show the outer circle, has Peck play a murderer, disguised by a stocking mask.) Thus, the particular actors Nunn selects to remain in the circle of crates and the amount of light he supplies help him shape his interpretation and the audience's response. Only some 10 per cent of the text is cut, including the usually deleted Hecate scenes, songs and dances, and the Siward and Young Siward references and speeches. With no scenery to be set into place beyond what can be effected by moving a crate into the circle, with actors' entrances and exits overlapping, Nunn escalates the pace of *Macbeth* in a 135–minute, intermission-free performance.

Nunn's position at the head of the Royal Shakespeare Company gave him the opportunity to do what few directors in commercial theatre can do: work with two sets of actors and one designer to produce distinct but related productions over a four-year period, from 1974 to 1978. His understanding of the play grew through this work. The first production starring Nicol Williamson and Helen Mirren was actually two productions: an elaborately dressed original in 1974 in Stratford that stressed religion and faith, followed by a stripped-down version at the Aldwych in London in 1975, with virtually the same cast, that stressed ritual. At the Aldwych especially Nunn had the elements that point to the 1976 production (black-painted brick walls and a chalk circle for playing), but both productions with Williamson had aspects that reappeared in the one with McKellen. Sue Dommett, a student of these productions whose remarks are keyed to the 1976 prompt-book, frequently notes the similarities (descriptive quotations, below, are from her work, unless otherwise noted). The 1976–78 version with Ian McKellen as Macbeth and Judi Dench as Lady Macbeth achieved more audience and critical acclaim than any other production had since Laurence Olivier played the title role in 1955. It moved from the studio workshop space of The Other Place to Stratford's main stage, then to the Warehouse and the Young Vic in London, and finally Thames Television taped it in a television studio and aired it in 1979. The performance on the small screen – because television, that hybrid medium, can lean more towards its stage side, less towards its film side – captures something of the mood of the stage version, but the stage version is considered superior by Nunn and by many who have seen both. Only rarely is the screen audience allowed a glimpse of the actors in the circle, never of an audience (for none was present during the taping), and movement is constrained by the frame, forcing some changes in blocking. Since Dommett provides very full information about the stage production, it can be visualised, with a little help at times from the video version.

Nunn's achievement is a unified view of the play, with ensemble acting creating a seamless interpretation. The smooth integration of the natural and the supernatural is part of this unity. Yet Nunn faced squarely the problem of the Porter's scene (II.iii.1–40) by wrenching it completely out of the time and place that the rest of the production inhabits. Played by Ian McDiarmid as a music-hall comic, the Porter is as out of place and yet as welcome as the bizarrely entertaining witches of early productions. Though the director imposes his will on the production, the audience has the sense that each actor responded fully to that direction and made it his or her own. Of the production, Nunn himself says: 'I had a very high-level cast, I had the benefit of my own experience over the previous two years, and I had extremely inventive leading actors who were convinced of the thinking that had already been brought to bear upon the play' (Thames TV Poster, 1979). A chief point is that, while Nunn knew what he wanted, he persuaded the actors to want that also and allowed them their own means for getting there. The Welles Voodoo *Macbeth*, in contrast, always was Welles's, with the actors as sometimes recalcitrant puppets. While there is no discounting the influence of Nunn's inspiration, one sees his production without thinking of him. The actors are primary – helped, to be sure, by Nunn's direction and by John Napier's overall design.

The circle setting encloses a community of actors, a community of characters, with the audience outside that circle looking in but often spoken to and drawn in. The circle is suitable for a communal rite, for purging Scotland of the evil that infects it, evil in the person of Macbeth and, to a lesser extent in this production, Lady Macbeth. The conundrum of Scotland is that piety and goodness are insufficient to protect the realm from Macdonwalds and Swenos without the violence of its warriors, its Macbeths and Banquos. And thus the ending, the turning over of the kingdom to Malcolm, is something less than the joyous

[129]

occasion productions often make it. Welles's production ends on a low note for morality but an exultant note for witchcraft because the powers of evil have, if anything, consolidated their power and are ready to work their will on the next generation. In Nunn's production, where the witches lack power, the thanes themselves recognise that Malcolm is not the leader they need; that in generating a Macbeth the community has revealed a sickness at its heart; that in its Macduff as warrior, Malcolm as king, it has duplicated the situation of the earlier insurrection. No wonder the men subside at the end into brooding contemplation.

Nunn creates the community of Scotland through the presence of the thanes, Angus, Macduff, Lenox and Rosse and others. While the community may be morally sound, it is physically powerless, and there are few warriors. Neither Lenox nor Rosse looks like a fighting man: Lenox acts the role of chamberlain, attached to Duncan's person, robing him and caring for him. Rosse enters in I.ii with an attaché case, as if he were a civil servant. These thanes' costumes suggest proper British morning dress, all black with touches of white at the neck, and their behaviour is explicable through the social roles their costumes imply. Rosse's voice expresses his deep feeling for Scotland when he describes the battles to Duncan (I.ii.48–64), and again when he speaks to Malcolm (IV.iii.164–73); nevertheless, out of fear rather than overconfidence, Rosse leaves his kinswoman Lady Macduff in that same rawness that Macduff had left her. And though Angus, a thane, is the messenger who comes to warn her explicitly, he does not remain to help her. The decorous costumes and circumspect behaviour are seen in the other thanes as well.

Though their deportment betokens the reserve appropriate to civil servants, their warmth implies rich currents of feeling in the community. Fellow feeling, conveyed through physical contact, informs many relationships. After the murder, both Lady Macbeth and Macbeth caress Donalbain to comfort him as he learns of his father's death. Though they are deceitful, one surmises that such caresses are customary. Banquo lovingly wraps Fleance in a blanket (the *that* of 'Take thee that too' (II.1.5) instead of the belt or scabbard to match the sword of line 4, as in many other productions). Because Macbeth evinces deep affection for his community and they for him, in this production there is a special poignancy often lacking in other productions when he says:

I have liv'd long enough: my way of life
Is fall'n into the sere, the yellow leaf;
And that which should accompany old age,
As honour, love, obedience, troops of friends,
I must not look to have; but in their stead,
Curses, not loud, but deep, mouth-honour, breath,
Which the poor heart would fain deny, and dare not. (V.iii.22–8)

We have seen the community from which Macbeth divorces himself. The production studies the implications of weakness aligned with morality, strength with depravity, within a kinship structure. Shakespeare was fascinated by cousins, by sons once removed; competition among cousins can lead to usurpation, and ironically – or predictably – the competition is among those who should be closest: blood relatives in a community where such relationships count: 'The near in blood, / The nearer bloody', as Donalbain says (II.iii.138–9). In many ways, McKellen's sometimes icy Macbeth is among the most charming in memory, the one with the closest, easiest relations, by turns genuine and untruthful, with the other thanes.

Communal rites, both sacred (by Duncan) and profane (by the three Sisters), are prologues to the first scene. The cast enters and sits on the crates, facing inward. Organ music creates a church-like ambience: 'The basic minor key harmonies are unobtrusive and the music uses chord progressions rather than a melody to achieve its effect. The impression is of a church before the service begins' (Dommett, p. 15). These same chords, somewhat soured, portend the intrusion of something unwholesome. The witches gather in a tight circle, holding hands and bowing their heads over two small twigs they have taken out of a bag. They begin keening, crying out and moaning, the sounds rising to a crescendo that culminates in a thunder clap and darkness. At the same time, Macduff helps a feeble Duncan to rise to his feet from the circle and kneel and pray. Donalbain kneels behind his father. The lights return and the first scene begins. The holy Duncan, in a simple white robe, with white fly-away hair, large cross and martyred demeanour, remains in prayer during the witches' first scene.

The two ceremonies of the prologue and first scene compete with and comment on each other, and the light enables the audience to see the surroundings, to note that Macbeth and Lady Macbeth – or the actors waiting to impersonate them – watch the proceedings intently. The youngest witch (Susan Dury, who also

[131]

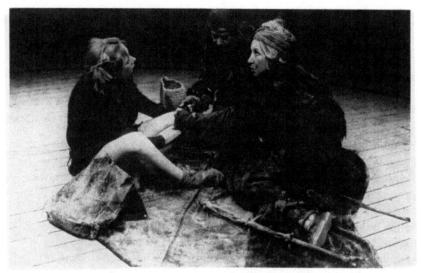

8 The Weird Sisters: Susan Dury, Judith Harte and Marie Kean, 1976

plays Lady Macduff) is a drooling, twisted woman with a limp, who has the gift of second sight. The second Witch (Judith Harte) asks her, 'There to meet with …?' and Dury answers 'Macbeth' (I.i.7), an answer that is news to Harte, though with a smile and a nod, she appreciates the rightness of its *being* Macbeth. In the witches' next scene, they remain crouched on the floor until the moment they are ready to leave, a position that emphasises their weakness. Later, their apparitions are papier mâché dolls. Thus, the witches are not the great instruments of Fate and witchcraft that they were in Welles's 1936 production, but at most descend to malicious mischief, their chanting over the cauldron a parody of the *Dies Irae* (they also mark Macbeth's naked back and forehead with crosses). They are dressed in dun-coloured rags, the third witch with bare head and legs, the first and second with ragged turbans that reveal their straggly hair – a travesty of the hair-enclosing turbans of the other women. Though audience attention is riveted on them, Duncan's murmuring of the *Agnus Dei* in the first scene counterpoints their utterances. As the witches complete their ritual, Duncan, the sacrificial lamb taking upon himself the sins of the community, beats his breast, 'mea culpa'. With two competitive ceremonies enacted, Duncan's appears at the beginning to be the more potent, partly because it overlaps and then follows theirs and thus seemingly overcomes theirs, and partly because the witches themselves are limited and weak. They are, though, a wonderful part of this production – especially through their presence around the circle. Nunn solves the problem of making the witches important theatrically without diminishing Macbeth's and Lady Macbeth's centrality.

Somewhat later (I.iv) Duncan receives on his frail shoulders the brilliant, heavily gold encrusted white cope that has been on view near the circle, and his kingship is thus confirmed just before he announces that Malcolm is to be his heir. This pause for spectacle eliminates what in the text is and what in performance could be rapidly sequential: the promise of further emoluments to Macbeth and Banquo and the immediate reversal of that promise, at least from Macbeth's view, as Duncan announces Malcolm's preferment – in the middle of the line in which he was expressing his joy in Macbeth's and Banquo's victories:

> My plenteous joys,
> Wanton in fulness, seek to hide themselves
> In drops of sorrow. – Sons, kinsmen, Thanes,
> And you whose places are the nearest, know,
> We will establish our estate upon
> Our eldest, Malcolm; whom we name hereafter
> The Prince of Cumberland. (I.iv.33–9)

The pause in the middle of line 35 in this production to allow Duncan to take on the kingly robe ritualises the elevation of Malcolm, making it a spiritual occasion and separating it from the prizes of war. In contrast, the Folio text does not have even the dash that marks a pause in the Arden edition, quoted above.

While Marvin Rosenberg in his *Shakespeare Quarterly* review (p. 195) said that both the saintly characterisation and the splendid robe were holdovers from the earlier Nunn productions (with Nicol Williamson in 1974 and 1975) and that 'both could easily have been dispensed with', it seems clear now that Nunn makes them central to this production: the saintly king is vulnerable in a world where wickedness flourishes. In this pared-down production, where all the other costumes are simple, the cope takes on the meaning of kingship and the value of the office for each of its wearers. Duncan and Macbeth are robed with it, Malcolm will be robed with it, and it remains on view when no one wears it – the king's raiment a fit emblem for garments that are, for different reasons, too large for all the wearers. Nunn certainly has licence to emphasise the saintly aspects of Duncan, for Shakespeare has him called 'gracious' by both Macbeth and Lenox, in the sense of especially deserving of and marked by God's favour. Significantly, though, no one uses the epithets *gracious* or *sainted* until after Duncan is dead (Macbeth in III.i.65, Lenox in III.vi.10, Macduff in IV.iii.109). Shakespeare's strategy here is similar to that in the major tetralogy where Richard II is esteemed by his enemies only after he is dead. But earlier, Macbeth himself praises the king when he debates killing him:

> this Duncan
> Hath borne his faculties so meek, hath been
> So clear in his great office, that his virtues
> Will plead like angels, trumpet-tongu'd, against
> The deep damnation of his taking-off. (I.vii.16–20)

The words 'meek', 'clear' and 'virtues' describing Duncan and his acts do not, however, so unequivocally indicate graciousness as they imply it when cojoined with 'angels' and 'The deep damnation of his taking-off'. Still, the heavenly proscription against regicide is not peculiar to gracious kings but applies to all kings, of every stamp, to the 'great office', rather than to the individual occupant of the seat of power. It applies to Macbeth, a legally installed king, as well – though Shakespeare turns every trick he can to make the audience forget that. Returning to the words specifically describing Duncan, the word 'meek' ascribes to Duncan an unkingly trait in a besieged Scotland, and it may be Shakespeare's oblique reference to the excessively milksoppish Duncan of the Chronicles – the one that the thanes conspired to overthrow for the sake of right (that is, warlike) rule in Scotland. Nunn ignores Shakespeare's invitations for ambiguity in the *character* of Duncan by idealising him from the beginning to give the audience an unambiguous contrast between good and evil. On the other hand, he preserves ambiguity in the *significance* of the contrast by suggesting an ambiguous notion of right kingship.

If Duncan is frail and the thanes ambassadorial or attendant rather than warlike, if they are fitter for civil service than warfare, Malcolm's weakness is understandable, endemic rather than personal. Much as the audience privately may value this sort of weakness – which is, after all, a disinclination to 'bathe in reeking wounds' (I.ii.40), an activity hardly the credential for living in a

[134]

civilised society – the weakness is also calamitous in societies where Macdonwalds, Swenos, assorted murderers for hire and witches, too, lurk about to undo civilisation. In our own time, in the West, we have separated the leader's moral innocence from the military power of the State (see Rabkin, p. 104). Since rarely is a Western government leader also a warrior, we are free to divorce the traits that, in reality, cohere in the leader: secret agents may engage in dirty tricks while the leader ostensibly stands clear, but that subterfuge remains an illusion. Shakespeare clairvoyantly dramatises that same division through Malcolm's description of the saintly English king (IV.iii.159) coupled with the apparently digressive scene where Northumbrian Siward willingly sacrifices his son to the maw of war (V.ix.12–19). Shakespeare successfully divides rule and killing between two characters, gracious Edward the Confessor and warlike Siward. Nunn obscures this division through eliminating Siward and his son – though he does retain in full Malcolm's description of the English king, which is ordinarily cut in modern productions. With no view of English soldiers – since the only characters shown in Act V are Scots – Nunn concentrates attention on the moral issues in one kingdom, where both experiments fail; that is, rule and killing separated (as in the time of Duncan) and rule and killing cojoined, as in the time of Macbeth. This is the tragedy: there is no way out until the society as a whole can abjure killing.

Nunn forces the audience to face the dilemma of a violent society so aptly expressed by Harry Berger in 'The Early Scenes of *Macbeth*'. Berger notes: 'In a society which sanctions violence ..., and in which ferocity and praise mutually inspire, intensify, each other, the success of outstanding warriors must always be greeted with muffled concern as well as "great happiness"' (p. 14). For what would these warriors do if they had 'no foreign foes to prey on?' (p. 11). Those who are eagles in war will not happily be sparrows in peace. Marilyn French, in *Shakespeare's Division of Experience*, similarly fixes the tragedy's meaning on the inability of the warrior Macbeth to renounce the behaviour that earns him praise on the battlefield when he turns to the domestic arena, which should be, she says, the female realm of nurturance:

Macbeth is not about ambition per se. It considers the question, why is murder acceptable in war and not at home? What is the difference? It depicts the cost to a man, a woman, eventually an entire culture, of extending to the community the masculine dominance of the public sphere, the cost of devaluing feminine ends. (p. 333)

While these comments by Berger and French do not apply to all productions of *Macbeth*, they are appropriate to Nunn's. Through his evocation of a community of Scotland, Nunn poses the same questions and potentially tragic answers that they explore: he asks, among other searching questions: What do we do with the eagles when there is no war? Do we want sparrows to lead us in a peace that could at any time yield to war?

Similarly, Nunn advances the implications of Malcolm's weakness, intimated in Shakespeare, whose Malcolm is rescued by the bleeding sergeant (I.ii.3–5) and has evidently left the field of battle, for he is with Duncan who knows little about the action on any front. Shakespeare's Malcolm is not a forceful participant but the object of others' actions. In Nunn's version, Duncan commands Malcolm to 'Go pronounce [Cawdor's] present death, / And with his former title greet Macbeth' (I.ii.66–7), rather than asking Rosse, as productions usually interpret the unexpressed stage direction. Malcolm, a young lad (Roger Rees) dressed like a college student in a white turtleneck sweater, hangs his head, evidently sickened by the task. Rosse, the courtier, immediately intercedes and offers, to Malcolm's relief, to undertake the responsibility. In the scene of the revelation of Duncan's murder, Shakespeare has left directors with an interpretative crux about Malcolm's and Donalbain's decision to run away (II.iii.121). Unless the thanes immediately treat them with suspicion, their departure is strange. The sole clue that Shakespeare provides is that no one speaks anything comforting and no one hails Malcolm as king, though he had been named heir. Instead, the men are going to convene in the hall as if an election is to take place. In contrast, the first time Prince Hal appears after his father's death he is called 'Your Majesty' (*2H4*, V.ii.43), and even before he enters, within a few lines of the announcement of the old king's death, he is referred to as the 'young king' (*2H4*, V.ii.9). Granted the situation is different in *Macbeth*, but in the final scene, as soon as Macbeth's death is announced, Malcolm is hailed as king. The thanes' silence after Duncan's murder may be a clue that can elucidate the departure of Duncan's sons – unless a production chooses to advance another notion. Nunn slips into the lacunae that Shakespeare leaves to underscore Malcolm's insufficiency.

The production builds a complex onstage reaction to the discovery of Duncan's murder that stresses the force of the community (II.iii.62–144). Macduff returns from Duncan's room barely able to articulate his tale of 'horror! horror! horror'. Before he can tell his grief, Macbeth comforts him with hands on both arms, looking full into his eyes with sympathy. Macbeth joins Lady Macbeth in comforting Donalbain while telling him that the king is dead. Only then does Malcolm hurriedly enter to be told the news by Macduff. Some productions make Macduff's line, 'Your royal father's murther'd', an attack on Macbeth's rhetorical flourishes in his metaphorical description of Duncan's death; not so in this production. All behave deeply connected to each other as they react in shock. Donalbain runs out to see for himself, but Malcolm, after his ineffectual 'O! by whom?', sits on the floor, incapable of action. Lenox, scarcely able to speak because of his tears, declares that 'Those of his chamber, as it seem'd, had done't', while Macbeth comfortingly strokes him. Lenox's grief effectively distracts the thanes from Donalbain's and Malcolm's, which should be the prime object of concern. Still, so far, the entire community is behaving like a united group. This alters as Macbeth announces he has killed the grooms, and Lady Macbeth, reacting to the sickening description of blood, faints. Now Malcolm and Donalbain, who has returned, separate themselves from the group, both with their movements and with their speeches to each other. Having lost trust for all the others, they stand apart. Nunn suggests their weakness by their youth and by their bare bodies, to which they clutch blankets. Macbeth has taken Lady Macbeth off and then returned, standing close to the other thanes, opposite the sons. The thanes, still united, react to the sons' distance by exiting to 'put on manly readiness, / And meet i'th'hall together' without offering the customary marks of affectionate concern. Banquo and Macduff do not even look at the young men. Rosse begins to approach Malcolm but thinks of something that stops him: is it suspicion? Nunn motivates their flight in these ways. No hostility is expressed toward them until they withdraw from the group. Malcolm is fainthearted for rushing off instead of exerting himself to marshal a well-disposed community and to affirm his rights.

Nunn's Malcolm has several other opportunities to show himself for what he is – a gentle, spiritual man who undertakes battle and warfare reluctantly, only when Scotland reaches its last extremity. In IV.iii, he is still dressed like the college boy, and his face expresses the same pained martyrdom we saw in Duncan. When Malcolm sullies himself by claiming lechery, Macduff barely suppresses an incredulous smirk. And when Malcolm describes himself as without any kingly virtues, he does it with such profound pain, such loathing for all he is saying, that it is a wonder Macduff believes him, because sincere revulsion for acts not yet committed joined to self-described depravity is puzzling. Still, Malcolm's testing of Macduff is reasonable in Nunn's production, because Macduff indeed has given – as have all the thanes – Malcolm reason to suspect him: 'You have lov'd him well' (IV.iii.13). Though Peck's Macduff is the most dour of Scots, making him difficult to read, his coldness to Malcolm and his haste in following Macbeth after the revelation of the murder justify Malcolm's doubt. Still, Malcolm so plainly needs Macduff that this testing makes Malcolm seem unable to mobilise warriors. Malcolm is no leader.

When Malcolm finally goes to war, he dons a greatcoat over his sweater, but Nunn's blocking denies Malcolm a change in his character. While Macbeth and Macduff fight strenuously, perilously close to the first row audience, Malcolm and the other thanes are, for the most part, motionless as they speak. Macbeth remains in centre stage during the scenes when Malcolm and the thanes approach Dunsinane (V.ii, V.iv, V.vi) while they stand at four quadrants of the circle. These Malcolm scenes are much shortened, too, and much less dramatic than they might be, since audience attention is held by Macbeth, in centre stage, slobbering over his juju dolls taken from the witches in the cauldron scene. (For the video, unable to show the whole playing area, Nunn achieved a similar effect by showing Macbeth in the foreframe while Malcolm and the others line up in the distance.)

Nunn does not rely on opposites only. Within the two extremes of eagle and sparrow – Macbeth and Macduff contrasting with Duncan and Malcolm – many multifaceted characters present themselves: for one, John Woodvine's Banquo, whom Rosenberg, after seeing two preview performances at The Other Place, described as 'Macbeth's equal in force, but brilliantly contrasting in design – lean, shrewd, hardheaded, observant of all around him. He protected the ambiguity in the role: to his untimely end, he was not committed either to an unqualified moral repugnance to Macbeth's act, or to an exclusively self-serving policy of accommodation'. Woodvine himself did not resolve the ambiguities for Rosenberg: "'Did Banquo have any plan, after Duncan's murder, for dealing with Macbeth?" [Rosenberg] asked him. Woodvine smiled: "Who knows what he would have done – if he had lived"' (Trevor Nunn's *Macbeth*, p. 196). After expressing his doubts about Macbeth (III.i.1–3) and after his suspicions are aroused by Macbeth's too-casual question about Fleance riding with him, Banquo nevertheless kneels and kisses Macbeth's hand before he goes riding, surprising Macbeth by this display.

Nunn's Lady Macbeth is another rich character with potential for good, though she chooses evil. Her development throughout the production points up the conflicts Nunn finds in the play. In Marilyn French's scheme of things, Lady Macbeth should – more than Macbeth – protect the sphere of nurturance. Shakespeare shows her effort to abrogate her femininity, to turn her milk to gall. Her assurance that she would have, had she vowed to do so, dashed out the brains of the babe who milks her is her supreme denial of nurturance. In spite of this denial, Judi Dench, following the interpretation of such nineteenth-century actors as Helen Faucit and Ellen Terry, polished to new brilliance with compelling acting the fragility and vulnerability of Lady Macbeth. Dench, in calling upon all the powers of darkness, violently wrenches her nature to unsex herself, unlike the terrible Lady Macbeth for whom these declarations are exultant liberation. The plot requires Lady Macbeth to encourage Macbeth to bring murders considered appropriate to the State at war into the domestic sphere. But in spite of this Lady's temporary access to warrior mettle, McKellen's Macbeth does not, after welcoming her partnership in murder, allow her a role in the masculine sphere. Ultimately, his excluding her, his insistence that she should remain out of the public world, leads to her madness. Because she has annihilated her feminine role, when he dismisses her she has nowhere to turn. Macbeth decisively rebuffs her in his first court scene, where her reaction shows what a blow his rejection is. 'Be innocent of the knowledge, dearest chuck' (III.ii.45), Macbeth says later; the partner in greatness is to stay out of affairs of State. Dench's Lady is to help him entertain his guests; she is to applaud her husband's deed once it is done. That is all.

Judi Dench's excellences, within the chosen interpretation, are legion. Dressed in a narrow black sheath, her head completely turbaned in black, her white face stark in the harsh light of her scenes and somewhat childishly pudgy, Dench has no resources of costume or setting to help her. Instead, she uses her face and body to give the nuanced delivery that is the mark of every great actor. Nervous, high-strung, she is repeating, when we first see her, phrases from the letter, which she has already memorised. She uses a box, which Angus has placed in the centre for her, to express the varying levels of her emotion, jumping up from it impatiently or subsiding onto it. The actors playing the three witches, Banquo, Macbeth, King Duncan, Macduff, Angus, Lenox and Malcolm all watch, the light allowing full sight of those around the circle. Beginning with the ninth line of the letter, Lady Macbeth starts off from memory with 'Hail, King that shalt be. Hail King that shalt be'. Then she returns to the first lines, repeating, still from memory, 'they have more in them than mortal knowledge' (2–3) as if, says Dommett, fascinated 'with the idea of supernatural intervention'. Her fascination deepens to conviction as she pauses before uttering firmly 'metaphysical aid' (line 29). Her chief motive is Macbeth's exaltation, though she speaks disdainfully of his 'human kindness' (17). Jumping up, she urges him to 'Hie ... hither', stressing 'golden round' through lengthening the vowels, almost singing them (25–8).

Alone again after the entrance and exit of Seyton, she pauses for a moment, looking at the letter, considering whether 'they [who] have more than mortal knowledge' will come to her aid to persuade her husband. But the letter has inspired her: if spirits come to him they may also come to her. She conjures the 'Spirits / That tend on mortal thoughts' (40–1) apparently by drawing them from deep within the ground, pressing her palm against the upward push of those powers. And when she begins actually to make contact with them, her feat so appals her that she recoils and cries out, sending a chill down the spines of those in the audience. A moment later she commits herself again to the unwonted task, falling down on the ground, pressing her outspread arms down as if to contain and control the powers she calls forth. As she speaks she begins to rise to her knees until at 'Hold, hold!' (54) she flings her arms up, her voice firm and certain. Her belief in these powers, inspired by his letter, has been confirmed by her contact with them. Their 'metaphysical aid' along with his abilities will lead to certain success.

If Judi Dench alone created a finely modulated Lady Macbeth, her collaboration with Ian McKellen shaped a stunning depiction of the pair. Dench and McKellen are well matched, the theatrical chemistry between them palpable. More than usually loving, Macbeth and Lady Macbeth embrace with the passion of two trying to become one. Her voice as she greets him is 'full of warmth and pride' . He has no words but can only embrace and kiss her over and over. As they begin to speak 'Macbeth caresses her breasts and back. Her voice is soft and low. Rapt in his pleasure at being with her he answers unthinkingly'. Since he has already determined to murder Duncan (I.iv.50–3), Macbeth's joy here is that his soulmate, without having to be told anything, is already so much with him in thought. He declares with certainty that they will speak further of this business. The thought of the deed they will speak of does give him pause now, and he does allow her to have the last word. Still, though the scene ends with her saying, 'Leave all the rest to me' (73), he takes the initiative by leading her offstage, bringing her, before he exits, to her place in the circle between two of the witches and opposite the third, where she awaits Duncan's arrival. The women make bird sounds as the king's party enter, Lenox and Macduff carrying on the frail Duncan. In the same ritualistic gesture of deference we have seen Macbeth perform very convincingly to both Duncan and Malcolm, she kisses the hem of Duncan's robe and his hand. As she answers his greeting, she acts, says Dommett, surprised that her voice is calm, but she does not speak again, her last speech being cut (25–8). Her nature, which she thinks has no milk of human kindness, is not up to the deception she has to practise to greet Duncan. She behaves as if she cannot believe that she can pull it off.

The next scene overlaps, as the thanes and sons, their arms around each other, exit, and Macbeth enters. In what is often her strongest scene, her persuasion of Macbeth, she does not so much convince him as give him a way to assure himself that the murder can be accomplished with impunity, for this Macbeth, though very much needing her approval, is not led by his wife. During his soliloquy before she enters, he moves restlessly, his eyes scanning 'the gallery spectators, involving them in the debate'. By the end of the soliloquy, Dommett thought that his perfect stillness meant he has made up his mind not to do the deed. He nods vigorously several times as he says 'falls on th'other' (I.vii.28): what stops him is his fear that his vaulting ambition will lead to a fall. Lady Macbeth begins speaking to him without the tone of motherly admonition so common in strong Lady Macbeths. He pauses in his decisive stride to the banquet to tell her his decision, then responds to her impatience, her scorn, by coming behind her to put his arms around her. She will not let him, 'furiously rejecting the embrace'. She spits out her words, walking away from him. With 'great dignity', he says 'I dare do all that may become a man; / Who dares do more, is none' (46–7). He cannot fathom her attack, is almost winded by its strength. Dommett says, 'without her love and respect life would be meaningless'. He is, however, about to leave, when Lady Macbeth pulls him around to face her for the 'I have given suck' speech. Though moved to admiration by her speech he is not convinced to change his decision. 'If we should fail?' is said gently, quizzically, more to appease her than for his own information – more to expose, gently, the unreason of her demand than to elicit her reassurance. He keeps trying to hold her, shushing her and shaking his head 'no' as she outlines the scheme in detail. After she discloses her plan to drug the grooms he begins to see that his ambition need not lead to a fall (in the videotape of the production he continues to shake his head 'no' here). His head up, embracing her, he communes more with himself than with her. After his admiring ejaculation 'Bring forth men-children only!' (73–5), he pauses, musing: 'Will it not be receiv'd ...?' (75–8), and during this pause he persuades himself. The pair exit kissing.

Even more in her next scene, Dench's Lady betrays the vulnerable core of the character. Waiting in the shadows beyond the circle while Macbeth speaks to Banquo and then to the invisible dagger (II.i), she enters 'backwards with short, hurried steps' to await Macbeth's return from the murder chamber (II.ii). The first noise uncovers the anxious person beneath the thin-shelled bravado. 'She walks nervously around the centre of the circle, wringing her hands' . The business of the knives underscores her anxiety. Directors have to decide what to do about the fact that Lady Macbeth does not remark on the bloody knives for some forty lines after Macbeth's entrance. In this instance, they are in full view all the while and her disregard for them exposes her absence of mind. The blood frightens her; his fear frightens her. She tries desperately to control herself, and through herself, him. 'She attempts to calm him with a rational explanation' about the two who 'address'd them / Again to sleep' by explaining with strained patience, 'There are two lodg'd together' (II.ii.24–5), but he tries her composure by insisting that she should tell him why he could not say 'Amen'. After snatching the daggers, going off to gild the faces of the grooms and returning, she speaks to Macbeth 'as if she [has] rehearsed her speech' to shame him into self-command. But she does not succeed. Totally self-absorbed, he will never listen to her again. With all the force she can gather, keeping her blood-spattered hands clear, she pushes against him with her body to move him off.

The demonic power that she had summoned to herself has vanished, and the connection between her and Macbeth disintegrates. After her faint in the disclosure scene, his caresses appear to nauseate her, and she falls forward, eliciting the second 'Look to the Lady' (II.iii.123). At Macbeth's (added) coronation ceremony, his investiture as king, he smiles at his Lady with his lips alone, while 'his eyes remain narrowed and dangerous'. Something has gone wrong in her scheme. When we see her as queen, she is adorned only with a modest gold coronet, a slender necklace and tiny earrings – a small change in material well-being, bespeaking the essentially egalitarian court circle. But into this community has come a viper. Even before Macbeth articulates his mistrust of Banquo, Lady Macbeth, though she addresses Banquo with apparent warmth, can barely conceal her suspicion. After Macbeth decisively rebuffs her, addressing his 'God be with you' (III.i.44) to her as an abrupt dismissal though she had approached him smiling, 'She steps back, involuntarily, as if he has struck her… .She glances back at him wounded but he is unresponsive'. Immediately, before she has time to leave, Macbeth addresses Seyton. Lady Macbeth 'looks round at [Seyton], with hurt disbelief that he is replacing her in Macbeth's confidence. Seyton meets her gaze.' Later, when she asks Seyton the whereabouts of Banquo (III.ii.1), 'their voices are controlled but their mutual dislike is obvious'. The competition between them had begun when Seyton, breaking in as messenger in I.v, reacted strongly to her exclaimed 'Thou'rt mad to say it' (31) as if he did not expect this tone from her.

Lady Macbeth's dejection during her last attempt to be a partner to Macbeth (III.ii) is a way-station to her madness in the sleepwalking scene. She has already forgiven him for spurning her, but, though she wants to comfort him, he moves away from her. Her attempts to advise him meet with anger. He does not want to have to explain his fears about Banquo; he expects her to know his thoughts. At last he accepts her embrace (after 'dear wife!', 36), but his obscure hints about 'A deed of dreadful note' (44) terrify her. Now all unwillingly she is held in his unloving grasp. At last, she moves away from him, crying.

The banquet scene gives Dench's Lady a last opportunity to impose her will on a disintegrating situation. The circle of crates is repositioned with guests moving them into the centre of the stage; there are no onlookers for this scene. While Macbeth and Seyton (who has the words of the First Murderer here, though he was the Third Murderer in III.iii) are in close conference at the banquet, Lady Macbeth sits at some distance. As they speak, the two men together perform a wine ritual, Macbeth proffering the cup to each thane, then Seyton wiping the rim with a white cloth, a parody of the communion ritual. She calls Macbeth away from their close conference: 'My royal Lord, / You do not give the cheer' (III.iii.31–2), the rest of her speech being cut. After Macbeth begins reacting to the invisible ghost, a ghost of the mind, and after Rosse tells all to rise, she tries 'desperately to keep control of the situation and her own fear'. Though she tries to shame Macbeth into control, he frightens her. She has the nerve, though, after her commonsense avowal 'When all's done, / You look but on a stool' (66–7) to sit on it. He yells for all to look, plucking them by the sleeves. In panic, she screams out 'Fie! for shame!' (73), then 'claps her hand over her mouth, aware of the scene she is making'. At last, the ghost being gone, Macbeth becomes calm and opens his arms to her on 'Come, love and health to all' (86). Relieved, a nervous smile on her lips, she goes to him, and once more the thanes sit. In moments, though, he sees the ghost again and throws the wine cup in a wide curve, the dregs of red wine arcing out. He clutches her as she rises, burying his face in her body. She stands helpless as with his dagger he stabs violently at the empty stool, his face twisting. His saliva mixed with the reddish wine, looking bloodied, drools out of his mouth. Ironically, he falls into a seizure; just such a one as she had used to excuse him upon the first vision. This time, he does not regain composure when the ghost leaves. He questions the thanes closely, thrusting his twisted, drooling face into theirs. Hysterically, she interrupts when he seems about to disclose too much. Rosse kisses Macbeth's hand in leave-taking and Lenox is about to when she screams at them 'Stand not upon the order of your going' (118). He attempts a ghastly smile and waves his hand in bitter mockery of genial hosting. Her 'A kind goodnight to all!' (120) is full of desperate pain, and 'she sobs, slumping down on her box'. Total weariness almost overcomes her. He has to pull her to her feet, and speaks 'We are yet but young in deed' (144) as his fingers pinch her face. He almost drags her out, walking towards a spotlight so that their shadows loom huge on the stage. 'The music recalls the introduction to the *Gloria* before Macbeth's coronation but it is discordant and loud. Her feet go from under her. Blackout.' Powerlessness and ineffectuality, delayed somewhat by his discomposure, overcome her now.

The sleepwalking scene holds no surprises except the number of changes Dench can ring on the predominant emotion of soul-wrenching despair. Entering without even the simple jewellery that marked her investiture as queen, she remembers everything horrible, nothing hopeful. Eyes glistening with tears, she tries to obliterate a stain on her hand, biting and mouthing it, then stares searchingly at the hand she holds to the candle, the better to see the irremovable stains. Her voice rises to an incredulous shriek as she cries, 'Here's the smell of the blood still' (V.i.47). Her wretched sigh is a yowl of pain and despair, eliciting the doctor's comment that her 'heart is sorely charg'd' (50). Though Nunn keeps Malcolm's epithet 'fiend-like Queen' (V.ix.35), Judi Dench makes her a loving wife, a tender helpmeet who stoops to murder because she knows what her husband wants and deserves. Her mourning for Lady Macduff uncovers the softer nature hidden beneath the façade: 'Where is *she* now?' (V.i.40–1). Sympathy is mixed with hopelessness: 'she' at least may be in heaven, but where will she herself be? This is a Lady Macbeth who is not oblivious to the evil of her enterprise but who has overcome her conscience to help her husband. Speaking of *his* scruples, she was, we finally realise, commenting on her own. She arouses both fear and pity, because she is so believable a victim of self-delusion.

An audience's pity for her shades into dislike for him because he rejects her. Macbeth speaks about her with the doctor without evincing much feeling (V.iii.37–9). And when her death is announced (V.v.16), he thinks more of his own mortality than hers. Though Dommett says that 'his voice registers his appalled realisation of what life will be without her', I do not hear that tone on the videotape. In his explanation of the speech in *Acting Shakespeare*, his one-man stage show, taped for broadcast, he does not mention Lady Macbeth as a factor in Macbeth's desolation. When he betrayed the community by treacherously killing Duncan, he effectively extinguished all feelings. By killing Duncan, he had killed the better part of himself. It is himself he mourns. In still another valid interpretation, Robert Cushman says in an *Observer* review (18 September 1977):

> Ian McKellen's Macbeth is worm-eaten from the start ... Our first glimpse into him comes when he tells Banquo, 'Your children shall be kings'. Envy is already there and, once loosed, it is a consumer. The note is sounded again in Mr McKellen's most scornful high tones, once he is king; he has done it all 'to make *them* kings? The *seed* of Banquo – kings?' It sickens him.
>
> Envy reaches backwards, too, colouring the despair of 'Duncan is in his grave'. The words, and the mind behind them, are rancid; and it is this mood that takes possession of the last act. Everything disgusts him, and his only reason for fighting to the death is the thought of subjection to Malcolm is the most disgusting of all. (quoted in Dommett, p. 249)

Though Dommett and Cushman disagree, divergence of interpretation signify the richness of the character that McKellen builds. Much is mysterious about his Macbeth: might he have remained a good man? Is goodness in anyone a choice rather than an innate trait? His duplicity is illuminated for the audience; never has a Macbeth so successfully hidden his feelings about Duncan's naming of Malcolm as his heir. That he truly loved Lady Macbeth at first is unequivocal. Though he is himself the architect of his fate, he childishly clings to the misshapen puppets that the witches give him after their prophetic warnings. Similarly, during the cauldron scene he leans, childlike, against the bosom of the First Witch, who eyes him unfeelingly. Example after example might be offered of McKellen's intelligent approach to the nuances of the character. One remembers that abrupt nod towards Duncan's chamber, as he says, 'Whiles I threat, *he* lives' (II.i. 60), rolling up the shirt-sleeve of his right hand for the task; the mesmerised concentration on Duncan's blood on his hands afterwards; his slicked-back hair and the heel-clicks of the dedicated soldier; his false bonhomie with thanes and murderers; the idiocy of his drugged nakedness in the cauldron scene (IV.i); the desolation of his despair in most of the fifth act, with a swinging bare bulb lighting up his grotesquely convulsed face. No other actor has so well depicted the existential *nausea* of a man who has chosen evil. His performance achieves what Macready strove for – psychological truth in every moment, fully motivated action and thought, convincingly conveyed to the audience, who will be all the more persuaded by his reality because they disagree about precise motives, just as differing opinions are provoked by any complex individual.

The ending is inconclusive. As such, the production could have been an example for Stephen Booth (pp. 90–2) and James L. Calderwood (pp. 34–6), who both comment on inconclusiveness in *Macbeth*. The side of righteousness, represented by saintly Malcolm, has won. But this Macduff has been the most unreadable of men, taciturn, outwardly unbending. Angus, Rosse and Lenox are as impotent as ever. Macduff might, one supposes, have undertaken to free Scotland from Macbeth's rule without Malcolm – except that he needed those thousands of English soldiers that Malcolm had available to him. Macduff's voice falters when he says, 'Hail, King of Scotland!' (V.ix.25), which only Rosse (not *All*) echoes. The very last image is of Macduff, Lenox, Rosse and Angus sitting dejectedly in a tight circle, the insignia of office visible on the stacked crates where Macbeth had placed them. Malcolm speaks from the edge of the circle, and then exits alone. Significantly, he says nothing about raising the thanes to earls; nothing is gained. One by one, the thanes exit. The last to leave, Rosse and Macduff exchange empty glances. The problem of right rule in violent times remains, even in a society that values morality.

Ron Daniels's 1999 ensemble production

Ron Daniels, director of *Macbeth* for Theatre for a New Audience (New York City, spring 1999), grasps the tragic terror of *Macbeth*: characters think that they are their own masters and that they shape their fate, but they are subject to inscrutable forces.[5] He links those forces in this production to Vodou rites, but his genre is Greek tragedy, with its reluctant and obscure oracles that provoke men and women to try to speed or avert events. Any attempt to circumvent fate will be useless because the supernatural forces mould events as *they* wish. Is it for the good, ultimately? It may seem so for a moment, but that could be an illusion: the ambiguity of fair and foul is the engine that drives the production. Macbeth (Bill Camp) may be the only character who comes to know that he is struggling with fate: 'Come fate into the list', he cries (III.i.70). His nobility lies in this self-knowledge; he senses he cannot win but will 'try the last' (V.viii.32). But the Weird Sisters do not go to meet Macbeth merely to act upon *him*; all the characters are part of the deterministic weave, and in this production all have more weight than they have in many others.

Daniels is a native of Brazil, where Vodou is practised in some quarters.[6] His depiction of the religion is unlike Orson Welles's exoticism, seen from the outside, but a glimpse of a vibrant, living religion. Vodou practitioners gifted in contacting inscrutable forces (ancestors, saints, gods), in trance-like states, transmit messages to seekers. Daniels is also much influenced by Ted Hughes's strangely compelling work *Shakespeare and the Goddess of Complete Being*, a grand unified theory of almost all the works of Shakespeare, from his earliest poems to *The Tempest*. Hughes in his mythology, based on 'Venus and Adonis', sets aside Shakespeare's realism in favour of the symbolic elements linking Shakespeare's works as he understands them. Daniels distributed copies of Hughes's *Macbeth* chapter to his troupe of actors, made available lavishly illustrated books on Vodou, and showed a documentary film on Vodou by the experimental film-maker Maya Deren.[7] In her film, Vodou trances take place within a circle of bystanders casually engaged in their own concerns. That is, no rapt or respectful audience of observers watch the supernatural manifestations of the priest or priestess; instead people go about their business in a party atmosphere while the trance proceeds on a different plane. Daniels infused his production with this connection between the spiritual and the quotidian.

The director's legerdemain, often entertaining in itself, empowers the attentive audience to grasp the meaning of the play as he sees it. Foremost is his blurring the distinction between the real and the theatrical. Actors pour blood over James Farmer and make him into the Bloody Sergeant before our eyes. Characters exit from one scene unable to see characters entering for succeeding scenes. Doubling of roles also contributes to the theatricality, especially when actors are easily recognisable in their various guises and are, nevertheless, like Reg E. Cathey (Banquo, Porter, doctor, Weird Sisters' minion), brilliantly in character whatever their role. Actors fill the entire theatre space, entering or retreating down two centre aisles, down two side aisles and through five doors around the shallow disk-shaped stage floating above black sand. Actors who become characters before our eyes, overlapping scenes, doubling of roles and entrances made through an auditorium have been commonplaces of productions since the 1970s, but here the theatricality fits the conceit: Daniels both invites the audience to be a part of the action and also insists that they view it with detachment, as do the spectators and celebrants at a Vodou ceremony: the audience members are the bystanders at the ceremony of *Macbeth*.

The elegantly simple set design by Neil Patel provides effective spaces for action, for downstage confidences to the audience, and for separations between those taking the centre and those watching from the edge. Skirting the upstage curve, a wooden wall (with three doors) could be rolled open to reveal beyond it stairs leading up to Duncan's chamber and for Lady Macbeth (Elizabeth Marvel) to descend in her sleepwalking scene. The lighting mixes natural and psychological effects, sometimes reflecting the soul's anguish, sometimes spotlighting individual characters, sometimes freezing the action – as when spots freezeframe the banquet guests while Macbeth queries his trusted servant Seyton, who had been the third murderer as well as the Bloody Sergeant. At other times, light washes the audience as well as the stage. Sound effects (by Akin Atoms) punctuate the action mimetically as well as symbolically. To say that the language is clear and precise and that every word can be heard and understood is simply to state the bottom line requirement for any decent production. But the actors do much more, fully inhabiting their roles in most of the performances I saw.[8]

Daniels dared much; he had a vision, and his concept was more significant than the minor accidents that may have prevented it from being actualised perfectly at every instance. Some budget shortfalls led to solutions that, to some observers, improved upon the original idea. When the producer insisted that Daniels should choose between effigies for the cauldron scene or twelve real trees for Birnam, Daniels chose the former: Vodou over nature. The silver rattles that stood in for Birnam trees created a riveting sound effect, and the artifice worked better for the short Birnam scene (V.iv) than a skimpy realism would have done.

The three Weird Sisters, as usual, were the key to the director's intention, and these women, who opened and closed the production, were Vodou women who had no purpose separate from that of the spiritual forces acting through them. The youngest (Careena Melia, hereafter *Careena*), a tender novice, bare-shouldered in white gown, eager and skittish, submits willingly to her schooling. The middle Sister (Starla Benford, hereafter *Starla*), a round-bellied matron garbed in brilliant red, has seen it all and participates with some detachment because she is not responsible for learning or teaching. The oldest (Rajika Puri, hereafter *Rajika*), a graceful, fluid-bodied, black-swathed wise woman, gently leads the rites. These actors are all superb in their roles, reflecting through their ethnicity (Irish American, African American, and Indian, respectively) the all-embracing dimensions of their religion, the Triple Hecate of virgin, matron and crone. As the play opens, each enters to adorn and demarcate the sacred space with *vèvès*, Vodou's ritual symbols. Affectionate touches and glances throughout the Sisters' scenes mark their collegiality. Rajika, as leader, examines and approves the others' designs, and, as they all gather over the lit grate at the centre, the dialogue begins.

In the third scene, they meet again for their important business. To make themselves conduits for the prophecies they will relay to Macbeth, Rajika administers to all a potent topical drug that makes the novice reel and even produces a shudder in the phlegmatic Starla. Rajika tells her story of the sailor's wife less out of spitefulness than from a wish to entertain herself and to distract Careena, writhing from the effects of the drug. But as she enters into her story, Rajika's eyes glint with the image of her malicious mischief. Returning to playfulness, she plucks from the air an imaginary pilot's thumb and shows it to the credulous Careena who screams, then laughs at herself in chagrin, Starla looking on with sceptic disdain. Without altogether erasing the menace in the text, they show they are channels for magical powers, rather than powers of darkness themselves.

When Macbeth and Banquo enter (to strobe lights and then a spot on Macbeth alone, bare-chested, the blood of battle still on their bodies and clothes), the Sisters' minions (played by all the actors not otherwise engaged) gather below the downstage edge of the disk. The director shows his strong touch with the disappearance of the Sisters in the third scene. Careena, almost desperate from the poisonous effect of the drug, is running wildly across the stage. Macbeth catches her by an arm ('Stay, you imperfect speakers', I.iii.70), causing her to collapse and, from his perspective, to disappear. As the others move to help her up and off, to Macbeth and Banquo they also disappear. The audience sees the three, still in character, still affected by the drug, slowly move to positions by their doors, where they watch discreetly for a moment before they exit.

The cauldron scene, right after the intermission, was the climax of the production, visually and dramatically. Daniels meant it to be the final rising action of the first act to be followed by the killing of the Macduff babies, but the first act would then have been too long for audience comfort. Coming out of their three doors, the women gathered with their cauldron at stage centre, each ladling herself some of the repulsive brew after her recipe speech. Now their minions are on the disk with them, watching solicitously, reaching out a hand to steady them as they react to the potent drug. Though only Starla was visibly pregnant, all three will give birth to the masters who will speak (through the women) the prophecies to Macbeth – Rajika, as the eldest, with a minimum of fuss (a baby head dripping with red streamers); Starla, squatting, with exultant pushes (a bloody baby), and Careena with terror and agony and then triumph (a crowned baby with branch). For the show of kings, the minions (who had exited smoothly with the babies) re-entered bearing carnival effigies – enormous, glowing, crown-topped poles within which the men move, hidden by streamers. In retrospect, we realise that the prophetic masters too were carnival effigies, jewel-encrusted, vivid doll babies.

Fleance held the mirror showing 'many more', and Banquo stepped outside his streamers to point 'at them for his'. After Macbeth fell in a faint, Rajika, saying lines frequently cut, calls upon all to 'show the best of our delights ...' (IV.i.125–32). The king effigies and Sisters dance on stage, and, at a sharp signal from Akin Atoms on the sound platform, move into the audience, almost touching people with flowing streamers. It looked dangerous and exciting, attractive and repellent. Then the carnival disappears but the effigies remain positioned upstage right and left, a reminder of what is promised to Banquo's issue, contradicting the impression we may have had that the effigies are Macbeth's narcotic-induced vision.

In the play this scene is our last view of the Sisters, but in this production they continue to exert their quiet force. After Macbeth, Seyton and another muffled character murder Lady Macduff (Starla Benford) and her two children, they leave the dead baby on the stage. Careena, who had entered a centre aisle and had watched the murder, silent, and sad – perhaps even grieving – approached the baby, spread a fine cloth and, tenderly lifting its body, wrapped it and took it away. The minions wash the blood from the stage and wipe it dry even as Malcolm and Macduff enter and position themselves for the beginning of their scene. The ritual sacrifice and the ritual cleansing are the turning point of the play, and what we see in this next scene is in a different key altogether. Touches of blue in the costumes of the Malcolm group reflect heavenly purity (in contrast to the deep red touches in the costumes for Macbeth and his Lady in the coronation scene).

After the play's last words, Daniels ends with what may be the Sisters' most potent image: they solemnly enter the space as Malcolm and the Scots exit into the aisles, stop and turn. The women are weary, their work is done for a time, and there is no exultation. They glide to Macbeth's head lying on the lit grate at centre stage, stoop over it and move their hands over it – in prayer? benediction? supplication? – and then turn palms up into an intense solitary beam of light that shines down on the head for a few seconds before dimming to black. The light comes from above as well as from below. The iconography is mysterious and spiritual. In the *Playbill*, a programme note from *Shakespeare and the Goddess of Complete Being* suggests Daniels's agreement with Hughes, who states,

> Throughout mystical tradition, beheading signifies 'removing carnal consciousness, replacing it with spiritual consciousness.' In general, beheading means to be reborn with a new, other consciousness. This meaning is constantly refreshed and re-enforced by recurring as a common, archetypal event in ordinary dream life.

Like Ninagawa, Daniels sees the possibility for redemption for Macbeth, who, in this version, acted as much from necessity as will. The tragedy then lies in all the characters' human inability to understand the forces that control their lives. Since this is simply the human condition, however, the performance does not single out Macbeth as the tragic hero. Duncan, Macduff and Banquo are similarly tools of fate. If the audience recognise this truth, they will experience in this production the pity and fear that Aristotle considered the aim of tragedy.

Without flamboyance (except for the show of kings), Daniels made the three Sisters the most important single image of the play: they are the Triple Hecate that Hughes celebrates as aspects of the Goddess mythology. Unlike Welles, whose witches, Hecate and minions dominate, Daniels maintains a careful balance between his Vodou women and all the others.

The kingdom is in crisis. The gracious, kindly old king's time has passed, and yet his adolescent sons are not ready to take on the kingship. An interim period, a dreadful wash of sacrifice and blood, allows Malcolm to grow into his role. Duncan (Graham Brown) tries to forestall his fate; perhaps sensing it, he tries in his gentle way to pull the kingdom together, wrenched by traitors and invaders. He orders the death of Cawdor to cauterise the wound to the body politic – shocking his thanes and sons who are not used to such forthright action by their gracious king. When Duncan offers gifts to bind his thanes to him, he perhaps encourages Macbeth to think that he could have all.

Duncan's actions, as well as his frailty, hint at his tenuous awareness and an awkward resolution. His naming of Malcolm (Daniel J. Shore) as his successor seems here a move of desperation, and it surprises all the thanes, though they quickly (except Macbeth) move to acknowledge the new Prince of Cumberland. Clearly, the person named to succeed could as well have been Macbeth. But only if war is a society's permanent condition is the warrior a better choice than the gracious son of a gracious king; naming Malcolm is a bid for peace and serenity.

Rightful succession is also the issue in the testing scene (IV.iii.18–139), which many productions cut almost entirely, and for good reason when they cannot make anything of it. But for Daniels, the scene is pivotal. He meant it to open the second act where it would have immediately created a disjunctive vision, separate from the sacrifice of Macbeth that begins in the cauldron scene and that will converge with Malcolm's apotheosis at the end. Placing the intermission before the cauldron scene made his job more difficult.

Macduff and Malcolm are part of the design set in motion in the third scene with the Sisters and sealed in the cauldron scene. This Macduff (Stephen Pelinski) is a man who never thinks beyond orderly progression, from father to son. He served Duncan. He returned to Fife rather than see Macbeth crowned. He sought out Malcolm instead of taking arms against Macbeth himself. With no ambitions for himself, he thought he could persuade Malcolm to take what was his, the throne of Scotland. While he did not think he was sacrificing his own family, he was taking a chance that he would be a permanent exile: 'These evils thou repeat'st upon thyself / Hath banish'd me from Scotland' (IV.iii.12–13). He was not worried about his family because Macbeth had so far murdered men only ('Each new morn / New widows howl, new orphans cry' IV.iii.4–5). The crucial point of the scene is that Malcolm's probing of Macduff is also his testing of his own mettle. Before Macduff arrived, Malcolm knew that there were 'goodly thousands' ready to march into Scotland, but he was not yet sure who he is, and whether he is ready to be his father's successor. But when Macduff passed the test by finding his own edge of incorruptibility – his inability to support a king without any king-becoming graces – suddenly Malcolm can return with Macduff at the head of the English force: 'Old Siward with ten thousand warlike men / Already at a point, was setting forth. / Now we'll together ...' (IV.iii.134–6). That he was testing himself as much as Macduff is suggested by the questioning tones in his dialogue: What *is* a good king? What kind of people must a king have around him to succeed? When Ross arrives, Malcolm, relieved and enthusiastic, tells him, 'We are coming thither' (IV.iii.189). No more testing then. The actors brought to their roles a sense of their characters' struggles with each other and with what they believed is right and true. Because Shore is a most sympathetic Malcolm, in spite of his craftiness, and Pelinski a noble follower, the audience can accept the ending in this production as a moment of gracious resolution – unlike some other productions that cannot work up any positive reactions to Malcolm and can express only pity for Macduff. Daniels's is not a production that questions kingship *per se*.

The troupe acted as a team: with all the actors paid the same wage, there were no stars (though several have been stars in other productions). This could easily have been a director's piece, and to a large extent it was, of course, because Daniels's vision was the initiating force: Jeffrey Horowitz, the artistic director of Theatre for a New Audience, had asked Daniels to choose the play he wanted to work on. Daniels chose *Macbeth* because he felt he had something to say about it. But he drew his actors into discussions of their understanding of every line. He accepted their ideas and expressed his wishes as enthusiastic requests: 'I would *love* it if you could ...' He often praised their interpretations. He gave each actor opportunities to find his or her character and to believe in it. During the rehearsal process, depositions by each actor in character, facing the others as a jury of questioners, brought out the background and motives of each. Some of these sessions were very difficult for the characters as they tried to defend their actions. The result was firm bonds among the actors who worked most closely together. Both James Farmer as Seyton and Bill Camp

[154]

as Macbeth learned about their relationship from the depositions, and their acting reflected it. Stanislavsky worked in this instance.[9]

Always the messenger, Ross (Jonathan Hammond) in this production is a time pleaser, a man who goes along with Macbeth as far as he can. When he visits Lady Macduff, he is full of nervous guilt and altogether unconvincing in his assurances: 'Things at the worst will cease, or else climb upwards / To what they were before' (IV.ii.24–5). Moments after he leaves, he throws in a crumpled message urging her to flee: 'Be not found here. Hence with your little ones.' Daniels's compression of the two messengers (Ross and another) into one exposes the torment of a man trying to be on both sides at once. When he brings the news to Macduff, his shame and guilt show as understandable uneasiness. Earlier, in the scene after the discovery of Duncan's murder (II.iv), Daniels had Lady Macduff, her son (Kyle Russell) and babe in arms enter to greet Macduff and remain upstage while Macduff conferred with Ross. The former decided to go to Fife, the other to Macbeth's coronation at Scone. The failure of Ross to respond to the little family in that scene along with his effusive comfort in the later scene showed that his concern for them was forced – perhaps by guilt.

The production cut the Old Man in II.iv, keeping the focus on the thanes and their interactions. The Porter scene (II.ii), particularly the part before Macduff's entrance, is another that is frequently cut and perhaps it should be because audiences seldom understand the allusive jokes. Reg E. Cathey's Porter clarified the text by developing for each beat a different facet of the drunken man's musings and by engaging the audience as he moved down the aisle and singled out the farmer, equivocator and tailor. It's an over-the-top performance that never failed to captivate the audiences I observed. As Banquo, in contrast, Cathey was dignified, concerned about Macbeth, his friend, and also about himself. Their last exchange before the murder was serious and meaningful, with intent gazes long held and with firm handgrips. Right then Macbeth had a choice to make; it still was not too late to be of Banquo's party rather than murder for more. Daniels had Cathey (against the sense of the lines) suppress any hints that Banquo has any doubt about Macbeth (II.i.26–9) or that Banquo might have ambitions of his own (III.i.1–10). Though Banquo worries about night thoughts that assail him (II.i.7–9), Cathey's Banquo shows that a good person can successfully thrust aside such thoughts. Daniels is not above a grand gesture or two: one in this production was the symbolic appearance of Banquo, naked except for a bloodied ruff, at the banquet scene, an image avoided for matinées with invited school audiences, showing perhaps that the nudity was unnecessary. However, the nudity was part of the meticulous attention to presentation in this production, including the elegant gold sashes for Duncan's men (Macbeth and Banquo along with the others) and the large ruffs that choke the new king and queen in their formal scenes and that make their embraces awkward and impotent. Banquo's nudity and his bloody ruff are symbolic of his death and his descendants' accession to the throne of Scotland and later, through King James VI of Scotland, to the throne of England: an ascent through sacrifice.

But attention to every aspect of a production must reach an apogee in the roles of Macbeth and his Lady, and in them the production found its center of distinction.

Bill Camp's Macbeth is a charmer but with a serpent under a thin skin; rage was there from the beginning, festering beneath the smooth façade from old frustrations and imaginings of entitlement. His compunctions about the murder are barely discernible. Mostly he hesitates out of fear – of being caught, of losing more than he stands to gain. Once he makes his decision, he is single-mindedly villainous, his regrets a convulsive reflex, motivated more by fear for himself than by contrition. Daniels expresses the softer aspects of Macbeth's nature in Lady Macbeth: the two together make one whole. Elizabeth Marvel's Lady is loving, strong, focused and ruthless. Rage is foreign to her; it does not motivate her. She is scarcely aware that it lies beneath her husband's surface. They are an attractive couple with a strong emotional and erotic bond. When he says 'We will talk further', she nods in agreement: he is not putting her off, but exercising a necessary precaution, with which she concurs. When the king's retinue arrived, she was loving to all, especially Donalbain, who leapt into her arms to be caressed. Her warmth is not a mask; it is her genuine self which she forces aside to achieve her husband's goals. In some ways, he is softer than she is: when she says that she has given suck, he raises his finger warningly as if to say 'Don't talk about that!' He seems more pained by their loss of babies than she is. Her gaze is all forward, towards the future; his constantly slips back to the past. After the murder, she is exultant, thrilled with their new status – looking ahead to the glory of ruling. He looks back at what he has done and refuses to let her embrace him. Descending the stair from Duncan's chamber after she has smeared the grooms with blood, she seems pleased with herself as she looks at the blood on her hands. She urges Macbeth to move ahead, to preserve himself by washing and putting on his nightgown, but he follows her reluctantly, caught up in the deed.

In a chiasmus different from most others I have discussed, their transformation into the other is in worldview rather than in power, for they have always been equals. She, the one who looked forward, who urged Macbeth to look to the future to success and triumph, cannot stop looking back at what they have done (especially the murder of the Macduff family), and he, who before and immediately after the murder of Duncan looked back longingly at a life of wholeness and camaraderie, can do nothing but move forward without learning anything from the past. Even when he knows he has sacrificed everything meaningful to him such as 'troops of friends', he must continue on his path. He takes on her demonic singleness of purpose; she questions their purpose. She would have 'dash'd the brains out' of her smiling infant had she so vowed (I.vii.58); Macbeth does dash the brains out of the Macduff child. During her sleepwalking scene, she rips down her white nightgown to expose her breasts, tearing at them and at her womb. She had asked the unseen powers to unsex her (I.v.41). Now she wants to unsex herself lest she bring into the world any babies whose brains will be dashed out. Macbeth has lost all interest in sex and progeny. By his penultimate scene, Camp's Macbeth, a peevish bully, was virtually catatonic (sleeping when not raging). His dissolution allowed for the smooth dominance of Macduff and Malcolm.

Critics, with Clive Barnes among the few exceptions, did not much like the production, though they praised individual actors and elements. Reading the selection of reviews in the Theatre for a New Audience press kit, I am struck with how much they differ from each other. To one, Bill Camp's Macbeth was the only good thing; to another, only Elizabeth Marvel's Lady Macbeth saved the show. One singled out Daniel J. Shore for special praise; another dispraised him. One thought the sound the most impressive aspect; another found it obtrusive and too eclectic to convey any meaning. Similarly for every single aspect of the production, from set to costume to staging: some reviewers selected for admiration the very items others damned. I have seldom seen such disunity among a sheaf of reviews. Many reviewers did not even mention the three Sisters. Most did not, it seems to me, understand the production. I suppose the director has to take some blame for that, but the reviewers should share it also. In all the productions I have studied, I have found that the more a director strays from the model created by David Garrick and Mrs Pritchard, the less the production will be understood by the reviewers. The audience, which has no such preconception, can respond more spontaneously. Daniels's is not a Garrick–Pritchard production. His view of the three Sisters is not negative: they are merely Other, in touch with a non-human sphere. Macbeth is not the noble soldier who is subverted by his powerful termagant of a wife, but a man with powerful ambitions and an aversion to the sweetness of Duncan's court: the three Sisters release a hateful misanthropy that was in him all along. Lady Macbeth is a strong, resolute partner, who, like several other Lady Macbeths, does not understand that one murder will lead to many others, and who, unlike other Lady Macbeths, loves her husband too well to let herself understand his inner anger and cannot survive his descent into madness.

Daniels's *Macbeth* was an original, provocative and worthy attempt to capture an aspect of this difficult play. An intelligent *Macbeth* like this one – well-acted, sensitively directed and ably produced, with many thrilling moments – is a welcome addition to the roster of productions from which we can learn something meaningful about this play and about ourselves (and thankfully the videotape at Lincoln Center preserves one performance). Of course, the question may arise – 'But is this Shakespeare?' Though we cannot know Shakespeare's intentions with any certainty, to assume the weird women's benignity would be foolish. Shakespeare does invoke white magic in *The Winter's Tale* (V.iii.94–111) and, had he meant to do so in *Macbeth*, he certainly could have done so clearly. However, there is something to be said for extending his great theme of reconciliation, so poignantly invoked in the late plays, to *Macbeth*, to a spiritually healed Scotland. Both Ron Daniels and Yukio Ninagawa look for and find ways to expand *Macbeth* so that it can embrace Shakespeare's vision of forgiveness.

Ninagawa Macbeth: fusion of Japanese and Western theatrical styles

PAUL A. S. HARVEY AND BERNICE W. KLIMAN

Surprisingly, *Macbeth* received its première in Japan comparatively late, in Tokyo in September 1913, translated by Ogai Mori, a famous novelist and translator, and directed by Sojin Kamiyama. The play was performed sporadically up to the late 1930s, most notably in the productions of Shoyo Tsubouchi (translator and director) in June 1916 and of Kaoru Osanai and Sugisaka Aoyama (directors) in February 1927. After a hiatus during the Second World War, two major *Macbeth*s stunned audiences: Akira Kurosawa's film adaptation, *Throne of Blood* (1957, discussed in Chapter VI), and the Tsuneari Fukuda's (translator and director) Bungakuza troupe *Macbeth* (1958). Following these, *Macbeth* became one of the more frequently performed Shakespeare plays. Altogether over one hundred different *Macbeth*s appeared in the twentieth century, along with many revivals. *Macbeth* has played in Japan every year from about 1970, and since 1990 an average of five or more different productions have appeared every year. To date there have been at least sixteen published translations. If all this seems surprising, then it should be said that in terms of frequency of performance and translation in Japan, *Macbeth* falls a very long way behind *Hamlet*.[10]

The performances themselves reflect Japan's rich theatrical diversity: Kabuki adaptations by Tsubouchi, focusing on Lady Macbeth (1894–15; see Arai), and Kohei Hatakeyama (1905), setting the play in Korea; Noh elements in Kurosawa's film adaptation and a Noh version of the play in English by Ueda Munakata Kuniyoshi (1987); experimental productions by Sho Ryuzanji (1988), Takeshi Kawamura (*A Man Called Macbeth*, 1990), Tadashi Suzuki (the English-language *Chronicle of Macbeth*, Melbourne 1992) and Kazumi Shimodate (*Osorezan Macbeth*, 1998, Edinburgh, 2000, an adaptation translated into a northern Japanese dialect). Numerous orthodox productions have played through the years, with Tsuneari Fukuda's being considered the most literary of the modern translations. So many different Japanese *Macbeth*s make it impossible to point to one particular style or interpretation as *the* Japanese *Macbeth*.

Incorporating elements of Kabuki, Bunraku (puppet theatre) and experimental theatre, Yukio Ninagawa's *Ninagawa Macbeth* can, in some sense, represent the pinnacle of all. One of the most extensively traveled Japanese theatrical productions ever, it has generated wide acclaim, and Ninagawa has become the best known of the handful of talented Japanese artists who regularly direct Shakespeare. Born in 1935 in Kawaguchi City north of Tokyo, a heavy-industrial working-class area (see Gallimore and Takahashi), he, like Kurosawa, aspired to be a painter but failed to win a place at Tokyo National University of Fine Arts and Music. A regular theatregoer through his teens, he was inspired to become an actor by the production of Kobo Abe's first play, *Seifuku* (Uniform). He won a place as an apprentice actor in the Seihai troupe at the age of twenty-one (1956) and remained with them until 1967 when he started directing, forming his own company, the Contemporary People's Theatre, in 1968. He was a leading figure in the Tokyo left-wing underground theatre movement, opposed to traditional costume drama. He directed plays on a shoestring in small obscure venues, finding an audience among the disaffected youth of the late 1960s and early 1970s. He started directing Shakespeare in 1974 with *Romeo and Juliet* for the Toho company, starring the Kabuki actor Koshiro Matsumoto (then Somegoro) as Romeo. The partnership with Toho proved successful, largely because of the producer Tadao Nakane, who went on to produce most of the major international Ninagawa stagings including *Ninagawa Macbeth*. Working with Nakane (who later founded the production company Point Tokyo), Ninagawa moved into commercial theatre and started directing Western classics on a large scale: in addition to *Macbeth*, he has directed *Medea*, *Peer Gynt*, *The Tempest*, *Midsummer Night's Dream*, *Lear* and *Hamlet*. The international reception of his *Macbeth* propelled him to star status in Japan, and for more than a decade his name on a billboard has been enough to guarantee a full house for most performances. Viewed in the West as an arthouse director, in Japan he is known for spectacle and accessibility. His achievement in the last twenty years has been to reach new audiences with Shakespeare at a time when theatre audiences have been shrinking and to show the world beyond Japan that a Japanese voice can speak through the medium of European theatre in an arrestingly beautiful way.

The first reactions to his *Macbeth* were not auspicious. When it was performed in Tokyo (February 1980) at the Nissei Theatre, reviewers were unsympathetic and audiences stayed away (see Takahashi, 11 October 2000, p. 24). Later, Nakane, who had arranged in 1983 for a hugely successful tour in Europe of Ninagawa's 1978 *Medea*, decided to try to repeat the success with *Macbeth* at the Edinburgh Festival. *Ninagawa Macbeth* first played in Amsterdam and then for four performances in August 1985 in Edinburgh, winning glowing reports from British critics. This success led to an extended run at the Lyttleton Theatre (National Theatre, London, 1987) and a tour of the USA and Canada (1990), with performances at Ottawa National Arts Centre and the Brooklyn Academy of Music, New York. It was taken to Singapore (1992) and also revived in Japan, touring to major venues throughout the country as far as Okinawa. It was last revived in 1998, playing to a full house at the new Opera complex in Shiga, Biwako Hall. Together with *Medea*, it was perhaps the most successful of the postwar Japanese theatrical productions abroad. European and American critics were dazzled by the striking combination of Japanese theatrical elements and classical Western text (albeit in Japanese).

In addition to reviews, scripts, interviews, programmes and a variety of printed materials, the video of the Bunraku Theatre performance in Osaka, March 1985, has provided details of design, blocking and acting. Its Macbeth, Mikijiro Hira, and Lady Macbeth, Komaki Kurihara, both performed in the original 1980 production. In later performances Masane Tsukayama and Kinya Kitaoji played Macbeth but Kurihara stayed with the production. The video is more than a fixed-camera record: it employed half a dozen cameras, and able direction by Ryuzo Matsumoto ensured that closeups, blocking and alignment made good televisual sense. Its weakness is that it tends not to show the whole stage very often.

The performance was strikingly unusual from its opening moments. Japanese temple bells sounded. Two grey-faced women, bent almost double with age, carrying lunch-boxes (*bento*) on their backs, made their way through the audience to the stage, which was closed off by a huge Japanese-paper lattice screen, with shutters extending one quarter of the stage from left and right. They climbed steps up to the apron of the stage, made an obeisance, prayed, then laboriously drew back the shutters as lightning flashed behind the screen. They sat down at either side, left and right, unpacked their lunch-boxes, and proceeded to eat while the performance unfolded. Picnic lunches are common at Kabuki or Bunraku performances. As the main stage darkened between scenes, spotlights caught them downstage far right and left, outside the 'playing' space – eating, weaving elaborate cats' cradles, sewing, weeping, listening with inward turned eyes. They represented the commoners who are outside the main action, their role to witness and endure, filtering the enactment through their custodial care of these memories. They framed the action, eroding the glamour of ambition and energy by barring the audience's direct gaze. Only for the battle scene in Act V did they rise again during the performance, to shut the battle behind a translucent screen. The abiding Old Women, in their rags, counterpointed the ephemeral elegance of the warrior class and the machinations of the supernatural at centre stage.

Huge screens filled the proscenium arch, and decorative gold panelling above the screen had a peacock with outstretched wings, and cloud motifs. (On setting see Mulryne.) The programme informed the audience that the stage was meant to represent a Buddhist altar, an idea that came to Ninagawa when he was praying at his own family altar for the repose of his brother and father. The altar, he said, would bring the story, set in a distant period far away, closer to the Japanese, linking it to their ancestors. Ninagawa made ingenious multivalent use of it, as is typical of all his work. By setting the play within the hallowed space for remembrance and worship of ancestors, he not only domesticated the foreign play but also made a statement about Japanese history. In his book *Fighting Theatre*, he comments: 'it's as though a perfectly ordinary person saw desperate action in war, and it were said to him, "You, perhaps ... will become [Thane of Cawdor or the equivalent]"' (101, Harvey trans.; see also Takahashi, 4 October 2000, p. 24; and Minami, et al., pp. 212–13). Though the production (like Kurosawa's *Throne of Blood*) was set in the turbulent sixteenth century, Ninagawa invited us to consider the more recent past, hinted at in his comment in *Fighting Theatre*. He meant us to ask: could Macbeth himself represent prewar imperial Japan, destroyed by the enticement to an overweening ambition? This latent interpretation became explicit at the end of the play, when Malcolm gave his final speech in the high-pitched ringing tones that characterised radio broadcasts from the war period. As he spoke, the Old Women replaced the shutters, as though closing the doors on that period of history; his last words were heard from behind the closed, darkened screen.

At the same time, Ninagawa stated that when he was planning the production he was also thinking of an incident when members of the extreme left-wing group, the Red Army (similar to Italy's Red Brigades), carried out an ideological purge at their retreat in the Japanese hills in Karuizawa that led to fourteen deaths (February 1972). It was a shocking incident for left-wing Ninagawa and his generation and resulted in his political disillusionment. Shortly after, he formed a new theatre company that he called The Sakura [cherry tree] Company, a name taken from the title of a short story by Kijiro Kaji, *Underneath the Cherry Trees*, whose first line is, 'There is a corpse buried underneath the cherry trees.' The theatre's name commemorated the dead Red Army members, and for Ninagawa, who frequently cited the line about cherry trees and corpses in reference to the production (see Ninagawa, *Note*, p. 154; Takahashi, 3 August 2000, p. 24), *Macbeth* spoke to the tragedy of comrades killing comrades.

As is typical of Ninagawa's method, personal and public symbolism are intertwined. Before the altar, together with our surrogates, the Old Women, we grieve for the enormity of loss in war and conflict, for long-past wars, the Second World War and the blood bath in the Japanese hills only a few years before the first performance – for the loss of idealism. Macbeth wading in blood was to have a wide political reference.

However, this interpretation of the production was unnoted by most critics. Undoubtedly, for most of the foreign audience who came to see *Ninagawa Macbeth* in its travels round the world, the most impressive aspect of the production was the design by Kappa Seno. Notwithstanding the deeply serious political frame that Ninagawa had placed around the play, he did not stint on visual opulence. Critics responded enthusiastically to what Michael Billington, the *Guardian* newspaper critic, describes as Ninagawa's 'aesthetic grace' (p. 286). Billington's review of the run at the National Theatre described the production as 'achingly beautiful ... In his hands the play seems less an anatomy of evil than a lament for the waste and destructiveness of vaulting ambition; and through it all runs what Virgil calls "the sense of tears in mortal things".' The production was indeed astonishingly beautiful to look at. The *shoji*, the huge sliding screens, which became semi-transparent when backlit, were the single most important design element – concealing, revealing or teasing with partial views. Exquisitely made, the screens fitted closely their whole length, opening and closing with a smooth action that had taken many hours to perfect (Dawson, p. 56). Frontlit (as they were at the beginning of the

[163]

performance), they rendered the stage completely opaque, a sealed space that we could not penetrate. When they were backlit, we were granted a partial access to action taking place behind them. Viewed through the screens, the action was distanced from us but, owing to the lighting, glowed with remarkable fulgence, achieving at times a magical lantern effect. For some of the scenes, this effect was stunningly beautiful. Only when the screens were open did the audience have direct access to the action, but even then the Old Women always mediated. Sumio Yoshi's lighting designs also guided our emotional response. Lady Macbeth for the sleepwalking scene, for example, appeared in the distance, her figure slashed by the shadow-bars of slatted screens, a visual metaphor for the punishment her mind was inflicting on her.

The screens divided up the acting space and by so doing provided an interpretative commentary. For the second witches' scene (I.iii) the screens remained closed, with the witches dancing and cherry blossoms falling: we were separated from the action as though it was happening in another world to which we were denied entry, the world of the supernatural. At the disappearance of the witches, the screens opened, the barrier vanishing with the witches. The barrier was in place again when the apparitions paraded behind the closed screens, backlit, as Macbeth and the witches stood on the narrow front apron (IV.i). The screens were closed for the beginning of the play as well as for the beginning of action after the interval, as though Ninagawa wanted to hold us initially at a distance from the play. With Duncan's arrival at Macbeth's castle (I.vi), the screens divided the space between the outside and inside, with a suggestion that the inside of Macbeth's castle was analogous to the supernatural world we had witnessed earlier. The screens were closed upon Banquo's murder (III.iii), which was backlit, with flurries of cherry blossoms falling like snow, the whole sequence suffused with a glow that accentuated its poignancy. The banquet (III.iv) began behind closed screens, which were then flung wide apart by Macbeth, as he rushed out in terror. The screens were closed and backlit as the forest of Dunsinane paraded across the stage (V.vi) – lending the scene a dreamlike ambiance. The two Old Women on either side of the stage, intrigued by the moving trees, came up to the screens and peered in, only to be startled as the screens suddenly began to slide open. The screens and the Old Women created the effect of a play within a play, giving the production a metatheatrical aspect. The enclosed boxlike stage into which we peered also suggested parallels with the cinema or television, calling to mind Kurosawa's film version of *Macbeth* twenty-five years earlier. One faced, as it were, the white wall of the cinema screen, which split open to reveal in three dimensions the shapes of light upon its surface. The device allowed the director alternately to distance and bring forward the action, changing the way we conceived of the space before us, much as a cinema camera can manipulate space through closeups and long shots.

Ninagawa also had screens to close the back of the stage. Duncan entered for the scene in which he would greet Macbeth (I.iv) through sliding screens painted with an exquisite ancient cherry tree in bloom. The king sat in front of the screen, on a throne placed before the suit of armour he had worn in his previous scene (I.ii). The helmet with golden horns, above the armour looked like a disk shining above his head like a halo. He was gorgeously attired with gold *haori* (outer garment) over a diamond-patterned gold kimono. His head was shaved with a topknot in the recognisable samurai style. The screens at the rear formed a picture-image from ancient Japan: such elaborately painted screens are features of Japanese palaces and castles.

The stage was arranged on three levels: the upstage highest, with four steps down to the midstage and down two steps to the downstage area extending over the screen runnels to the front edge of the apron. Tiered staging is one of Ninagawa's favoured designs. He arranged the players for Duncan's first scene (I.ii) in a descending upside-down V, from the highest level mid-upstage, on diagonals to the lowest level. This established a hierarchical relationship, with Duncan occupying the apex of the pyramid and his courtiers descending to left and right. Ninagawa employed this design for the second courtier scene (I.iv), for the banquet scene (III.iv), and again at the end for Malcolm (V.viii). After Duncan's murder, his armour remained in the same place, the apex of the pyramid, symbolising the ever-present crime of his murder. It was the fixed reference point for stage action, which Macbeth had to negotiate during his many upstage entrances and exits. Just beneath this stage position Macbeth was finally killed.

The distinct sets were unified, as were the costumes, by the cherry blossom theme. At the beginning when the three witches cavorted, their large arm gestures mimed the wide-limbed cherry tree that dominated many of the scenes. The blossom-laden tree

and its representation on a painted screen, the delicate and continuous fall of petals in many scenes (a staging technique borrowed
from Kabuki) as well as their traces on the platforms of the
interiors, provoked reflection on evanescent beauty, on the un-
stoppable cycles of nature that speed us to our deaths. A feature of
the production was the sheer quantity of cherry blossoms;
normally in Kabuki petals drift from the flies individually, but
Ninagawa deployed them as if they were snow. Scenes involving
action of any kind took place under falling blossoms, or beneath a
huge cherry tree, or beneath swathes of cherry blossoms hung
from the flies. The effect of all these blossoms was overpowering.
In Japan blossoms are associated with sexual activity, and the fall
of the petals with the loss of love, with the transience of earthly
happiness. Ninagawa's yoking of murder and cherry blossoms is
typical of his iconoclastic method in general.

For Macbeth's scenes within the castle with Lady Macbeth, and
alone, the stage was bare, apart from one or two significant props.
The English scene (IV.iii) was distinguished from the other
interiors by wooden statues of gods from the Buddhist pantheon
set about the stage. These are guardian deities that one can see in
the temples in Nara or Kyoto. They would never, of course, be
found within a Buddhist altar (in which one finds statues of
Buddha); they stand in the temple's display halls. The English
court was thus set within a Buddhist temple rather than in the
altar of the other scenes. While one observed Macduff or Malcolm,
behind them the statues also came into view, establishing a visual
link: these were the forces of goodness.

Throughout the performance, the range of sound effects made
a powerful contribution: emphatic speech rhythms, whether brus-
que and guttural or whining and pathetic (as was Lady Macduff's
voice); gongs, Buddhist chants and natural sounds of thunder.
Ninagawa most significantly interwove three pieces of Western
music: Gabriel Fauré's *Requiem* (1887, op. 48), principally the
Sanctus; Brahms's String Sextet No. 1 in B flat major (1860, op.
18); and a few phrases from Samuel Barber's Adagio for Strings
(1938, op. 11). The Fauré sounded repeatedly throughout the performance, its soothing *Sanctus* at the beginning as the Old Women
made their way to the stage to pull back the screens. The repeated
phrase, 'Sanctus, Sanctus', pointed to the life to come that Macbeth had rejected when he opted to kill Duncan – 'We'd jump the
life to come' (I.vii.7). The Fauré quieted tension with transitions

between scenes. Being a mass for the dead, it spoke also to the notion of grief and its assuagement. Western reviewers heard in it a redemptive note. The most startling moment was the *Pie Jesu* from the *Requiem* lovingly sung as Macbeth lay dead, curled in a foetal pose. Startling juxtapositions of divergent theatrical styles shook the audience into attentiveness and awareness, prodding them to accept the uneasy juxtaposition of unrepentant wickedness and forgiveness, engaging their participation in a ritual of loss.

Ninagawa's method provided both stress-inducing dramatic tension at the same time as its antidote. A good example of this technique was to be seen when Lady Macbeth played Barber's Adagio on her cello, with impressive plangency: the mellow harmony of the music was shattered by the messenger shouting his announcement of the arrival of Duncan, and by Lady Macbeth's rasping answer. It was as though the arrival of Duncan and Lady Macbeth's response to it (harsh-voiced as a raven) prefigured the later tragedy. The Brahms, a passionate secular piece, was heard most notably during and after the scene in which Macbeth and Lady Macbeth met for the first time, following the letter-reading (I.v). Unlike the Fauré, this piece heightened tension, the passionate violins suggesting emotional crisis (as in III.ii). The Brahms also figured effectively in the dance-like choreography of Banquo's murder, the sound of the music swelling louder and cherry blossoms falling thicker as Banquo was dispatched. Brahms also introduced the sleepwalking scene and accompanied the final fight (V.viii).

Although the production's design aspects won most praise from the foreign critics, Ninagawa also carefully constructed and directed the Shakespearean text and the characterisation of the two protagonists. Because the witches (played by men) were stylised creations who seemed to represent Fate, because the murderers through their black Ninja costumes and subservient demeanour were ciphers and because the other characters were depersonalised, Macbeth and Lady Macbeth held an unchallenged position at the emotional centre of the drama. Though he had the larger part, they were equal in power throughout the play, the relation of the warrior and his consort impeccably realised. No rupture divided them. Thus, his sorrow at her death was moving and his determination to fight admirable: he overcame his demoralisation to act as he deemed right and as, he believed, the Fates expected, defending the position he had won so wrongfully.

Ninagawa adopted the Yushi Odajima translation of *Macbeth* (first published in 1983, three years after the first performance; see Ninagawa, *Note*, p. 149). Odajima's translation is distinguished by its modern colloquialism and by witty Japanese versions of Shakespearean puns. Odajima went on to translate the entire *Works*, and for the last twenty years his translations have been ubiquitous. In this production, Ninagawa made changes to render the play more accessible. He retained the names of the individual characters, but 'Scotland' (in the case of Macduff's cry 'Scotland! Scotland!' IV.iii.100) became *Fatherland*, 'England' *Southern Country*, and 'Ireland' *Western Country*. These changes allowed the action to be sited in an imaginary non-specific locale congenial to Japanese audiences. Kurosawa did much the same in *Throne of Blood* by putting a frame about the film and setting it in the distant medieval past. Other of Ninagawa's changes were in line with this distancing. To make it easy for the Japanese audience to follow the story, Ninagawa removed culturally specific terms and details, such as 'Bellona's Bridegroom', replaced by 'Macbeth becoming reborn as the god of war'. When Duncan walked down-stage to pat the seated Macbeth on the shoulder and to say 'make thee full of growing', he did the same for Banquo, but he didn't embrace either. This choice was again culturally specific – an embrace would have been wrong. The most significant of the culturally specific cuts, which are common in Japanese adaptations of Shakespeare, are those which dilute the Christian emphasis of certain passages. Conspicuous was the loss of 'I had most need of blessing' through "Amen" / Stuck in my throat' (II.ii.16–30). These fifteen lines emphasise Macbeth's regret, fall from grace, and despair; they vitally underscore the Christian background. Ninagawa retained in this scene the lines on Macbeth murdering sleep, which gained greater emphasis from their isolation. Ninagawa speeded the pace and diminished the text's density.

Odajima replaced the phrase 'like a poor cat in th'adage' with the original proverb 'like the cat who would eat fish but would not wet its feet', which works well in Japanese. In general the changes made to the text were in the interest of pace and comprehensibility: to make the play accessible to larger numbers of Japanese, for whom Shakespeare retains the reputation of being 'difficult'. The loss of cultural background is an inevitable part of the translation process, though some of the cuts are regrettable.

Ninagawa reduced the witches, and the reason for this was

again cultural: no direct equivalent for them exists in Japanese. In their last scene (IV.i), the items for the cauldron gave way to a dance prior to Macbeth's arrival. Ninagawa cut the lines on Aleppo (I.iii.7–10), delivered in the first performances. Cuts to the witches after the beginning of the production probably occurred owing to a perception that they were among the dramatically weaker elements. The Porter was also reduced, his interaction with Macduff removed. The script removed Hecate's scene (III.v) – a standard cut – and placed Lenox and Lord in conversation (III.vi) after the cauldron scene, a standard move. The cut and transposition meant that the cauldron scene (IV.i) followed, after the intermission, directly on the banquet scene (III.iv), giving Ninagawa a strong ending for the first act and an equally strong beginning for the second. The production was very Macbeth-centred, for the cuts to the witches and the Porter served to narrow the spotlight upon Macbeth. The scene in the English court (IV.iii) was severely cut to speed the pace – it is too long for most productions. The Scottish rebel army (V.ii) was cut to a few lines, again to improve the pace, though at the cost of losing some of the choric quality of this short scene. One other significant area was the alteration in Banquo. With his lines on sleeplessness cut (II.i.6–7), he was presented as a bluff, straightforward hero, a contrast to Macbeth, who monopolises angst-ridden complexity. By making the production Macbeth-centred, Ninagawa also took advantage of Hira's prestige and popularity.

Ninagawa's sculpting of Macbeth's character can in part be seen in the cuts made to some of his speeches. In Macbeth's great soliloquy 'If it were done', the lines on 'pity striding the blast' (I.vii.21–2) are cut. The reason is again partly cultural, since the lines make little sense in Japanese (being difficult enough in English), but the cut also accords with Ninagawa's diminishing of Macbeth the poet. Macbeth's sensitive eloquence, something he shares with Hamlet, or even Othello, is replaced by an intense but less verbal alienation. Following his line 'My mind is full of scorpions!' (III.ii.36), he gives the lines about the shard-born beetle, but the line and a half about Hecate and the bat are cut (III.ii.40–1). This is cultural, the reference to Hecate being obscure, but it also takes from Macbeth his eloquent word-painting of the forces of darkness. A similar effect occurs when, with the removal of 'witchcraft celebrates / Pale Hecate's off'rings' (II.i.51–2), we lose the parallel between Macbeth and the forces of darkness he describes. Following 'To be thus is nothing' (III. i. 47), the lines are also cut in which Macbeth discusses his fear of Banquo, Banquo's royalty of nature and Macbeth's genius rebuked. This cut contributes to Ninagawa's aim to diminish Banquo's role in the play, but it also eliminates the opportunity to witness Macbeth's perceptive assessment of a rival.

Although important matter is lost in cultural adaptation, a great deal is also gained. Ninagawa shaped the resources of traditional Japanese theatre to enhance the characterization of Macbeth – principally with Kabuki stylisation. The production was unusual in that it boldly mixed different theatrical styles, anathema to purists but executed with great panache here. This stylistic bricolage has become Ninagawa's hallmark. Hira's speaking style was modern, but it borrowed various elements from Kabuki: his facial make-up pattern, some of his moves on the stage and some poses, such as the *mie*, or bravura pose, when the actor holds a gesture motionless for a few moments, like a statue, to the applause of the audience. While the cuts to Macbeth's speeches removed some of the interiority of the character, an exterior poeticism replaced it. Since Kabuki is an exceedingly visual art, it supplies aesthetic satisfaction by costume, dance and movement in a way that the Western stage cannot ordinarily emulate. On the other hand, through the amalgamation with a Western text, Ninagawa also achieved something that cannot be emulated by traditional Japanese stage forms. As Anthony Tatlow points out,

Ninagawa has developed an acting practice that employs a gestural language whose strength depends on its consciousness of body as the primary site for exploring the emotions, but that has been able to shed, or escape from, the standardised conventions because its engagement with a 'foreign text' encourages it to reimagine its own tradition's proxemic conventions. (p. 73)

Macbeth's first appearance was striking. Macbeth and Banquo arrived on horses (white for Macbeth and black for Banquo), gracefully operated by two men each, with great attention to detail in their steps and in flicks of their manes. Cherry blossoms fell while the witches hailed the two soldiers. Both Macbeth and Banquo were dressed as elegant samurai, Macbeth in a white kimono with a black corslet, and a circle of rope round his neck, from which hung twists of paper, holy charms from a Japanese shrine (called *nusa*). His make-up distinguished him from the other characters. He had sharply angled eyebrows and white face-paint, with a thin red line extending either side of his nose to beneath his eyebrows. This was like the *kumadori* make-up worn for major Kabuki roles, designed to create a visually bold effect. He wore a wig usually seen in historical drama or Kabuki or Bunraku plays, the hair swept back from the face and bound on the crown of the head, cascading back to form a pompom. The message was that Macbeth was potentially villainous (the make-up with the steeply arched eyebrows), had a high social status (the armour, horse, samurai hairstyle) and had a dandy's concern with appearance (the loose pompom of the bound hair). There was something of the outlaw about him.

His second scene (I.iv) offered a greater opportunity to examine him closely: he was dignified, polished and elegant, physically more beautiful than most Macbeths, by no means openly villain-ous, a man with a conscience, also exhibiting evidence of anxiety and nerves in hands trembling, shiftiness in the eyes and a slight tremolo in the voice. In terms of Kabuki style, he would be classi-fied as 'wagoto', that is to say the softer more feminine Osaka style, rather than 'aragoto', the Tokyo masculine style. He was distinguished from Banquo by his larger reactions to various lines. He grabbed at his sword hilt to indicate intensity of feeling. Hira, speaking with measured eloquence through the scene, clarified Macbeth's development in thought. As he gave his long aside his eyes shifted meaningfully to signify that he was considering his options very carefully (I.iii.127–48).

Gifted with a rich bass voice, Hira placed great emphasis on the declamation of his soliloquies, lowering his voice an octave to give the speeches weight and resonance. For 'If it were done' (I.vii.1), he entered upstage centre, in golden *hakama* (Kabuki trousers) and a silver-grey kimono. These garments signalled that Macbeth is still good here; he has not committed murder, and the brilliance of the cloth reflects that integrity. It is symbolism Nina-gawa adopts later for Macduff and Malcolm, both of whom wear golden kimono. Macbeth spoke his lines leaning forward, with his right hand inside his kimono, a gesture from Kabuki indicating pensiveness. He wheeled round after he walked past Duncan's armour (poised upstage centre), as though he thought that it had moved. He was neurotic, on edge. He spoke his first line frowning fiercely, staring fixedly at the floor. The speech gathered in inten-sity and volume until he mentioned Duncan, 'his virtues / Will plead like angels', at which point he turned away, striking his head, and squatted.

For the next scene (II.i) Hira made a bravura entrance, walking backwards, holding up a large red kimono, which hid him completely. This was an effect borrowed from Kabuki and notable for its bold symbolism, the red representing the blood to be spilt by his murders. When Banquo challenged him, he turned, framing himself within the red kimono, worn over the silver-grey kimono of the previous scene. Ninagawa emphasised the suspicion between the two men as they conversed: Macbeth made to embrace Banquo on the line, 'It shall make honour for you', but Banquo waved him aside. Left alone on the stage, Macbeth wheeled, flicking off the red kimono, and squatted, composing himself. The taking off and putting on of the red kimono indicated Macbeth's indecision as to whether he will robe himself in blood, as he must do if he is to kill Duncan. Against the sense, Hira gave the lines a rapid-fire delivery, presumably to convey Macbeth's nervous tension; but Macbeth should be hesitant during this speech. Hira conveyed well the psychological tension, looking exhausted on the phrase 'it is the bloody business' (II.i.48). A temple bell tolled. Macbeth shouted out 'Yoshi!' (Right!) and picked up the red kimono that he had cast to the floor. He closed the scene with a half-*mie* on 'that summons thee' (II.i.64), his body poised in front of the suit of armour, half-way up the steps, his left hand holding the red kimono, which trailed down the steps beneath him, a great swathe of red, like a pool of scarlet blood. Then he exited through the sliding doors centre back. The scene encapsulated the great strengths and weaknesses of Ninagawa's work: Macbeth would surely *not* be shouting out anything before he enters to kill Duncan. Visually, however, the *mie* on the steps made convincing sense, summing up the action in a memorable way.

Ninagawa built on this characterisation following the murder. Macbeth returned, close to desperation (II.ii). Macbeth's psychological distress was not rooted in a Christian conscience. The Japanese context presented the murder as a crime against feudal loyalty to a greater extent than in the original. Shock and revulsion were the keynotes as Macbeth stumbled on, hunched over, speaking more slowly than before, his voice broken as he called out, 'I have done the deed'. He held up bloody hands as he howled out the lines about murdered sleep. To make him relinquish the long-bladed knife, Lady Macbeth had to strike his hand with her

9   Yukio Ninagawa's production of *Macbeth*, 1990

fist. Left alone, he looked at his hands in despair and said, 'What hands are here?' When Lady Macbeth returned from smearing the grooms, he pressed her bloody hands up to his face, and kissed them, staining his face red: the death-laden eroticism was intense. He spoke 'Wake Duncan with thy knocking!' desperately. The murder had transformed Macbeth into a shattered wreck.

This scene contrasted sharply with the next; the Macbeth who returned to make his rhetorically rich but empty peroration on the death of Duncan was calm and poised (II.iii.89–94). He wore a light green *yukata* (light cotton kimono), which produced a strong visual contrast with the blood of the previous scene. Ninagawa coded the production with reds and greens, but not simplistically. As Macbeth explained that he couldn't stop himself killing the grooms, a rainbow prism shone upon him, with red and green, a slash of rainbow colour, on the stage-left wall. Presumably the colours were a visual correlative for the choice that Macbeth had faced: whether to go ahead with evil or to stop. Towards the end of his speech, when Macbeth went downstage to comfort Malcolm and Donalbain, Lady Macbeth, who wore a white *yukata*, performed her faint: it was clearly done to divert attention from Macbeth's insincerity about killing the grooms. She looked at him

[173]

meaningfully, counting on him to play his part in their duet of deception, getting him away from Malcolm and Donalbain. These two were played young, with youthful voices and with floral kimono that reflected their youth. They remained on stage at the end of the scene – stumbling up to the suit of armour upstage. Malcolm stood in the rainbow spotlight, a visual link being established with Macbeth, suggesting that Malcolm would be faced with similar choices of good and evil. They ran off the stage down the aisles.

Following Macbeth's coronation (III.i), Macbeth and Lady Macbeth reappeared with different visual identities. Macbeth was puffy-looking, with a hard mask-like expression, though his white face paint had gone. He moved slowly, swaying slightly, as though aged by the recent events. Both he and Lady Macbeth had new coiffure. Building on the earlier visual representation of him as something of an outlaw, the designer Jusaburo Tsuimura made him look like a pirate king with pigtails hanging down just to the side of his eyes; pirates in the eighteenth century wore such pigtails. Aside from the pigtails, his hair was, like Lady Macbeth's, brushed up away from his face over a long white comb placed horizontally against the crown. The brushed hairstyle was not native Japanese but an amalgam that Tsuimura created for the silhouette-effect of horns (he called the style *ryujin*, meaning 'dragon man'). Macbeth wore a beige inner kimono and a dark green outer gown, with a baroque brown ruff-frill collar; the visual impression was of excess. In this scene his interaction with Banquo was cold and sinister. As Macbeth walked off at the end of the scene, he addressed an imaginary Banquo, speaking with mock solicitousness, 'tonight you have to find the right path, if you want to go to heaven', rather than with Shakespeare's urgent 'must find it out tonight' (III.i.141).

In the banquet scene (III.iv) Macbeth revealed a new side, when he was generous to the assassin who had failed to kill Fleance. He put his arm around his shoulder, comforting him with the comment that 'at least the grown serpent is dead'. Macbeth was good to his own. (Kurosawa in *Throne of Blood*, in contrast, had his Macbeth strike the assassin dead.) His exquisite formal black kimono with a large cherry blossom pattern and brilliant orange *obi* (silk band for tying the kimono) symbolised his self-possession, which the appearance of Banquo's ghost completely shattered. He dashed out in terror through the screens to return dishevelled, with his kimono half-off, trailing behind him. On his return he fell to the ground in a paroxysm of fear, while Lady Macbeth dismissed the guests very sharply. Hira delivered 'Blood will have blood' with desperation, but his Macbeth gained in strength and resolve by the lines 'returning were as tedious as go o'er' (III.iv.137). One of the great strengths of Hira's performance was the modulation he achieved between the extremes of terror-struck reaction to the ghost, or the psychological reaction following the murder, and the fought-for self-control that is won back. The end of the banquet scene demonstrated this development when Hira struck a *mie* and gave the line, 'We are yet but young in deed' (III.iv.143).

When Macbeth revisited the witches (IV.i) he wore once again the rope and the holy charms around his neck as at the beginning, but he wrapped himself in a black cloak, and his make-up rendered him gaunt and drawn. His hair was loose, symbolising his state of mental disarray. Macbeth flung open his black cloak to expose an elegant silver-grey flecked kimono, a gesture that invited appreciation of the visual splendour of the garment but did not contribute to plot or character. Here, one can note Ninagawa's prioritisation of visual effect, even at the expense of context. The freezing of the action to draw attention to costly ornament and decoration that Ninagawa took from the Kabuki theatre characterised Macbeth's final appearances, where the gorgeousness of the kimono contrasted with the claustrophobic isolation in which he finds himself.

For the final scenes, Macbeth again wore his hair loose. In the scene of the fleeing of the thanes (V.iii) he sat disconsolately on the throne, his feet tucked up beneath him, on an otherwise almost empty stage. With a forearm greave on his left arm only, he was in a state of semi-preparation. When he said 'then fly, false Thanes' (V.iii.7), he squatted upon his heels on the throne, looking like a large colourful toad or spider. He gave the lines 'my way of life' (V.iii.22–6) a self-pitying sadness and weight, hand on heart. Using the same phrase that he had pronounced earlier when braving fate, he called Seyton to say he would fight. The production balanced his self-pity and stubborn valour. With a broken voice he begged the doctor to heal Lady Macbeth (V.iii.39), again lapsing into despair, and then, in a fit of anger, knocked the doctor down and kicked him.

The scene when Macbeth learns of the death of Lady Macbeth and of the moving grove (V.v) was a tour de force, with all Ninagawa's penchant for visual impact on full display. As Macbeth entered, he carried a single candle that he used to light other candles, which looked like dozens of fallen stars. On hearing the women's cry, Seyton dashed off, then returned and, grieving, announced Lady Macbeth's death. He left Lady Macbeth's silver kimono with the red lining centre stage. Macbeth stroked it, picked it up, kissed it, and put it on as he said that 'she was going to have to die at some time', and he thought that he would have been told such news eventually: this is translator Odajima's interpretation of 'She should have died hereafter: / There would have been a time for such a word' (V.v.16–17). Hira's Macbeth said the lines to console himself – death is inevitable, it was going to happen anyway. Wearing his wife's kimono, Macbeth began 'Tomorrow and tomorrow', his lower lip quivering and tears filling his eyes. Disgust erupted on 'Out, out, brief candle!', at which he fell to the ground, blowing at the circle of candles around him. He spoke 'Life's but a walking shadow' with a quavering voice, fighting his grief. He broke down and wept between saying 'full of sound of fury' and 'signifying nothing' (V.v.26–7). The Japanese translation changed Shakespeare to 'even though the bawling out of sound and fury is terrible, / It has no meaning at all'. At 'terrible', Macbeth started sobbing – he had become the idiot, the fool of time, grief-stricken. He spoke 'there is no meaning' as a profound truth, a revelation. At this point the servant entered to announce, from outside the candle-circle, that the forest was moving. An article in the *Mainichi Newspaper* (5 October 2000, p. 24) suggested that, when Macbeth learned that the cherry trees had started to move, Ninagawa had a recording playing the sound of the police firing tear gas at the students in Yasuda Hall at Tokyo University. The destruction of Macbeth was connected to Ninagawa's personal symbolism of the destruction of 1960s left-wing idealism. In this context, Malcolm would represent the right-wing establishment. Ninagawa commented later that he felt that the 'Tomorrow' speech exactly mirrored his feelings at the time (Takahashi, 5 October 2000, p. 24; Odajima and Ninagawa, p. 101). Here again Ninagawa iconoclastically refuses to separate moral categories.

Hira was good at the volatility that Ninagawa required, swinging between defiance and despair, and, at the end of the scene, to shock and horror at the wood moving. He stared, hand up to his face palm outwards to shield himself from an imaginary sun on 'I 'gin to be aweary of the sun' (V.v.49), dark finger shadows forming across his face. Desperation with 'Blow wind! come, wrack!' was followed by martial resolution as he slowly closed up his fist and stiffened to give the final line. The visual impact of the scene was impressive, with the single figure of Macbeth surrounded by candles (expressing the 'brief candle' from the speech itself). The stage was otherwise in darkness. These candles represented the victims of his tyranny, and he stood lit by the flames of his many killings, Lady Macbeth's death being simply the latest result of the decision taken to kill Duncan. The sound of battle approached, and the scene closed with Macbeth holding up one candle, which was the last to flicker out, figuring his own imminent death.

Macbeth's final scene (V.viii) was powerfully achieved. The screens were closed initially, distancing us from the action. Cherry blossoms were still falling, though the cherry tree (for V.vii) had been removed. Macbeth ran in and was encircled by assailants whom he kept at bay, like a bear fighting off mastiffs. The screens pulled open as he dispatched half a dozen of them. Macduff entered upstage left and spoke rather than shouted, 'Turn Hell-hound'. When Macduff stated that his was a caesarean birth, Macbeth tottered, lamenting his trust in the witches. He squatted down, refusing to fight. Threatened with being made a side-show, he gathered up resolution and for the third and last time, using the same Japanese phrase as before (*saigo made tatakauzo!*), said that he would fight to the last. The contrast with his earlier adroit swordsmanship was striking. The storm of blossoms continued as a giant red moon started to glow on the upstage backdrop. His sword lost, Macbeth was struck a great blow by Macduff from the upstage steps (from just below where Duncan's armour had stood), with the sound effect of a sword whipping through the air – at which point all sound was cut, and the blossoms ceased falling, a powerful *coup de théâtre*. Macbeth died, curling into a fetal position. He did indeed regain audience sympathy and achieve heroic stature in these last scenes (following the nadir of Lady Macduff's murder) though not perhaps as much as Ninagawa might have wished.

Unlike Mikijiro Hira, who performed only in the earlier per-formances of *Macbeth* (Tokyo, Osaka and the Edinburgh Festival), Komaki Kurihara performed in every one: more than any other single performer, she made the production hers. She characterised Lady Macbeth as a hard, fierce woman, moody and somewhat unpredictable, alternatively harsh and tender towards Macbeth, caring deeply for success. Her obsessive neuroticism planted the seed for her later madness. Ninagawa did not use a chiasmus effect because they were co-conspirators from beginning to end.

Her first scene is the celebrated letter-reading entry (I.v). The stage was cleared, apart from single candles on black iron stands arranged on diagonals from upstage centre, two on either side, the kind of candles found in old Japanese manor houses. The back of the stage was closed off by large unpainted sliding doors through which Kurihara entered, holding her kimono open in a triangular shape. She wore a red outer kimono with a green cherry blossom pattern and green lining and a beige inner kimono. As with Macbeth, red and green typified moral choices; the cherry blossom pattern, also worn by Macbeth later in the play, was a thematic motif in the design. Here the green clashed unpleasantly with the cherry blossoms. Her coiffure was severe, unattractive, with long locks hanging down to left and right like Medusa serpents; her white face and red lips a startling contrast. She took the letter, folded concertina style, out of her kimono and flicked it open in a deft gesture. Reading the letter with a fierce emotionless delivery as she walked forward, she looked straight out into the auditorium; she then folded it up carefully and placed it back inside her kimono, smiling with pleasure. She spat out towards the audience the speech that followed; this was a tough Lady Macbeth. Her lines on Macbeth's character beginning 'Yet do I fear thy nature' (I.v.16–20) were scathing. But towards the end of the speech Kurihara's voice softened and her expression brightened as she said 'thou'dst have, great Glamis' (22–5). Here, she arrived downstage, where the black lacquered cello lay. Visually, the conjunction of kimono sleeve and black-lacquered cello (lacquer being prototypically Japanese) was lovely. She continued with the second half of the speech, and, laughing out loud rather theatrically, she called up the spirits, confirming our impression of her hardness. At 'unsex me here', rendered in the Japanese as 'make me no longer a woman', she closed her eyes and flicked open her kimono slightly, in a restrained gesture of sexual abandonment that went against the sense of the lines. As she finished the speech Macbeth arrived through the sliding doors, moved downstage behind her, and from behind moved his right hand roughly inside her kimono over her left breast, his left hand remaining on his sword. The action underscored the sexual bond between them, pointing to Macbeth's aggressively phallic masculinity. In the ensuing conversation, Lady Macbeth spat out that Duncan would not see the morrow. She moved away from Macbeth and said that his face was like a book, finishing the speech with a harsh tone and a curt, impatient delivery. She moved off quickly after the end of her speech, leaving Macbeth gripping his sword, contemplating action, and looking anxious. She stood a moment upstage, looking back at him and smiling, establishing her dominance over Macbeth.

Her dominance was also in evidence in their next scene (I.vii). She replied to Macbeth's uncertain 'If we should fail?' by striking him hard across the face. She was incensed as she commanded him to gather up his courage: she was fiercely single-minded, almost terrifying. As with Hira, Kurihara was good at modulating the delivery, and her tone softened when she outlined the plan, with her right arm extended, displaying the red lining of the kimono, symbolic of the blood to be spilt. When she came to the 'guilt / Of our great quell' (in the Japanese the speech ends with 'and that will settle the matter'), she spat out the words impatiently, with an edge of desperation. Macbeth reacted with admiration. His face softening, he gave his lines slowly and thoughtfully. As he said 'what the false heart doth know' he looked round and smiled. They laughed together and proceeded back up the stairs, centre-stage and out. He was a different man from the one who had appeared at the beginning of the scene. Her strength of purpose had pushed him towards the deed. The scene made manifest their mutuality.

The scene after the murder (II.ii) was directed rather eccentrically, with Lady Macbeth literally reeling as she said 'that which hath made them drunk hath made me bold' – she did not know how drunk she was. She descended the steps diagonally, stumbled as she said, 'Death and Nature do contend about them, / Whether they live, or die' (7–8) and laughed. A noise made her shriek and clap her hands to her ears. She looked upset, distracted when she said, 'Had he not resembled / My father as he slept, I had done't' (12–13). The beginning of this scene takes her a step closer towards madness. When Macbeth showed his bloody hands (46), she asserted control ('Infirm of purpose!').

Their first meeting alone after the coronation (III.ii) displayed their co-operation. The stage was bare apart from a small screen placed midstage right with a kimono draped over it, a chair and the cello midstage centre, and a Japanese-style small floor mirror, downstage centre. A maid combed Lady Macbeth's hair; both sat on the floor, as if on tatami matting. After the maid left, Lady Macbeth looked deep into the mirror. Her make-up was softer, accentuating her femininity. She uttered in despair, 'Nought's had', weeping. It was a critical moment; she had moved further towards the madness of Act V, Macbeth stood in the wings, listening, but when he entered she hid her feelings. She spoke to him while still looking into the mirror, in effect addressing herself. Macbeth gave his speech descending from upstage, omitting the lines about scotching the snake, going straight to 'let the frame of things disjoint' (16) and thus increasing the feeling of crisis, which escalated to 'He [Duncan] sleeps well' (23). Then he whirled his kimono about him and dropped down on to the midstage, making the cherry petals swirl up. His restlessness saddened rather than frightened her, but she tried to cheer him; her sombre look appeared only when his face was averted from hers. In turn, he tenderly covered her with her robe as she reclined. A warm intimacy still existed between them when she asked him to 'Be bright and jovial' (28) at the banquet, and he agreed. However, Macbeth then rushed over to seize the mirror, and, lifting it, stared into it, crying out, 'full of scorpions is my mind, dear wife', wailing that Banquo and Fleance still lived. Warmth continued between them in this scene, with 'Be innocent of the knowledge, dearest chuck' (45) played with them close together, Macbeth stretched on the floor, Lady Macbeth with her hand on his arm. From this position Macbeth gave the speech, 'Come seeling Night'. They gave a strong sense that they were confederates. While giving the lines 'Things bad begun', he took the kimono from the screen and dressed Lady Macbeth in it, over the red kimono she was already wearing, The outer kimono was dark red with large white cherry blossoms – the blood theme clearly stated by the red, together with the erotic ambivalence of the white cherry blossoms, symbols of sexual fulfilment and its rapid decay. Cherry blossoms and death, the production's visual theme. The beauty of the kimono contrasted with Macbeth and Lady Macbeth's increased moral degeneration. They exited together.

In the banquet scene (III.iv) Kurihara presented a strong and, again, impatient Lady Macbeth, snapping at Macbeth with exasperation, dismissing the guests with harsh and authoritative abruptness. At her final scene – the sleepwalking scene (V.i) – the doctor and maidservant entered from stage left, midstage, and moved downstage to observe. Lady Macbeth entered stage left, upstage, carrying a candle and staring fixedly at it. Her hair loose, she knelt midstage right, at the edge of the steps, and leaned forward to wash her hands, pouring water as if from a jug into a basin, all the while rubbing at her right hand obsessively. Her voice harsh and strained, she used the same tone of voice with which she had upbraided Macbeth, sounding insane. Without lipstick and with her face and hands made-up in pale green, she looked ill. The change from her previous scene was considerable. Her voice shook as she cried out that she would never have thought the old man to have had so much blood in him. Then she threw herself about in distress, falling to the floor and tumbling down the steps. She rose and tossed her hair forward, wiping her hands in it and muttering, 'What, will these hands ne'er be clean?' (41). She gave a long protracted groan, rather than a sigh, then fell to the floor and lay there, the red lining of her kimono turned outward so that there was a large red pool over her abdomen, suggestive of a huge wound. She wept as she talked about Banquo's murder. As she left the stage, she spoke to an imaginary Macbeth, castigating him; turning back, she shrieked out, 'Hurry up!', an addition to Shakespeare. It was a dazzling performance, with commitment and variety in voice and action.

A criticism that might be made of the production (and of Ninagawa's work in general) is that he overloads the palette. His is a baroque extravagance that seems to know no restraint. But to say this of Ninagawa is to miss the point. He achieves much of the effect he is striving for by filling the dramatic space with symbols that operate with dream-logic and by making large, extravagant statements. Could one say that his production of *Macbeth* was simply too beautiful? Surely *Macbeth* requires a starkness, a restraint, in order for its power to be truly unleashed. But this was part of his point: underneath the cherry blossoms, corpses are buried – death and eroticism are intertwined. Clarity failed at certain points: was Malcolm to be a good king? The high-pitched tones of his delivery at the end suggested that perhaps he would not be, though in the English scene the visual juxtaposition with the Buddhist deities suggested that he would; and his bright golden-hued kimono (similar to that worn by Macduff) also suggested a noble, uncorrupted nature. These loose ends did not really matter, however. Ninagawa, unlike many directors of Shakespeare, is an artist rather than an interpreter: he shaped the medium of Shakespeare's play to forge a new work of art that had a meaningful relationship with the original but that took the audience into an entirely new domain. For all its seriousness, the production was far from solemn. The Porter, his salacious comments cut, was himself the image of obscenity, with bare buttocks and a truncheon hanging between his legs. The cavorting horses were a witty delight. Ninagawa's fusion of Japanese and Western theatre, of urgent political purpose with aesthetic brilliance, was something to be profoundly thankful for.

CHAPTER VI

The production: visionary directors on film

Visual poetry in Akira Kurosawa's *Throne of Blood*

Akira Kurosawa's *Throne of Blood* (*Kumonosu-Djo*, The Castle of the Spider's Web, 1957) is among the most satisfying films based on a Shakespeare play. Rather than create a performance or an interpretation of Shakespeare, Kurosawa has lifted *Macbeth* from its original culture and transformed it into a film of medieval Japan. The entire text of Shakespeare is gone (and what text is in the film is merely a list of flat correspondences), but Kurosawa creates another interesting and compelling whole that takes its place. With his indebtedness to Japanese picture scrolls of the Middle Ages, Japanese myths, medieval battle literature, Noh drama and more, Kurosawa provides luminous images for the simple themes he develops.[11] Although *Throne of Blood* is different from some Shakespeare films with their uneasy marriage of dramatic and film conventions, *Throne* successfully alludes to Japanese dramatic traditions within a completely filmic structure.

Though Kurosawa recreates and adapts rather than interprets Shakespeare, comparing the two yields insights, not so much about Kurosawa's success or failure in producing a performance of Shakespeare's *Macbeth* as about the artistry of both. Comparisons invite us to see what the concerns of each are; just where Kurosawa differs, there we can detect what his purpose is, what he wants the emotional effect of his work to be. We relate Shakespeare to Kurosawa for the same reasons we compare Shakespeare to Holinshed: to illuminate the artist's choices.

This chapter concentrates on Kurosawa's poetry. There is, of course, no verse in *Throne of Blood*. Where speech appears at all, it is often, as one critic notes, a rough, brutish, guttural, barked-out language that is far from the sonorousness and fluidity of

Shakespeare's. But there is visual poetry, a term that is only some-what metaphoric. At the first level, there are visual equivalents to Shakespeare's words. The film illustrates 'Fair is foul, and foul is fair' with shafts of sunshine amidst the rain of Labyrinth Forest. And four messengers who come, one after another, to His Lordship (Duncan) represent 'thick as hail, Came post with post' (I.iii.97–8). But in a second, higher level of visualisation, Kurosawa captures the images, rhymes, rhythms, compactness and above all the intensity of poetry. These, Aristotle says, and not verse, are the essence of poetry.

Words can serve only to remind the reader of Kurosawa's striking images – not to capture them: His Lordship's arrival at North Castle in the sunlight; Asaji (Lady Macbeth) disappearing and reappearing with the drugged wine, a smug smile on her face after she has persuaded her husband to do the murder; Washizu (Macbeth) sitting on the mat as the old woman tells him his child is stillborn; the same old woman tearfully throwing her body before him to prevent him from violating the taboos of childbirth, he only slowly comprehending that he must not go to Asaji and the dead child. Such references as these may be multiplied. All convey meanings aside from their intrinsic beauty. His Lordship's arrival marks the end of sunlight; Asaji, in her unearthliness, is associated with the forest spirit; Washizu is isolated, his attempt to change fate unsuccessful.

Visual rhymes, that is, repetitions and parallels, like the rhymes of verse, bind and please while they deepen meanings. Fog, mist, smoke from torches, dust from hooves and feet play a leitmotif throughout the film, symbolising the self-deception men practise to shield themselves from the truth. The cawing crow, heard as a bad omen by the servants, a good omen by Asaji, parallels the displaced birds of the forest, seen as a bad omen by an aged retainer, a good omen by Washizu. The birds have fled as the trees that will fulfil the prophecy about Washizu's destruction are hewn down. Self-deception allows one to rationalise the super-natural. Rain is twice associated with the forest spirit. The structure of her hut is recaptured in the screen behind Washizu in the forbidden room while he is waiting for Asaji to bring him the spear and again when he is caged by the arrows of his retainers. Earlier, Forest Castle folk have shot arrows at Noriyasu and Kuni-maru (Malcolm and Donalbain), trying to escape from Washizu. Expediency motivates both attacks, the just and the unjust. The crescent moon echoes the crescent-decorated helmet, the symbol of His Lordship's power, just before Washizu kills him. Later, though Washizu ostentatiously keeps the helmet with him, he never wears it.

Michael Mullin ('*Macbeth* on Film') identifies three styles in film, all of which Kurosawa employs: naturalistic, realistic and expressionistic. The rhythms of the film are marked by stasis and violent action (a Noh hallmark), as for example the tensely rigid council with the banners flapping wildly behind them. The rhythm builds up a relentless suspense and tension. When Washizu and Miki (Banquo) are lost in the Labyrinth for fully four minutes of real film time – representing many more minutes of elapsed time – we find the film dictating its pace to us. We must yield to it. The film pulsates, slackening and tightening. Realism and heightened actions work together to create this rhythm as they spiral forward together and meet at the film's end when Washizu's stylised death throes contrast with the archers' realistic and comical fear of their dying quarry. Three naturalistic conversations among Washizu's retainers contrast with the highly formal scenes that follow. The first, an idyllic scene, takes place in the sunny courtyard of North Castle. The men are happy and think their master must be also. Ironically he is not, because in a troubling confrontation Asaji's steely logic is driving him to kill His Lordship. A second realistic conversation takes place in slightly overcast weather in the tower of Forest Castle. Washizu's men think that he has 'lifted them high'. Now if only he had an heir, they say. Ironically, Washizu will soon learn that Asaji is pregnant, the news that will result in his downfall. Finally, with wind howling and rain pelting down, the retainers crouch near the gate under shelter, talking of the 'long-time' rottenness of the foundations, the rats that are leaving and the men who have committed suicide because of Washizu's suspicions. This scene is immediately followed by the news of the stillborn child. Through the opposition of these natural and stylised scenes Kurosawa delicately exposes the gradual dissolution of Washizu's confidence. A Noh performance generally consisted of five tragedies, devoted to gods, heroes, women, contemporary or general subjects, and demons, interspersed with farcical prose segments called Kyogen. Together they formed a dramatic whole. We see this same concept of contrasting styles at work in *Throne of Blood* (see Keene).

It is in the nature of film to leave out a great deal. With a few shots (the highlights of what would be full action onstage) and with the powerful effect of montage, where the juxtaposition of shots produces a more powerful whole than the sum of its parts, film frugally conveys its narrative. But Kurosawa's film goes beyond this ordinary terseness to achieve the budlike density of poetry. Of many examples, two can illustrate. In the first sequence, Asaji disappears to get the pitcher of drugged wine; reappears with it; next, the drugged guards sleep with the pitcher at their feet; she approaches them; Washizu waits in the forbidden room; she enters with the spear; he grasps it from her hands and stalks out. We do not see her offer the wine to the guards, we do not see her take the spear, we do not see the murder, and we do not hear one word throughout the sequence. We are allowed to piece it together, powerfully exercising our imagination, much as Shakespeare allows us to visualise the murder by keeping Lady Macbeth onstage while it takes place offstage.

Another example: Asaji tries unsuccessfully to convince Washizu to assassinate Miki. Finally she tells him she is with child. We next see Miki's bolting white horse, which is to take Miki to the banquet. There Washizu is to announce that Miki's son, Yoshiteru (Fleance), is his heir. Yoshiteru tries to persuade his father to stay away from the banquet, but Miki does not listen. The horse is finally saddled. Later, when Miki's men are talking, one says that he missed going to the banquet because of the horse. In the background the white horse returns riderless into the courtyard. We do not see Washizu agree to the murder, we do not see any compact between Washizu and the murderers, we do not see the murder, and the murderers do not come before the banquet scene to tell Washizu that Miki is dead. Using the visual image of the horse, Kurosawa can omit narrative details (see Blumenthal).

Most importantly, Kurosawa, through his themes, characterisations and cinematic style, captures the intensity of poetry. Like Shakespeare's Macbeth, Kurosawa's Washizu commits a crime against society, but in Kurosawa (as in Polanski) corruption at the heart of the society is the destructive force. First, His Lordship had – in 'self-defence' – killed his own lord. Second, out of expediency rationalised as the good of the castle, Miki joins with Washizu, for only Washizu, Miki says, can hold the castle against Inui, the enemy of their province. Third, Yoshiteru, Noriyasu and Kunimaru join forces with Inui, whose aim apparently has been to take Forest Castle for himself. Fourth, Washizu's men remain loyal because of his persuasiveness in projecting success, not through any deep-seated sense of his moral authority. They kill him, again out of expediency, when he seems doomed to fail.

Most productions of Shakespeare's play, in contrast, represent Macbeth as an aberration in his society. The end for Scotland can be a healing, a return to normality. The Malcolms, Macduffs, Lenoxes, Rosses and Siwards of most performances outweigh the Macdonwalds, Cawdors and Macbeths. In contrast, Kurosawa depicts a warrior society fuelled by ambition and willingness to kill. The corruption of his society, however, does not mitigate Washizu's offence – though it does make that offence less special and less tragic. Washizu, like Macbeth, commits a crime against the moral order of the universe. Shakespeare's Macbeth understands this. He realises he has given his 'eternal jewel' to the 'common Enemy of man' (III.i.67–8).Though Washizu perhaps lacks understanding, clearly he suffers. Even before Miki's ghost appears, he is glowering from fear, anxiety and self-disgust. He readily applies the dancer's words about vain ambition to himself. (Compare Shakespeare's affable Macbeth at this point.) He says only one word, 'Fool!', after the child is stillborn, but in this expletive he conveys his realisation that he vainly fought his destiny.

Differences in Kurosawa's society from Shakespeare's lead to a reversal of characterisation and awareness. In *Macbeth*, Lady Macbeth thinks that one murder is all that is necessary. This is the pathos of the character. But Macbeth knows that one is not all. Once he and Lady Macbeth have committed the crime against society and the moral order, they are led relentlessly to all the other crimes. In *Throne of Blood*, however, one murder would, it seems, have been enough. When a society is corrupt, it can tolerate a certain level of crime. Washizu's hopes not to kill again after the first killing might have been realised if familial ambition had not pushed him into the murder of Miki. The tower scene at Forest Castle, where the retainers express satisfaction, seems to imply that Washizu goes wrong only when he tries to circumvent the prophecy, not when he fulfils it. On the other hand, the lowering sky in that scene suggests that there is a moral order in nature contradictory to the corrupt social order. The sympathetic reaction of nature – mists, rain, horses, the rats that leave, the vice-like hold of Labyrinth Forest – reveals that the moral order has been disrupted. In other words, although society is corrupt and Washizu is just part of that corruption, there is a higher order of values – just as there is in *Macbeth* – which all recognise and which affirms the values of loyalty over treachery, candour over duplicity.

That is why, in spite of the corruption of society in *Throne of Blood*, Washizu commits crimes against himself. Washizu fears the spirit as a manifestation of his own desires; he tells Miki he has dreamed of what the spirit has told him. (The phlegmatic Miki accepts this matter-of-factly.) Macbeth, too, finds in the witches' words an echo of his own thought. Washizu, like Macbeth, views himself as noble and loyal. He mouths the words 'we must be loyal to our lord'; 'we must trust friends', just as Macbeth says, moments before he enters wholeheartedly into Lady Macbeth's scheme, 'I dare do all that may become a man; / Who dares do more, is none' (I.vii.46–7). Washizu's extreme behaviour after he kills His Lordship, like Macbeth's, proves that he has acted against his better self. He allows fear and ambition to overcome loyalty, just as his men act out of self-preservation in killing him. Though the characters in *Throne of Blood* resemble those in *Macbeth*, methods of characterisation differ. In *Macbeth*, characters frequently describe other characters. We know about Duncan and Banquo, for example, largely from Macbeth:

> this Duncan
> Hath borne his faculties so mild, hath been
> So clear in his great office, that his virtues
> Will plead like angels (I.vii.16–19)

> Our fears in Banquo
> Stick deep and in his royalty of nature
> Reigns that which would be fear'd: 'tis much he dares;
> And, to that dauntless temper of his mind,
> He hath a wisdom that doth guide his valour
> To act in safety. (III.i.48–53)

In Shakespeare, words define characters. But in Kurosawa, characters reveal themselves by their inner feelings that flow in some mysterious way through masklike faces and – often – quiet bodies (as in Noh). For example, when Washizu and Miki meet at the gate of Forest Castle to conspire after the murder of His Lordship, Miki's disgust at and awareness of Washizu's crime show in his face and glance.

In terms of exploring her character's inner life through body language and demeanor, Isuzu Yamada's Asaji is remarkable. It is difficult to see how she does it, but we know what she is thinking.

[188]

Her downcast eyes, for example, lift upward to Washizu only once during their initial conversation as she looks full face towards him for the first time. He has just said that treachery does not live in his heart, and she replies, 'I know better'. Toshiro Mifune's acting as Washizu is done, as someone has said, with teeth and eyes – and, I would add, with feet and knees. But her acting comes from deep within her. Washizu is a coiled spring, tense in stasis, violent in quick action. She is like the black stars that have collapsed into themselves. Her curious dance of fear and exaltation in the forbidden room, an aberration for her since she exerts control through apparent passivity – marks the beginning of madness and is equivalent to Lady Macbeth's line, 'Had he not resembled / My father as he slept, I had done't' (II.ii.13–14). Asaji's submissiveness and subservience contrast sharply with her power. Her intelligence is a chief moving force in the film. It is she, for example, who reminds Washizu to ask the murderer of Miki about Yoshiteru; Washizu was ready to dismiss the man without learning what they most need to know. After she learns that Yoshiteru is still alive, her face says everything: it is all over. She has no more ideas, no more plans. Her logic of suspicion and betrayal has finally failed.

Finally we come to a most important aspect of the film that contributes to its intensity, Kurosawa's cinematic style, as complex and varied in its way as Shakespeare's verbal style. Framing the action, a voiceover chorus chants the eternal message, 'ambition kills'. This chant distances us, as do the many long shots and extreme long shots and the transitions that are clearly artificial, such as wipes (where one image replaces another much as a window shade pulled down replaces the scene out of a window). All of these counter the real, here-and-now quality of film. Yet the vision of a distant past refers to us too, for the chorus says, 'What once was so now is still true'. A shot of Washizu from in front of Miki's empty place at the banquet offers an example of camerawork sensitive to nuance and style. The camera moves toward Washizu, focusing on his disquiet, then dollies back again, revealing the inward-turned chalk-white ghost of Miki. Visual framing is frequently significant, as when the camera shoots Washizu and Miki through the crescent of His Lordship's helmet on the coffin at the gate of Forest Castle. Fast motion shots in the Labyrinth Forest mirror the frenzy of Washizu and Miki; slow-motion shots of the evergreen trees moving forward in a sea of fog convey the supernatural eeriness of the Birnam Wood sequence.

The telephoto lens, with its flattened perspective, captures in closeup the seemingly floating action of the funeral possession or the soldiers moving towards the castle. Deep focus shots produce skilful understatements, as when Miki's men talk in the foreground while in the background the riderless horse returns to the court-yard. There is no need for Kurosawa to cut from one group to the other. Rather, we are aware of the reactions of the men at the same time as we recognise the meaning of the horse's return. Another example is the shot near the end before the scene of Asaji's madness, when the castle is under siege. In the close fore-ground is a tripod, behind it a guard. Through the open sliding screens, in the far distance we see Washizu sitting alone, his retainer behind him holding the badge of office, the crescented helmet. The large space between Washizu and his men in the courtyard suggests his isolation.

One final set of shots might be mentioned. When Washizu finally falls down dead, arrows sticking in his body, in a high angle shot we see a fog-filled space between him and a dark curve of silent men looking on. Immediately Kurosawa crosscuts to the forest to a frozen shot of similar composition, fog-filled space and a curve of equally silent men around it. These two shots linking the inside and the outside of the castle – and thus the motives of each group – immediately precede the last shots of the film. A telephoto closeup from a different angle plunges us into the determined movement and noise of the attackers, with Noriyasu telling the forces how to proceed. A cut to the castle shows us the object of their march. But the object shot holds longer than we expect it to, and as mists shroud the castle we hear the battle no more. Instead the chanting voices again place the unfinished action in the past, and the film ends as it began.

Kurosawa's visual poetry is but one aspect of this austere and beautiful film, but it is the aspect that brings *Throne of Blood* close to the glory of *Macbeth's* language.

Roman Polanski

Roman Polanski was born in 1933 in Poland, just six years before the Nazi invasion that broke up his family. He survived because after his parents were taken to concentration camps, where his mother died, he ran away from the Cracow ghetto and was raised by Catholic families. After the war, he began as an art student and as an actor on stage and film, then studied at Łódź film school for five years, producing his first feature, *Knife in the Water*, in Poland in 1962. The many countries where Polanski has worked – Poland, Britain, the USA and France – are witness to the international character of his films. His first commercial success was *Rosemary's Baby*, in 1968. Though *Macbeth*, which appeared in 1971, was not a commercial success, it is a major Shakespearean film, frequently screened, discussed and written about.

The film is bound to offend many with its cruel imagery, its exploitative nudity and its evocation of his personal tragedy – the brutal killing of his pregnant wife, Sharon Tate, by the Manson gang just a little over a year before he began the film. Still, the work is fascinating not only for Polanski's understanding of the violence at the heart of usurpation but also for his sure cinematic touch and his dedication to clarity, coherence and unity that nevertheless allow for the ambiguity so looked for by modern audiences. Thirty years later, the film looks better than ever; its artistry makes it a classic though its debt to its own time is evident (the 1968 Soviet invasion of Czechoslovakia, violent repression of anti-Vietnam activists in the United States in 1968 and 1969, and release in 1971 of *A Clockwork Orange*, by Kubrick, to name just a few events of those times). The last decade of the twentieth century and the awful events of the beginning of the twenty-first corroborate the film's political prescience.

Polanski problematises the tragedy and the audience's relation to events by showing that the society, rather than the supernatural or the personal, determines the outcome: Like Kurosawa's Ashizu and Asaji, Polanski's Macbeth and Lady Macbeth act as their world has shaped them, and they are hardly unique within their sphere. In Kurosawa, resignation to the way things are, rather than a tragic vision, suffuses the whole. Polanski, however, sees the tragic figure in society itself. As Polanski depicts it, at the heart of Scotland is its predilection for violence. In this respect, Polanski and his co-adapter Kenneth Tynan appear to use Shakespeare's sources, the Chronicles, as much as they use the play itself. Shakespeare's text, however, flatly contradicts only a few of their choices; it provides ample warrant for some, and leeway enough to accommodate others.

The film's Scotland is not Renaissance England but a much cruder time and place when a curious mixture of barbaric selfishness and natural goodness appals the senses: the time, indeed, of the Chronicles, the eleventh century, when Scottish society had not worked out a system to contain violent upheavals – had not, in other words, become civilised – but was on the verge of doing so. The film explores this edge. The film is a *tragedy* because the society whose downfall seems imminent at the end has something of potential good in it; Some, like Lenox whose comportment denotes nobility, we would want to trust with leadership; others, like Malcolm, seem to improve over time. Still others, like Macbeth's attendant Seyton, mysteriously mix loyalty and amorality. It is also a tragedy – rather than a misanthropic diatribe – because, obliquely, Polanski does hold up a distorted mirror to another kind of society.

Polanski sears our eyes with violence. Murder is savage, and the film medium, by making it possible to depict it in graphic detail, does not obscure this unalterable fact as stage performances can. As productions from Davenant until the early twentieth century elevated Macbeth in stature, they minimised the violence of the play, not only by cutting lines that refer to violence and by muting onstage reactions to violent behaviour but also by moving offstage even the murders of Banquo and Macduff's child. So much was the violence suppressed that Bradley, writing around 1900, could say that *Macbeth*, like *Hamlet*, is notable for the 'absence of the spectacle of extreme undeserved suffering' (p. 264). Polanski not only keeps the murders of the innocents in view but embellishes them. It seems that Polanski will stop at nothing to make sure we see what murder is – the blood, the violated and torn flesh, the dismembered body parts.

Rape is to be expected when a castle is surprised and its inhabitants killed. Shakespeare has Rosse say to Macduff:

> Your castle is surpris'd; your wife, and babes,
> Savagely slaughtered: to relate the manner
> Were on the quarry of these murther'd deer
> To add the death of you. (IV.iii.204–7)

Polanski has filled in what Rosse was disinclined to relate, what most productions glide over, and what most audiences are reluctant to let themselves think – the *savage manner*. While Polanski does not retreat from the idea, he does mitigate somewhat the visual effect by showing the rape of a servant in the background of a frame that concentrates on Lady Macduff's face in close shot. The sound of women's screams and the laughter of men, more

than the sight itself, tells the horror. Just before, the two murderers' laughing leers and the attempted kiss by one while the
other watches as he awaits his turn hints that Lady Macduff, too,
will be raped; but the sequence ends with flames engulfing the
castle.

Although Polanski rubs our noses in violence, the film continually exhibits a curious restraint. As often as he shows murder in
progress, with the life flowing out with the blood, he retreats from
the spectacle: we do not see the opening battles we hear; we do
not see the king's grooms killed; we see the bear and dog of the
bear-baiting entertainment for the banquet scene after they're
dead, not the killing itself (though an early script had planned to
include it; see Kliman, 'Gleanings'); we do not see the slaughter of
Banquo's two murderers but only Rosse pushing the son into a
watery dungeon to join his father in death; we do not see the
death of Lady Macduff, nor her two small babes dying, and we're
barely aware that her son has been mortally wounded until we
see, with her, his blood on her hand. True enough, we do see
many dead and witness many deaths, often in ugly detail and with
astounding variety, the weapons ranging from spiked ball to
dagger to axe to sword to arrow. In the wash of all that blood, it is
easy to overlook how much more bloody the film might have been.
Polanski tells us frankly that this business of greed and treachery
is violent, and all the poetry in the world cannot obscure that. But
given the film's seeming predilection for horrors, he holds back,
because violence for its own sake is not his point. Relying on our
own imagination to fill the gaps he leaves, he has, as it were, an
acerbic laugh at our expense. All right, he seems to say, you cringe
from the violence I show you, but do not you yourself have those
same violent images in your mind? Aren't you quite able to imagine
what I hint at? He reminds us that the audience is complicit in the
violence, for don't we *want* Macbeth to get on with Duncan's
murder? Since the play's *genre* leads us to anticipate violence, we
want the murder so that the play can go on. Like Lady Macbeth,
we do not realise, perhaps, that this one murder will, shall, must (in
the words of Davenant's witches) lead to more violence: Polanski's
violence simply exceeds the audience's initial expectations.

He foregrounds violence as an artistic linkage through the film
as a whole. Take, for example, the visual pointing of lines. Cawdor's
death is actualised so that we understand how Polanski interprets
the lines describing it: 'Nothing in his life / Became him like the

leaving it' (I.iv.7–8). But Polanski goes beyond mere illustration, for Cawdor's death is an emblem of fair and foul, bravery tainted by treachery. With firm strides, the shackled man climbs the castle steps to the ramparts, stands resolutely at the edge for a moment to say wryly 'Long live the King' and then jumps vigorously to hang by the very collar and chains that have bound him; he does not confess his treasons or ask for forgiveness.

Fair and foul are mixed in visual images, many of them, as Jack Jorgens notes, repeated and echoed throughout the film, visual equivalents for the repeating poetic images of the play (pp. 161–74). Lofty scenes, as of the landscape surrounding Macbeth's Inverness (filmed on location in North Wales), and grimy, realistic scenes, such as the muddy, livestock-filled courtyard in that castle, vie with each other, just as gentility and depravity vie for ascendancy within the plot, as Polanski conceives it.

Though this is a film in which laughter rings out more frequently than in other productions, since *we* are not likely to laugh at all those 'jokes', the laughter serves to disrupt the surface of the film, sending mixed signals. Duncan's men laugh when the sergeant describes Macbeth's killing of Macdonwald: Macbeth 'unseam'd him from the nave to th'chops' (I.ii.22). This is not a joke that a modern audience is likely to enjoy. Other laughs are more innocent and might be more appealing to us: for example, Macbeth's and Banquo's echoing laughter about the prophecy as they ride away from the witches (their joking Polanski may have taken from the Chronicles, in which a long time intervenes between the prophecy and its fulfilment, so Macbeth and Banquo have plenty of time to joke about it). We can enjoy the laughter at Banquo's pun: recollecting Duncan's 'I have begun to plant thee …' addressed to Macbeth, Banquo responds to Duncan's 'let me infold thee, / And hold thee to my heart' (I.iv.31–2) by saying 'There if I grow, / The harvest is your own'. Other laughter is sardonic, as is the lords' when they obliquely discuss Macbeth's crimes (III.vi). Since we are apt to concur with their sentiments, we are responsive, but we may also wonder why these secretly disloyal lords are still there with Macbeth, so late in the day, for the scene is transposed to join with the sequence after the witches' cave (IV.i), and our question undercuts the humour. Other laughter within the film is wicked and sycophantic, as is the thanes' (who are his hired thugs, the rapists and murderers in IV.ii) in response to Macbeth's wild joking in Act V; their laughter is likely to disgust us. Laughter sometimes draws us in, sometimes distances us, disconcerting us as it shifts. Laughter is equivocal.

In his shifting surfaces, Polanski seems to have been inspired by Kurosawa's supremely *cinematic* translation of *Macbeth*. Like Kurosawa, Polanski uses space emblematically. As in *Throne of Blood*, extreme long shots show caravans of travellers along curving roads. Just as Kurosawa frames a sun-filled, peaceful shot for his king's approach to the castle where he will be killed, Polanski shows in rosy sunset Duncan's long, slow march to Inverness. Both film-makers also include views of common people traveling along these roads. In Polanski's film, shots of displaced persons define Macbeth's cruel reign. The long shots in both films expand the theatre of the narrative, encompassing a world. (Grigori Kozintsev, also an admirer of *Throne of Blood*, uses similar long shots in his *Lear* filmed about the same time as Polanski's *Macbeth*.) Polanski also defines his interior spaces much as did Kurosawa. Dunsinane, with its stoneworks and elegance, its huge halls and paved courtyards, its tapestries and bright windows, is a high step above Macbeth's Inverness, with its cramped banquet room, its muddy courtyard, its straw-strewn halls and chambers and its wooden structure, a rail of raw wood naturalistically suggesting recent repairs. Just so does *Throne* show Washizu's (Macbeth's) rise through the move to North Castle, his prize for killing a traitor, and thence to the Forest Castle, after killing his leader. Exactly what these men achieve is symbolically represented by the space and men they command.

Though there are many points of similarity, each ultimately uses them differently. For Kurosawa the landscapes match events (one of his indicators that Nature and society are connected), but for Polanski the cruelty of an uncaring nature is painfully evident, for example, in the golden, rolling landscape shown when Rosse and a flunkey (the 'servant fee'd' that Macbeth brags of keeping in all his thanes' houses? (III.iv.131)) open Macduff's castle gates to Macbeth's henchmen; in the castle of Inverness that has 'a pleasant seat'; in the hills of Dunsinane stretching towards the Wood of Birnam. Other landscape views are appealing to those who are drawn to the bleak austerity of Scotland. Polanski's designers served him well. Like Kurosawa, too, Polanski uses music brilliantly, associating particular sounds with particular places and psychic states; some of the discords of the Third Ear Band sound similar to aural manoeuvres in the Japanese film.

The rhythm of shots in the later film recalls that of the earlier: the suggestive montages, the natural flow from closeup to medium shot to long shot, the splitting of scenes into segments denoting the passage of time. Examples in Polanski can be found in the scene of the witches' prophetic greetings (I.iii) where Polanski splits Macbeth's aside spatially and temporally, implying Macbeth's long rumination on murder. Similarly, Polanski divides the letter scene (I.v) into three scenes: the letter itself (I.v.1–14), interposed between I.iii and the second part of I.iv; Macbeth's entrance (at I.v.54, unmediated by a messenger); and finally, the 'unsex me' speech as Lady Macbeth watches Duncan's approach (I.v.40–54). A montage creates the first banquet scenes – the hurried preparation: the squealing pig caught and carried (echoed later by the image of a recreant stealing a pig on his way out of Macbeth's Dunsinane); and the banquet itself: the wind blowing out the lights and frightening Fleance, the servant in closeup running with the torch to re-light the oil, and the escape of horses from the stable both to suggest Macbeth's state of mind and to objectify Lenox's description of unruly night, the casual views of musicians, Rosse, Banquo and others in the background. Equally compelling is the added coronation sequence, with Banquo's pained face (his soliloquy of III.i in voiceover), his silence during the cheer for the new king, Rosse's smiling face sometimes in the foreground, the white-robed figures that visually belie what lies beneath the surfaces. By cutting from one space to another within one scene or segment of the text, Polanski changes the pace of the work from the sense of a continuous flow of time, which stage scenes afford, to the disjunctive, abrupt and discontinuous segments of film time. However, in contrast to Kurosawa's pace, which lengthens and draws out the film images, the play in Polanski's hands moves as swiftly as it seems by its Folio length to have been meant to move. More than almost any other Shakespeare play, *Macbeth* indeed can be encompassed in two hours' traffic on the stage. Partly because of its pace, Polanski's version commands our attention and teases out a responsive *enjoyment* from many viewers, something very few *Macbeth* productions can claim. It is ironic that a production as violent as this one can force such responsiveness. But his violence is not gratuitous and reflects a deep abhorrence for violence as well as a mesmerised fascination with it.

Banquo's murderers are representative of the society Polanski

depicts. Poverty-stricken, this father and son strike one as two of
the better sort morally. Macbeth has them killed rather than
rewarding them, as Shakespeare implies Macbeth will when he
says 'I will put that business in your bosoms, / Whose execution
takes your enemy off, / Grapples you to the heart and love of us'
(III.i.103–5). Polanski's Macbeth makes no such promise; these
murderers, who have little stomach for their crime, are not his
sort. Rosse must be sent after them to make sure they kill Banquo
and Fleance, and, though they resent Rosse's coming in III.iii,
their manner of fighting shows the reluctance that explains this
precaution. In III.i also, their exchanges of looks indicate both
their disbelief of Macbeth and their powerlessness. We can con-
clude, with them, that Macbeth is lying when he says,

> know
> That it was he, in the times past, which held you
> So under fortune, which you thought had been
> Our innocent self. (III.i.75–8)

And

> Are you so gospell'd,
> To pray for this good man, and for his issue,
> Whose heavy hand hath bow'd you to the grave,
> And beggar'd yours for ever? (III.i.87–90)

Nevertheless, they are helpless to disobey him. One of Polanski's
quirks is to make his audience sympathise with these murderers,
but Shakespeare gives Polanski reason to interpret their desperation as resulting from their powerlessness:

> 2 *Mur.*   I am one, my Liege,
>   Whom the vile blows and buffets of the world
>   Hath so incens'd, that I am reckless what
>   I do, to spite the world.
> 1 *Mur.*   And I another ... (III.i.107–10)

Unlike the vicious murderers of Polanski's later scenes who do or
say nothing to exculpate their criminality, this impoverished father
and son earn the audience's pity.

Shakespeare fleshed out the story of Macbeth with the description from the Scottish Chronicles of the murder of a King Duff by
Donwald, at the instigation of his wife. Using information from
the Chronicles that Shakespeare chose to ignore in his work,
Polanski ends his film by intimating that the cycle of usurpation

[197]

will begin again. Macbeth is no freak in this society, but an every-man. To the same discords of the Third Ear Band heard when Macbeth had encountered the witches – and on the same kind of rainy, dark day – Donalbain, a limping man with shifty eyes, hears the witches' eerie singing and seeks its source. Presumably, he will listen to another prophecy that will challenge *him* to unfold his own destiny. Though the quizzical look on Donalbain's face as he follows the sound implies that his presence there is simply accidental on his part (or engineered by supernatural powers), viewers may feel that he has purposely sought out the witches. Either way, the result will be the same. And indeed, as the Chronicles tell us, the cycle of usurpation did continue when Donalbain wrenched the throne from Malcolm's sons (Bellen-den, II, 176). Ending in this way with Donalbain, Polanski artfully encloses the film yet suggests a continuing spiral of action beyond the frame, beyond the film, and certainly beyond Macbeth's death.

The most controversial device that Polanski uses to make the society rather than Macbeth the focus of the tragedy is his moulding of Rosse. Polanski is not the first to think of Rosse as a kind of evil genius in the play, as Kenneth Rothwell has noted ('Ross'). Indeed, if we watch carefully where Shakespeare places him we can find justification for Polanski's depiction of him. Rosse in Shakespeare is always close to kings or would-be kings, willing to comfort Lady Macduff with words, it seems, but unwill-ing to protect her, absent from the Scottish forces joining to fight against Macbeth but present at the conclusion to hail Malcolm. In other words, Polanski can find warrant in Shakespeare for his depiction of Rosse as a temporiser; Polanski simply fills in the details. (See Kliman, 'Thanes'.)

In this production, Rosse is the most despicable of self-servers – played by John Stride as a Billy Budd with the heart of a Claggart. Duncan dead, he cleaves to Macbeth, enthusiastically acting the role of the Third Murderer, helping to dispose of Banquo's murderers, obscenely betraying the family of his kinsman Macduff, and, beyond obscenity, pretending to pity Macduff for these same deaths. He will stoop to anything to climb, servilely lowering himself to boost Macbeth on to his horse after it seems that Mac-beth is rising in Duncan's kingdom. Ever the opportunist, he seeks Malcolm out – motivated partly by jealousy – after Macbeth bestows a chain of office on the lackey Seyton. Rosse, after

Macbeth's fall, smilingly hands the crown to Malcolm and is the one to shout 'Hail, King of Scotland!' In him Polanski personifies Duncan's comment:

> There's no art
> To find the mind's construction in the face:
> He was a gentleman on whom I built
> An absolute trust – (I.iv.11–14)

Polanski prevents us from applying Duncan's comment to Macbeth alone by following the remark about Cawdor with the first part of the letter scene (I.v) rather than with Macbeth's immediate entrance, as in the text. In this way, Polanski refuses the irony of the rest of line 14, 'O worthiest cousin!', addressed to Macbeth, immediately after the word 'trust'. We are thus led to share Duncan's bewilderment about the disjunction of appearance and character, and to extend the comment to such as Rosse. John Stride's Rosse is as open-faced, fresh and *honest-looking* as can be imagined. If his were motiveless malignity, he could be called an Iago, but his motive is self-aggrandisement, unmixed with any overwhelming wish to hurt others, always a by-product with him. Polanski's characterisation of Rosse is part of a pattern of depicting a flawed society; he treats several other characters similarly – among them Malcolm, Donalbain and Macduff.

Another strategy of Polanski that draws attention from the principals to the society is to reduce Macbeth and Lady Macbeth in stature. One of the ways that Shakespeare raises Macbeth in audience esteem is through his verse. With some of Shakespeare's most lovely images cut, the poetry is not much in evidence in the rush of action. Polanski's ravaging of the verse has little to do with film necessity or film equivalencies for poetic language; it is the expression of Polanski's vision, which refuses to acknowledge any distinction in monsters and denies preeminence to Macbeth and his wife. Action often masks what poetry is left, as for example when Macbeth, waiting for his Lady to return from gilding the faces of the grooms, speaks while in closeup he dips his hands into a bucket to cleanse them, pouring the resultant reddish liquid on to the ground. Watching the images (which are homely and local) reduces the impact of the poetry of his lines (which are grand and distant):

> Will all great Neptune's ocean wash this blood
> Clean from my hand? No, this my hand will rather

The multitudinous seas incarnadine,
Making the green one red. (II.ii.59–62)

This action accompanying the words is different from the visual pointing of lines for clarity, found elsewhere in the film, even to the brink of obviousness (the visible dagger for the dagger soliloquy, the shot of his feet as Macbeth says 'Hear not my steps' in II.i.57). In the Neptune speech, Polanski's visuals overcome rather than enhance the verbal images. Further, both Jon Finch and Francesca Annis are directed to act in a flat, colourless style that destroys verse. Of course, a *Macbeth* stripped of its poetry is not *Macbeth* at all, many say. Polanski clarifies a difficult text but does not thereby improve it, some assert. But he has his reasons for quelling the language. All this diminution of poetry serves his purpose of denying to Macbeth the status of a poet.

Polanski withholds from the murderer the seductive graces that draw an audience, if against their will. His is simply another and, in my view, a defensible reading of the text. Those who want a terribly heroic, a satanically compelling, even a noble Macbeth ignore those details in Shakespeare's text that contradict that supposed grandeur, as reflected in the poetic images. A mere thirty-seven lines after Macbeth states his noble credo – 'I dare do all that may become a man; / Who dares do more, is none' (I.vii.46–7) – he *is* persuaded to 'do more'. The film refuses to romanticise violence; the angst of a soul in torment remains, but it is as arid and sterile an angst as that of Claudius or Henry IV. Macbeth is no Iago or Richard III, taking pleasure in mischief or murder. But Polanski refuses to swing to the opposite pole; he does not see Macbeth as a superhero whose greatness of soul somehow raises him above normal standards of behaviour.

Macbeth and his wife are attuned to the social forces that they can appropriate for their own gain. Though *Variety* (15 December 1971) deplored the pallid casting choice of Finch and Annis, The *New York Times's* Roger Greenspan (21 December 1971) understood the purpose for diminishing the main characters, not only through the means already mentioned but also through making them young and lightweight. Numerous willing partners abet Macbeth in crime: the ever-loyal Seyton, Rosse and many anonymous men, including two besides Rosse who help to dispatch the murderers of Banquo. How special, how deviant can Macbeth's behaviour be when so many are willing to further it? In contrast, how alone Macbeth appears to be in Shakespeare's play, how shadowy Shakespeare's murderers of the Macduff family: they do not, like Polanski's, explicitly take their places in court.

Then, too, chance as much as volition plays its role, further diminishing Macbeth's tragic stature. At the last moment before Duncan's murder, Macbeth hesitates, seemingly unable to murder the sleeping, naked guest lying in the herb-strewn best bed. Only because Duncan opens his eyes, sees the knife and, after a shocked whisper 'Macbeth!', is about to cry out, does Macbeth kill him. Shakespeare, of course, did not show this moment of decision; the scene is an unShakespearean intrusion of violence that deflects attention away from Macbeth's response and puts the focus directly and unsympathetically on the bloody deed itself, forcing the audience to adjust its perceptions. The accident for Shakespeare is in the presence of Duncan under Macbeth's battlements, not in Macbeth's fear of being unable to explain the knife in his hand: as Lady Macbeth says all too truthfully, 'th'attempt and not the deed / Confounds us' (II.ii.10–11). (Fuseli, in his drawing for 'The Shakespeare Gallery: *Macbeth*', c. 1775–76, also shows the naked king vulnerable to the naked dagger, and maybe this picture was Polanski's or Tynan's inspiration, see Figs 10 and 11.)

Chance, accident – these operate, but fate and the supernatural are much diminished in importance, if not altogether absent, to keep the audience's attention on social forces. In Shakespeare, as some interpret the text, the witches function as a horrific embodiment of Macbeth's and Lady Macbeth's evil natures or as goads to evil. But Polanski reduces their correspondences to Lady Macbeth and their effect on Macbeth. Nevertheless, they are very important to his interpretation of Macbeth's character and the society in which he moves.

First, Polanski's witches are women who believe, it seems, that their magic can either predict or contain events – women who are, then, practising witches, not supernatural beings. In our first view of them, before the credits, one old woman and one ancient, blind woman, with a young scabby apprentice who can only mouth the charms and utter inarticulate animal noises, are discovered at the seaside, where they bury an oily hangman's noose and a forearm and hand in which they place a knife. The women know they are to meet Macbeth, and they know where, but they do not seek him out. Instead, they depend on his encountering them, and he does, as they sit under a crude lean-to near their cave. The harsh chords of the Third Ear Band's music, sound for the audience alone, are like distilled mystery and terror. It is the witches' rough, tuneless singing that attracts the attention of both Macbeth and Banquo, who have stopped for a moment to escape the rain. As the old women speak to Macbeth, they begin moving away from him. Only he – not Banquo – follows them, only he sees the young one lift her skirts in an obscene gesture, only he sees them disappear into their cave with a bang of a door. His answer to Banquo's query about their whereabouts – that they have disappeared into air – is not true; his readiness to deceive signals his participation in his own destiny. He knows where he can find the women but does not want Banquo to know. Polanski lessens the Sisters' power in several ways: the crudeness of their clothing makes them seem like desperate peasants who have turned to magic; their living arrangements, with sacks and barrows, goats and pails, domesticate them, much as the household details of Inverness, with dogs and chickens and pigs, domesticate Macbeth and Lady Macbeth. A Macbeth encountered by *these* witches can make his decision for regicide without them.

The air-drawn dagger, though we see it, seems to be what Macbeth assumes it to be – a dagger of the mind. Polanski persistently shows it from Macbeth's point of view. The thane sees it beyond the frame and then the camera pans to it; it disappears when Macbeth covers his eyes. It marshals him the way he was going because it is in his mind. Yet its eye-searing presence and the music accompanying it at the same time hint at the supernatural. We are, it seems, to keep in balance both natural and supernatural possibilities.

Polanski, who chose to be graphic in Banquo's murder, limits the supernatural still more in the depiction of the ghost. The murderer describes Banquo's throat as cut and says he lies in a ditch 'With twenty trenched gashes on his head' (III.iv.26). But we have seen Banquo killed with an axe blow to the spine. When Macbeth sees Banquo, the ghost appears as the murderer described him, not as he actually died. Thus, the image is in Macbeth's mind, is indeed 'the very painting of [his] fear' (III.iv.60), as was the air-drawn dagger. The ghost appears once in the scene (not twice as in Shakespeare) but goes through a metamorphosis in cross shots – that is, shots of him interspersed with reaction shots of others. First, the camera catches him from behind, his formerly brown hair grey, his hand grey. As he turns to face the camera, his whole

10   Detail from Fuseli's *Study for Macbeth*

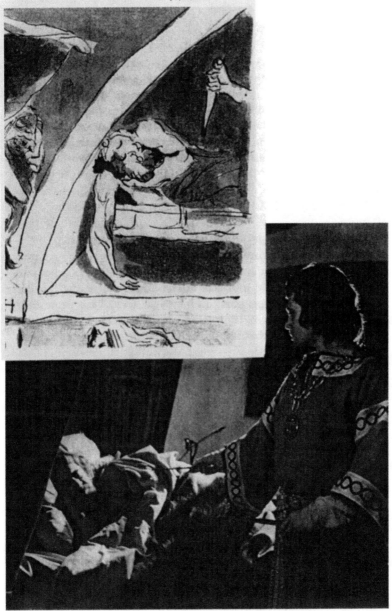

11   Roman Polanski's film of *Macbeth*, 1971

face has the pallor of death. The next shot shows him wounded and bloodied. The next has him confronting and chasing Macbeth in a dreamlike sequence. As Macbeth becomes more horrified, Banquo's ghost becomes ghastlier and ghastlier, moving huge and wraith-like in slow motion towards the camera, which gives Macbeth's perspective in a low angle shot that magnifies the phantom. The dream imagery for the ghost recollects an earlier added dream before the murder, when Macbeth, lying on his bed with open eyes, is helpless to prevent Fleance from raising and putting on the crown, helpless to prevent Banquo's hands from pressing on his throat (III.ii). Mental not supernatural forces account for the ghost.

Macbeth seeks out an opportunity to accost the witches by riding to their cave on his white horse (combining the theatrical tradition of the cauldron scene in a cave setting with an inversion of another hoary convention, the movie tradition of white horses for good guys). Throughout the sequence, Polanski mixes psychological and supernatural images. Macbeth drinks the witches' horrid brew and under the influence of the drugs has psychedelic visions, ending with an image of Banquo as he actually died, his head woundless, the axe stuck in his back. This vision is beyond Macbeth's knowledge. With psychological accuracy, however, the first apparition is Macbeth himself reflected in the huge cauldron, for since he has already suspected Macduff it is reasonable that Macbeth's own image should warn him against Macduff. But this reflection is succeeded by another that exceeds Macbeth's knowledge: the dissolution of his face into a retreating, trunkless, severed head. The second apparition is the bloody babe ripped from its mother's womb, the smiling midwife pleased with her success, a vague image that becomes significant to Macbeth only after Macduff's declaration that 'Macduff was from his mother's womb / Untimely ripp'd' (V.viii.15–16) recalls it to his mind (and a muted version flashes on the screen). The apparitions and the show of kings all appear to be a drunken dream; when he ends the vision by breaking Banquo's mirror, Macbeth is asleep in the now empty cave (the overturned goblet and cauldron a reminder of the drink that had drugged the grooms), awakened by drops of rain falling on his eyelids. Because Polanski mixes images that are psychologically apt with others impossible for Macbeth to have known, the result is ambiguity, extending to the witches themselves.

The final ambiguous image comes with Macbeth's death. Macduff strikes off his head, which falls and is eventually hoisted on a pole and carried to the ramparts. The sounds and the visual images suggest the point of the view of the head: the trunkless head faintly hears the jeering voices, faintly sees the mocking faces, with the camera shooting from its low angle of vision. Then abruptly, presumably as the head ceases to hear and see, sound and sight return to normal. This imagery, again, is not realistic.

Polanski cannot avoid supernatural predictions, because the witches' information about Macduff and about Birnam Wood surpass Macbeth's own knowledge – and possibly any human knowledge – but he tempers supernatural visions (as of the dead Banquo) with psychological realism. Macbeth's confidence in the prophecies about his invincibility is psychologically sound: Finch's Macbeth, like Shakespeare's, believes in such predictions only when it suits him. He acts to actualise the prophecy of his kingship, when, if he truly believed, he could have allowed chance to crown him, as he himself says. Then he tries to frustrate the prophecy about Banquo, as if that were possible. And finally, because of his faith in the prophecies about Birnam Wood and the man not born of woman, he waits passively for his enemies to surround him.

Though Finch is less daring than some Macbeths, he does not lack the courageousness that may be the character's chief claim at the end to an audience's grudging admiration. From the beginning of the film, this is a serious Macbeth: his grave looks give him stature, and the reactions of others to him enhance his dignity in our eyes. We see that Finch's Macbeth is young, but he inspires confidence in his ability to govern. It is reasonable that, in spite of Macduff's suspicions, Macbeth is elected to reign after Duncan. With his crown, walking easily among his thanes, he is kingly (III.i). As he steps deeper into crime and is more and more surrounded by those who murder for him, his face begins to age, and he deteriorates. At the end, when all the good men have left him, when even the bad men have deserted (killing the loyal Seyton with a crossbow to escape through the gate) and Macbeth is all alone, he is dignified in his contempt, steadfast in his belief in the drug-induced prophecies. Even after he discovers that his faith has been misplaced, he fights well and wins respect as a warrior from the watching soldiers and thanes. When the death blow strikes, a sword through his body, a smile flickers on Macbeth's ruined face. This moment is not unwelcome. He knows and has already said that he has lived long enough. Like Cawdor, he embraces his death.

While some contemporary reviewers, as noted, considered

Finch lightweight, his subsequent career, including his distinguished performance as Henry Bolingbroke in the BBC TV 'Shakespeare Plays' (1979, 1980), has made it possible to return to Finch's playing of Macbeth with new understanding of his gifts. He never allows himself to become bigger than the film, but his face, his movements, and his ease with the language mark him as a superb craftsman. As in the instance of vulnerable Lady Macbeths, a *character's* weakness can sometimes be evidence of an *actor's* skill. Polanski's is a Macbeth marked by excess of ambition, by understanding of the meaning of his crime and by loving regard for his wife without being in the least subservient to her. His gesture to those who admiringly chant his name as he approaches Duncan in I.iv is regal, but after Malcolm is named heir, when the men shout Macbeth's name again as he passes, his gesture represses their chant, for he knows what he is thinking as he looks at the hanging body of Cawdor across the courtyard. He unhesitatingly acknowledges the respect by others because it matches his own opinion of himself, and blindly, in fact, he accepts it as his due, not realising that the dedication of a Seyton is different from the 'mouth-honour' he receives from the others, such as the thanes who enjoy assignments to rape and murder. His one moment of elation coincides with his deepest befuddlement, when he believes that the witches' prophecies mean that he will never be defeated. Of course, this irony is built into the text, but Finch amplifies the effect with that rare laugh. Finch's complex characterisation of Macbeth makes him interesting, but he is not the tragic figure of the eighteenth and nineteenth centuries. The thane is simply the man within the society on whom the lens of investigation is focused for the moment.

Similarly, the devaluation of Lady Macbeth also avoids locating the tragedy in *her* character. The sexual energy that the two generate is not beyond matrimonial norms but, in fact, is another hint of domesticity, like the barnyard animals, cleaning rituals and so on that we find at Inverness. Yes, Macbeth carries her up the stairs to bed when he arrives home to tell her that Duncan is coming. Yes, they speak to one another in bed. But there is nothing lascivious in the camera's gaze. Their murderous plans are not kinky stimuli to sexuality. One might contrast Francesca Annis's womanly sexuality with the demonic sexuality – the orgasmic writhings – that other Lady Macbeths use to control their husbands (Judith Anderson and Jane Lapotaire come to mind).

Polanski's resolving of Macbeth's last doubts about murdering Duncan illustrates the relationship of the two characters. The film shows the banquet only hinted at in Shakespeare's stage directions for I.vii: '*Hautboys and torches. Enter, and pass over the stage, a Sewer, and divers Servants with dishes and service. Then enter* MACBETH.' Annis's hungry Lady stuffs food into her mouth between smiles at Duncan. Her plans do not unsettle her: she has said that Macbeth's letters 'have transported me beyond / This ignorant present, and I feel now / The future in the instant' (I.v.56–8), but the only thing she has imagined is herself and Macbeth as queen and king. She has not been transported beyond ignorance. Her childlike fragility suggests she is eager to play at being queen and to be the wife of the king, without much recognition of what it means. Pigs are regularly slaughtered in the courtyard; she imagines that getting rid of Duncan will be like that – and then to the feast. Precisely this inability to be transported beyond the present undoes her, beginning with the deaths of the guards. While she knew 'it must seem their guilt' (II.ii.56), she had not imagined how their deaths would happen, that she would have to

12   Jon Finch and Francesca Annis in Roman Polanski's
film of *Macbeth*, 1971

see it. For Macbeth, it is altogether different. He imagines, it seems, all of it, perhaps right down to his head on the pole. At the banquet, we hear his musings in voiceover, we see his fingers mechanically putting bits into his mouth, and underneath we hear the dim sound of the voices of the others. A sweet-faced Fleance, urged on by his father, who is ambitious for his boy, sings a ballad for the king. This pushiness might have spurred Macbeth's ambition, but suddenly the camera shows that he has already left the chamber. Alone, he muses on the balcony surrounding the courtyard, wanting very much to kill Duncan but hesitant to do it, self-deprecatory because driven by ambition rather than principle. When Lady Macbeth joins him outside, he tells her flatly that he has changed his mind and, when she speaks, demonstrates his lack of regard for her opinion by turning his back on her and returning to the banquet hall. Macbeth's peevish responses to his Lady and her frustrated tears as she continues to whisper to him while Duncan's grooms perform a sword dance reveal that she moves him only to anger. He steps further from her, pours himself a drink, and then into the frame bursts a cup – that of Malcolm, the heir, demanding to be served, sarcastically saying, 'Hail, Thane of *Cawdor*', putting Macbeth in his place. When the film was reformatted as a video (boxy instead of wide-screen), a view of Malcolm at the edge of the screen, scowling at Macbeth's success, is cut off. Polanski meant to show Malcolm's dislike of Macbeth in I.ii (see Kliman, 'Gleanings', p. 134). Macbeth's determination not to 'kiss the ground before young Malcolm's feet' (as he says later, V.viii.28) – instead of Lady Macbeth's persuasion – leads to Macbeth's decision, in the first act, to kill Duncan, as well as to his resolve in the last act to fight with Macduff rather than yield. Macbeth's ambition is fortified by his sense of rightful claim, earned on the battlefield, his superiority to Malcolm and his responsive ire at Malcolm's scorn.

The remainder of the segment strengthens the effect of Malcolm's decisive role in motivating the murder. Macbeth returns from Malcolm to his Lady with the only question that has kept him from proceeding: 'If we should fail?' Her intonation is Sarah Siddons's, 'We fail', with a sharp downward inflection, but the difference is that Siddons's Lady is ready to hazard all on this chance, while Annis's seems oblivious to the consequences of failing. Like a child, wiping tears from her eyes with the back of her hands, happy at last, she tells Macbeth how she will manage things. Her face changes to an anticipatory smile as Duncan, off frame, asks her to dance, which she does charmingly. Macbeth, watching her, in voiceover conjures her to

> Bring forth men-children only!
> For thy undaunted mettle should compose
> Nothing but males. (I.vii.73–5)

Her 'undaunted mettle' refers to her ability to smile at and dance with the man she intends to murder. What he does not recognise, it seems, is that she is not exactly deceitful, for in her unimaginative way she can divorce in her own mind the dance from the murder. Polanski's Lady for a number of reasons has not said anything about plucking her nipple from the boneless gums of her baby and dashing its brains out: she does not overwhelm a noble Macbeth by her terribleness (if she had, that would have obscured Malcolm's effect on Macbeth); she does not yet, we infer, know the tenderness of being a mother; and she is too childlike in appearance herself, it seems, to *be* a mother. Though Jorgens considered the couple to be sterile, their youth contradicts his opinion. In the text, Macbeth's fixation on Banquo's issue can suggest an expectation of fertility or barrenness – fertility if Macbeth acts to preserve his gains for his future progeny; barrenness if he acts out of jealousy. Finch's Macbeth leaves the motivation ambiguous.

For the scene preceding Duncan's murder (II.i), Polanski has a montage of images that mimes the partnership of Macbeth and his wife. In Shakespeare, Banquo and Fleance enter, then Macbeth and a servant; Lady Macbeth does not appear until the next scene. But in Polanski, we see her pour a drug into the wine vessel and begin to make her way towards Duncan's chamber, where an open doorway had revealed the grooms seeing Duncan safely to bed. Before she can proceed, from Macbeth's point of view we see Banquo and Fleance enter the courtyard on their way to a communal sleeping chamber near Duncan's chamber. A glance from her (a closeup of her expressive eye followed by a closeup of his responsive face and a return then to her face) tells Macbeth that he must delay Banquo until she gets into Duncan's chamber. Accordingly, he slides from concealment to accost the two, halting their ascent; under cover of their conversation she glides swiftly (like Asaji in Kurosawa's *Throne of Blood*) towards Duncan's room. Polanski interposes no servant to weaken the connection between husband and wife. Soon Banquo and Fleance enter the sleeping chamber, and after the air-drawn dagger points down the passage towards Duncan, we see her gently pulling the bell rope to tell Macbeth he should proceed. The mutuality of the pair continues in their first court scene (III.i) when Macbeth speaks directly to her the first part of what is his soliloquy in the text – his worries: 'To be thus is nothing, but to be safely thus: / Our fears in Banquo / Stick deep' (III.i.47–9). This Macbeth shares his concerns with his wife.

Content with being a queen, she shows no signs of worry when he begins to speak but becomes more concerned as he proceeds. When Macbeth asks Seyton whether the men he wants to see are waiting, her countenance remains open, signifying her acknowledgment of his kingly responsibilities. She has no curiosity about them. Since she voluntarily stops at the bottom of a stairway when he mounts, where she is joined by several others, we see only her back in long shot as he declares to those below him his wish to remain alone; thus, we do not interpret his statement as a rejection of her, as it is in many productions. Nor does she, as in the text, enter alone in the next scene (III.ii), seeking an audience with the king. Instead, she interrupts Macbeth's uneasy dream, having access to him at the most private of moments without needing a servant's intercession. Through this comparison of text and film, we realise how far Shakespeare has separated them by this point.

What divides them ultimately in the film is her madness, her remorseful guilt and his preoccupation with killing. They had thought that their love would endure beyond regicide, treachery and homicidal mania, but his thoughts leave him so cold that he cannot cry over her broken body in the courtyard, does not embrace her or have her moved from public view. Though he had called her in his letter his 'partner of greatness', Finch's Macbeth leaves no doubt that she is an adjunct to ambition and not his main motive: that is, he murders to raise himself, only incidentally to raise her. Her motive remains uncertain, whether her own advancement or his. But in keeping with the general plan to clarify without obliterating ambiguity, Polanski fills in the sketch of the Lady's movement from self-possession in the early scenes to madness and suicide, a progress that Shakespeare leaves open to interpretation. The text conceals much about her, some of which *must* be determined by performance (her age, her costume, her general demeanour) but some of which *could* remain indeterminate. For example, Shakespeare shows her in her sleepwalking scene to dwell painfully on past murders (V.i). We hear, too, that she has not been well and that her illness is mental (V.iii.37–46). But after the banquet scene (III.iv), since we do not see her fully conscious, we cannot determine for ourselves her state. She could be, like Siddons's Lady, sick but controlled except when asleep, not at all mad.

Polanski has his Lady appear twice in vignettes that show her madness. He adds a scene after Macbeth's visit to the witches' cave (IV.i), before the (transposed) scene of the disaffection of the lords (III.vi). At a bright window in the large hall, Lady Macbeth dozes over her needlework. Her gentlewoman, noting Macbeth on horseback below, wakes her. Starting with horror, Lady Macbeth looks at her hands, where drops of blood appear and then vanish. 'Precious Duncan's dead', she moans. Her gentlewoman leads her out under the cynical gaze of the lords, who are far distant from her in the huge hall. In Act V, after the sleepwalking scene, Polanski draws upon the description by the waiting gentlewoman in V.i to show Lady Macbeth, between V.iii and V.iv, take Macbeth's letter from the chest where she had placed it in her first scene and, wracked by uncontrollable sobs, read it again. Soon after, she falls or jumps to her death (V.v.7). The body remains there, a rough blanket thrown over the upper body, to be gazed at by Macduff and Young Siward when they enter the then deserted Dunsinane.

Between her invocation of the infernal spirits in voiceover in her second scene and her devolution as an active character in the last act, we thus see her gradual disintegration. The hints begin early. Her eyes glistening feverishly, she takes the bloody knives from Macbeth and determines to complete the job quavering with nervous strain and high-strung uneasiness. The blood on her hands appals her, though bravado and nervous excitement carry her through. These emotions are reflected again in her eyes when she watches with fascination the bear that is to be baited as entertainment for the banquet. Called out by the alarm bell after Duncan's death, she can barely speak for trembling. Her faint upon seeing the bloody grooms is genuine and does not protect Macbeth from further scrutiny by the thanes, as the faint sometimes can, for it takes place in the rear of a procession leading towards Duncan's chamber, with a shaky hand-held camera echoing her malaise. She sees the bloody grooms, her eyes meet Macbeth's, and she falls, but her servants, not he, attend her, and no one says 'Look to the lady' (said twice in Shakespeare). With a cut to a new view, Polanski shows that the remainder of the scene takes place after some time, for the lords, including Malcolm and Donalbain, Banquo, Macbeth and others, are standing watching as the doctor and his helper are completing the washing of Duncan's corpse. Malcolm and Donalbain do not speak under cover of her faint but only at the end of the scene. In other words, she has no effect on the outcome; Polanski has marginalised her by taking away her ability to influence events. By her next entrance in III.i, having recovered, she is confused by Macbeth's inability to look forward and be a king. In III.iv during the banquet, her voice a whisper, she tries to rally him, tries to bring him to a better recollection of himself and his position, but barely has an effect on him. The disappearance of the ghost and not her words calms him. She had little power over him from the beginning, and now this is apparent to her. She is a pathetic rather than a tragic character, and, fittingly, Malcolm does not call her a fiend-like queen nor does he refer to her suicide (V.ix.35–7). She is one of the powerless in the drama.

Polanski creates emblems of powerlessness through voice and nudity, as Bruna Gushurst has noted (p. 7). Those without power lack voice; those without power appear nude (including Macduff's son before he's murdered and the two murdered babies). Lady Macbeth's nudity in the sleepwalking scene makes her appear fragile and vulnerable. Sponsorship of the film by *Playboy* notwithstanding, the nudity has nothing in it of prurience. More inured to seeing nudity in films now than audiences were in 1971, we can more readily see how Polanski employs nudity beyond shock value.

Annis holds her very slender body in ways inimical to eroticism: she does not display herself or pose; rather her body, covered by her long hair, is painfully tense and nervous. The doctor, his reaction guiding ours, remains detached, even clinical. Her nudity is an inexplicable intrusion in the narrative – unless we accept Gushurst's explanation. Tynan's rationalisation (*Sound*, p. 102) is that people in those days slept nude, and the film claims historical accuracy in having Duncan, too, sleep in the nude, and in suggesting Macbeth's nudity under his white robe when called forth by Macduff and Lenox in the dawn of the murder. However historical and consistent Lady Macbeth's nudity, her gentlewoman would surely have moved to shield her from the doctor's gaze. But the nudity does show us to what she has come. If Macbeth's robes have become too loose for his frame, she cannot even put hers on. The body in the courtyard has on it nothing but a mean shift.

Similarly, the witches' nudity in the cave scene is not erotic. Any conventionally attractive bodies (judging by faces) are hidden from view by such aged, sagging bodies as we see on film only in pictures of concentration camps and insane asylums. The soft focus blurs their outlines, while close shots are always of faces, and the high camera angle further obscures the nudity. Furthermore, Macbeth's response focuses our attention on what they are doing and saying rather than on what they are not wearing.

Polanski's characterisation of victims as nude can be seen as a sexist posture; however, I would argue for what may appear to be an unlikely (and possibly inadvertent) feminism in Polanski's vision. Terence Hawkes sees two strategies for feminist readings of *Macbeth*: either Lady Macbeth out-mans the men, thereby subverting the patriarchal order, or the witches present an alternative to the patriarchal order (pp. 296–7). I disagree with the efficacy of his first strategy; productions that go that route thereby encourage misogynistic rather than feminist discourse. One of the manoeuvres of any 'ism' (sexism, racism, anti-Semitism) is to assign great power, much greater than ever realised in the society, to the hated group. The productions that make Lady Macbeth into a monster either demonstrate that she is an aberration from any norm for womanhood, or suggest that a woman can be a monster if her husband will not check her. In any case, the text strips Lady Macbeth of power by the end of the banquet scene. The productions that make her more manly than Macbeth simply appropriate the feminine in service of the masculine; the man wants to kill and the woman gives him permission, masquerading as the instigator. Making her powerless (as is Polanski's Lady Macbeth) does not seem feminist either, unless one values her highly strung nerves, her eventual sensibility to guilt and remorse, which the men (except the first two murderers and Macduff) seem incapable of feeling.

Nor does Polanski make the film feminist by expanding, as he does, the definition of manliness. The play is masculinist; that is, it is concerned with what it means to be a man, frequently defines manhood, and determines that manliness includes Macduff's show of emotion, 'But I must also feel it as a man' (IV.iii.221). The definition of manliness to encompass feeling expands man's nature but does not make for a feminist politics. A production might be feminist, however, if it were to expose the rottenness of the warrior society – all of it, from Duncan through Malcolm. One can say that Polanski's version does this.

The alternative, feminist vision, essential if the production is not to be merely misanthropic, belongs to the co-operative society of the witches. In 1986, Terry Eagleton (pp. 2, 4) called Shakespeare's witches heroines, enemies of the patriarchal order of violence and warfare. Years before, Polanski dramatised that interpretation. At first glance, Polanski's witches seem unlikely to occasion a feminist interpretation, and one ought not press the point too hard. But Polanski is contrary enough to assign home truths to unlikely sources. The blind witch stirring the cauldron makes all the others laugh uproariously when she says upon Macbeth's entrance into the cave 'By the pricking of my thumbs, / Something wicked this way comes' (IV.i.45–6), the film's first line from the cauldron scene. Outside their cave is a fragile wooden cross (a symbol never associated with the male society), and, inside, dozens of naked women. The sight of laughing, grinning, naked witches of all ages, from young adulthood to senescence, is unnerving because it makes them appear exposed in their humanity rather than all-powerful. Their laughter unites them *against* the visitor from that other society. Similarly, their first scene, the burial of the knife, rope and severed arm, can be seen as exorcism of the evils of the warrior society: the three women sprinkle herbs, pour blood, and spit – gestures to ward off evil. They are a community, and, for all their filth and poverty, they are self-reliant and care for each other. In the first scene each of the three undertakes her chore, each playing a role in the ritual burial, the young one helping the eldest as they retreat. They do not, as some witches do, scratch around among dead soldiers after the opening battle: that is left for one of the men to do. In the scene of prophetic greeting (I.iii), the old witch rubs the back of the young one, and Polanski omits all the witch-like talk before Macbeth and Banquo's entrance (lines 1–37 are cut), not letting us sense any competition among the women as in some other productions ('I *myself* have all the other', I.iii.14; 'Show *me*, show *me*', I.iii.27). In the cauldron scene, in an easy rhythm, first one then another woman steps up to place her charms into the cauldron after Macbeth's entrance: it is significant that though the cauldron is aboil they prepare his charm not in advance but in response to his

13 The three witches: Elsie Taylor, Noelle Rimmington and Maisie
MacFarquhar, in Roman Polanski's film of *Macbeth*, 1971

demands – *he* is the author of his undoing. They require nothing
fine for themselves, as their rags, their cave and their lean-to
show. Their golden goblet (is it the very one Malcolm thrust at
Macbeth?) is reserved for the visitor. Polanski certainly does not
offer the witches as an *attractive* alternative, but he has shown us
how little to be trusted are the beauties of person and setting in
the society of Duncan, Macbeth and Malcolm, in the faces of such
as Rosse. The women within the society – those briefly glimpsed
in Duncan's train, Lady Macbeth and the ones who shriek out
their sorrow upon the deaths of Duncan and of Lady Macbeth –
are marginalised women because they are thrust into the background within the society. Still, Polanski reserves for these women
significant evidence of human feeling within a community. The
witches have stepped outside this society, freeing themselves from
the margin, making themselves central in their own society.

   One of the ways they distinguish themselves from women
within male society is by eschewing all enhancements of face and
person. Some critics have attached the adjective 'attractive' to the
young witch (see for example Berlin, who refers to her 'good

looks' (p. 292)), and then have spoken about beauty and ugliness and the symbolic resonance – another instance of Polanski's actualisation of fair and foul. But to call the young witch 'attractive' (and the older ones 'ugly') plays into assumptions that to be young is to be alluring and that the audience is male. None of the witches makes herself sexually appealing: the camera focuses in closeup on women with hairy upper lips, toothless gums and conspicuous moles. Nudity itself is a violent rejection of teasing adornment. The film, which was produced at the time of the beginning of the women's movement, reflects the moment in history when women, to free themselves from sexist society, avoided make-up and burned bras.

Polanski's view of patriarchal society seems grim – he might say realistic. Certainly, he has caught the spirit of the Chronicles, with their everlasting litany of feudal war, with first one then another lord seizing the kingdom. A more poetic Macbeth is easier to accept, making our attraction to the murderer possible to rationalise: we respond to him, we say, because he understands his crimes and speaks of them in some of the richest language of Shakespeare's canon. Polanski lays bare the complicit violence at the root of our equal fascination with *his* view. For many of us, especially those denied the opportunity of seeing Olivier or McKellen, the Polanski *Macbeth* reigns supreme among versions reasonably close to the text. But Polanski earns that place not merely with violence but with withdrawal from violence, with cinematic excellence and with a coherent view shaped by the camera, by the narrative details, and without relinquishing ambiguity. He creates a compelling, Shakespearean drama in spite of a diminished Macbeth and Lady Macbeth because, like Welles, Kurosawa and Nunn, he has made the society the locus of his tragedy.

EPILOGUE

Making Macbeth wholly evil

The New York Shakespeare Festival's production at the Public Theater in New York City in 1990 did not employ the chiasmus structure found in so many versions since Shaw's, but director Richard Jordan struck a good balance between principals and directorial concept. Its perspective was unlike any other, however, in daring a wholly unsympathetic Macbeth. In stressing individual culpability, Jordan reminded the audience of the tyrants we read about daily; it seems more relevant now than it did in 1990. Interestingly enough, cast members I interviewed thought Jordan a tyrant also.

Jordan's Macbeth (the versatile Raul Julia) did not need witches to entice him to murder, and therefore, although they relished Macbeth's evil and pricked him on, he managed his own downfall – a choice usually adapted by productions that concentrate on Macbeth and Lady Macbeth, but here the social milieu was also important. Julia gained in horror with his *thinking* Macbeth, who coolly chose his path rather than being impelled towards it either by the witches or by Lady Macbeth or even by his own passions. He provoked curiosity: is it really possible for a rational person to commit such crimes as Macbeth commits? To find a kind of joyless pleasure in treachery? The sad answer is 'yes'. An audience can respond sympathetically to an evil thane if his remorse and sorrow induce pity, but, wherever Macbeth has such opportunities, Julia undercut them. In the 'yellow leaf' soliloquy (V.iii.22–8), the speech that most disarmingly invites audience sympathy through Macbeth's self-knowledge, he played it sardonically – distancing the audience's response. Nor did a larger-than-life stature put him beyond good and evil. The audience was invited to observe him with detachment.

His downfall was a paranoia that impelled him to sacrifice his wife and made him a tyrant. Jordan helped to shape the audience's perception of Macbeth's mistrust through Banquo's characterisation. Though after the murder Banquo suspected that Macbeth 'hath played most foully' for the crown, he decided like a true pragmatist to see what would be in store for him. He sincerely offered Macbeth his service and led the other thanes in All Hailing Macbeth as king. Nodding his agreement when Macbeth spoke of the 'strange invention' of Duncan's sons, Banquo warmly took in his two hands the admonitory finger Macbeth wagged at him to emphasise the half-serious warning 'Fail not our feast' (III.i.27). Had he accepted Banquo's freely given pledge of fealty, Macbeth might not have been deposed in war, the director implied. While denying 'king-becoming graces' (IV.iii.91) to Macbeth, Jordan suggested that evil can flourish when society winks at it.

For Julia to portray this Macbeth, he needed the Lady Macbeth that Melinda Mullins created. She emphasised her Lady's cheerful, good-natured qualities – more horrifying perhaps in a murderer than demonic terribleness. She was not domineering but a partner in the greatness she craved mainly for him. At the 'masterdom' she predicted for him (I.v.70), she knelt to him playfully. After Duncan's death, when she entered in the first court scene (III.i.11) dressed in a wine-coloured gown only somewhat more splendid than her former attire, she appeared content to sit at a low stool beside Macbeth's throne. Her ambition was entirely for him. An unthinking woman, she lost her reason not through remorse but because he disdained her after he was crowned. When they were alone for the first time after the discovery of the murder (III.ii), he spurned her solicitude with impatient gestures and tones, cruelly mimicking her advice when he told her to be pleasant to Banquo. She was no longer his partner – though she tried with her old playfulness and affectionate touches to reach him. Her sleep-walking scene was not a terrifyingly pitiful unfolding of the effect of guilt, fear and despair; instead, she replayed the times when Macbeth appeared to value her ideas. Her final words were calm and reasonable: 'Come, come, come, come, give me your hand. / What's done cannot be undone. To bed, to bed, to bed' (V.i.63–5). Those were good times for her, those moments after the murder when he had listened to her. To garner some sympathy for the pair, Jordan staged her suicide, and Macbeth spoke lines from the 'Tomorrow, and tomorrow' speech, bending over her body (V.v.19–28). Only with her death before his eyes could he shed his usual rationality, allowing his emotion to elicit an empathetic response in both the onstage and theatre audience. The waste – her death and what he had done to bring it on – was made pitiable through her physical presence and his anguish. With the news of the moving Wood preceding rather than following the suicide, her death more directly incited Macbeth to defy the enemy.

To those who look for the contemporary in Shakespeare, Jordan's *Macbeth* offered the play of our time. But though it was a well thought-out production, it did not satisfy many reviewers. They spoke for audiences who want to leave the theatre with something other than the cynicism and despair that current headlines engender.

NOTES

1 She appears in I.v, I.vi, I.vii, II.ii, II.iii, III.i, III.ii, III.iv and V.i, and is mentioned in II.i, V.iii, V.v, V.vii (or V.ix, as the last scene is divided in Muir).

2 On Kurosawa see below. For Ninagawa see below and Mulryne.

3 Bell's notations are worth following in detail; to supplement them I add remarks from other commentators, such as Campbell (pp. 166–87) and Boaden (*Siddons*, pp. 305–15), and from her own commentary on the role as recorded by Campbell (pp. 170–84).

4 The important question of how far they should be considered or followed in modern productions is discussed in Alison Latham and Roger Parker's *Verdi in Performance* (2001).

5 Artistic Director Jeffrey Horowitz founded Theatre for a New Audience (TFANA) in 1979. Since then TFANA has produced some of the best Shakespeare and classic theatre seen in New York, including *The Tempest*, *Taming of the Shrew* and *Titus Andronicus* directed by Julie Taymor and *Richard II* and *Richard III* directed by Ron Daniels.

6 *Vodou* is the spelling those sympathetic to the religion prefer. The spelling *Voodoo* reflects a 'lurid, celluloid image', according to Sallie Ann Glassman, *An Encounter with Divine Mystery: Vodou Visions* (New York: Villard, 2000), p. xiii.

7 Maya Deren (1917–61), an experimental film-maker, also wrote about Vodou.

8 Since I not only saw several performances but also sat in on many rehearsals, I was privy to intentions and saw how the director, choreographer (Kimi Okada), composer and musical director (Akin Atoms), speech and voice coach (Deborah Hecht) and actors shaped those intentions. It was a privilege to observe this humane director at work with his cast, and, though my objectivity has been compromised by my admiration for all the participants, my fly-on-the-wall view provided insights that deepened my understanding of the play in performance. I am grateful to Mr Daniels for his permission to observe the rehearsals.

9 Constantin Stanislavsky (1863–1938), the Russian director, teacher and actor, taught that actors had (among other things) to understand the inner life of their characters – 'Method' acting.

10 Two collections of articles indispensable to the study of Shakespeare in Japan are edited by Takashi Sasayama, J. R. Mulryne and Margaret Shewring, and by Ryuta Minami, Ian Carruthers and John Gillies. Akihiko Senda has our thanks for help with translations; Ryuta Minami's essay in the former collection and the introduction in the latter collection have been important resources. We also received help with reviews and visual materials from Point Tokyo, Tadao Nakane's production company. We have made use of the Arden CD ROM of the *Complete Works* for this chapter (Kenneth Muir, ed. *Macbeth*, 1951).

11 An earlier version of this chapter appeared in *The Literary Review* 22 (Summer 1979): 472–81; thanks to the editors for permission to publish here. For excellent discussions of Kurosawa's use of space and parallel structures see among others: Davies, pp. 152–66; Donaldson, pp. 74–91; Jorgens, pp. 153–60; Manvell, pp. 101–13; Rothwell, *History*, pp. 191–200; and for indebtedness to Japanese cultural tradition see Zambrano.

APPENDIX

A Some significant twentieth-century productions of *Macbeth*

Details of asterisked productions are given in Section B below.

	Director, manager, and/or actors	
1900–11	F. R. Benson, Mrs Benson	Stratford-upon-Avon
1910	E. H. Sothern and Julia Marlowe	New Haven
1911	Herbert Beerbohm Tree, Violet Vanbrugh	London
1920	J. K. Hackett, Mrs Patrick Campbell	London
1928	Barry Jackson	London
1930	John Gielgud, Martita Hunt	London
1933	Theodore Komisarjevsky	Stratford-upon-Avon
1934	Charles Laughton, Flora Robson	London
1936	Orson Welles	New York*
1937	Laurence Olivier, Judith Anderson	London
1941	Maurice Evans, Judith Anderson	New York
1942	John Gielgud, Gwen Ffrangcon-Davies	London
1947	Michael Redgrave, Ena Burrill	London
1949	Antony Qualye	Stratford-upon-Avon
1952	John Gielgud	Stratford-upon-Avon
1955	Glen Byam Shaw, Laurence Olivier, Vivien Leigh	Stratford-upon-Avon*
1957	Akira Kurosawa	Japan*
1962	Donald McWhinnie, Eric Porter, Irene Worth	Stratford-upon-Avon
1966	Alec Guinness, Simone Signoret	London
1967	Peter Hall, Paul Scofield, Vivien Merchant	Stratford-upon-Avon
1974	Trevor Nunn, Nicol Williamson, Helen Mirren	Stratford-upon-Avon*
1976	Trevor Nunn, Ian McKellen, Judi Dench	Stratford-upon-Avon*
1980	Ninegawa	Japan, video 1985, Brooklyn 1990*
1986	Adrian Noble, Jonathan Pryce, Sinead Cusack	Stratford-upon-Avon
1988	Christopher Plummer, Glenda Jackson	New York

1990	Richard Jordan, Raul Julia,	
	Melinda Mullins	New York*
1999	Ron Daniels, Bill Camp,	
	Elizabeth Marvel	New York*
2000	Kelsey Grammar, Diane Venora	New York

B Major actors and staff in the twentieth-century productions discussed

New York, Lafeyette Theater, 1936

Director: Orson Welles Designer: Nat Karson
Lighting designer: Feder Music director: Virgil Thomson

Macbeth	Jack Carter	*Lady Macbeth*	Edna Thomas
Duncan	Service Bell	*Lady Macduff*	Marie Young
Malcolm	Wardell Saunders	*Witch*	Vilhelmina Williams
Hecate	Eric Burroughs	*Witch*	Josephine Williams
Banquo	Canada Lee	*Witch*	Zola King
Macduff	Maurice Ellis	*The Nurse*	Virginia Girvin
Seyton	Larrie Lauria	*Porter*	J. Lewis Johnson

Hallmark Hall of Fame Television Broadcast, NBC, 1954

Director: George Schaefer Designer: Otis Riggs
Costume designer: Noel Taylor
Transmitted in colour and black and white

Macbeth	Maurice Evans	*Lady Macbeth*	Judith Anderson
Duncan	House Jameson	*Lady Macduff*	Margot Stevenson
Malcolm	Roger Hamilton	*Banquo*	Staats Cotsworth
Macduff	Richard Waring	*Donalbain*	Peter Fernandez

Stratford-upon-Avon, Shakespeare Memorial Theatre, 1955

Director: Glen Byam Shaw Designer: Roger Furse
Lighting designer: Peter Streuli

Macbeth	Laurence Olivier	*Lady Macbeth*	Vivien Leigh
Duncan	Geoffrey Bayldon	*Lady Macduff*	Maxine Audley
Malcolm	Trader Faulkner	*Witch*	Dilys Hamlett
Donalbain	Ian Holm	*Witch*	Mary Law
Banquo	Ralph Michael	*Witch*	Nancy Stewart
Macduff	Keith Michell	*Porter*	Patrick Vymark

Kumonosu-Djo (The Castle of the Spider's Web), *Throne of Blood*, Japan, 1957

Director and producer: Akira Kurosawa
Designer: Yoshiro Murai Composer: Masaru Sato
Black and white film

Macbeth/Washizu	Toshiro Mifune	*Lady Macbeth/Asaji*	Isuzu Yamada
Fleance/Yoshiteru	Akira Kubo	*Banquo/Miki*	Chiaki Minoru
Malcolm/Noriyasu	Takashi Shimura	*Duncan/Kuniharu*	Sasaki Takamaru

[223]

Hallmark Hall of Fame Television Broadcast, NBC, 1960

Director: George Schaefer   Designer: Edward Corrick
Costume designer: Beatrice Dawson   Music: Richard Addinsell,
Muir Mathieson
Camera: Fred A. Young
Colour film made for television and for cinema release

Macbeth	Maurice Evans	*Lady Macbeth*	Judith Anderson
Duncan	Malcolm Keen	*Malcolm*	Jeremy Brett
Donalbain	Berry Warren	*Banquo*	Michael Hordern
Macduff	Ian Banner	*Seyton*	Trader Faulkner
Porter	George Rose	*Physician*	Felix Aylmer

Stratford-upon-Avon, Royal Shakespeare Theatre, 1962

Director: Donald McWhinnie
Designer: John Bury

Macbeth	Eric Porter	*Lady Macbeth*	Irene Worth
Duncan	Clifford Rose	*Lady Macduff*	Diana Rigg
Malcolm	Brian Murray	*Witch*	Norah Blaney
Donalbain	Barry MacGregor	*Witch*	Yvonne Bonnamy
Banquo	Peter Jeffrey	*Witch*	Frank Marqussi
Macduff	Bill Travers	*Seyton*	Ian Richardson

British Broadcasting Corporation – Television, 1970

Producer: Cedric Messina   Director: John Gorrie
Designer: Natasha Kroll   Costume designer: John Bloomfield
Music: Christopher Whelen

Macbeth	Eric Porter	*Lady Macbeth*	Janet Suzman
Duncan	Michael Goodliffe	*Lady Macduff*	Rowena Cooper
Malcolm	John Alderton	*Witch*	Daphne Heard
Donalbain	Robin Browne	*Witch*	Sylvia Coleridge
Banquo	John Thaw	*Witch*	Hilary Mason
Macduff	John Woodvine	*Gentlewoman*	Rosamund Burne
Seyton	David Spenser	*Porter*	Wolfe Morris

Film produced in Great Britain, sponsored in part by Hugh Hefner, 1971

Director: Roman Polanski   Script: Kenneth Tynan
Designers: Wilfred Shingleton, Fred Carter
Costume designer: Anthony Mendleson
Music: Third Ear Band   Camera: Alastair McIntyre

Macbeth	Jon Finch	*Lady Macbeth*	Francesca Annis
Duncan	Nicholas Selby	*Lady Macduff*	Diane Fletcher
Malcolm	Stephan Chase	*Witch* (young)	Noelle Rimmington
Donalbain	Paul Shelley	*Witch* (blind)	Maisie MacFarquhar
Banquo	Martin Shaw	*Witch*	Elsie Taylor
Macduff	Terence Bayler	*Gentlewoman*	Patricia Mason
Seyton	Noel Davis	*Porter*	Sydney Bromley

Stratford-upon-Avon, Royal Shakespeare Theatre, 1974

Director: Trevor Nunn   Designer: John Napier
Lighting designer: Nick Chelton

Macbeth	Nicol Williamson	*Lady Macbeth*	Helen Mirren
Duncan	Frank Thornton	*Lady Macduff*	Jane Lapotaire
Malcolm	Eric Allan	*Witch*	Patricia Hayes
Donalbain	John Price	*Witch*	Jane Lapotaire
Banquo	Barry Stanton	*Witch*	Anne Dyson
Macduff	Malcolm Tierney	*Porter*	Ron Pember

Stratford-upon-Avon, The Other Place Theatre, 1976

Director: Trevor Nunn   Designer: John Napier
Lighting designer: Leo Leibovici
Music: Guy Woolfenden

Macbeth	Ian McKellen	*Lady Macbeth*	Judi Dench
Duncan	Griffith Jones	*Lady Macduff*	Susan Drury
Malcolm	Roger Rees	*Witch*	Judith Harte
Donalbain	Tim Brierley	*Witch*	Marie Kean
Banquo	John Woodvine	*Witch*	Susan Dury
Macduff	Bob Peck	*Gentlewoman*	Judith Harte
Porter	Ian McDiarmid	*Seyton*	Tim Brierley

Thames Television Adaptation of 1976 version, 1979

Producers: Trevor Nunn, Verity Lambert   Director for TV: Philip Casson
Designers: John Napier, Mike Hall   Costume designer: Lyn Harvey
Lighting designer: Luigi Bottone   Camera: Peter Coombs
Fight director: Peter Woodward   Music: Guy Woolfenden

Macbeth	Ian McKellen	*Lady Macbeth*	Judi Dench
Duncan	Griffith Jones	*Lady Macduff*	Susan Drury
Malcolm	Roger Rees	*Witch*	Judith Harte
Donalbain	Greg Hicks	*Witch*	Marie Kean
Banquo	John Woodvine	*Witch*	Susan Drury
Macduff	Bob Peck	*Gentlewoman*	Judith Harte
Porter	Ian McDiarmid	*Seyton*	Greg Hicks

The Shakespeare Plays Series, BBC Television/Time-Life, 1982

Producer: Shaun Sutton   Director: Jack Gold
Designer: Gerry Scott   Costume designer: Michael Burdle
Lighting designer: Dennis Channon   Fight director: Malcolm Ranson
Music: Carl Davis

Macbeth	Nicol Williamson	*Lady Macbeth*	Jane Lapotaire
Duncan	Mark Dignam	*Lady Macduff*	Jill Baker
Malcolm	James Hazeldine	*Witch*	Brenda Bruce
Donalbain	Tom Bowles	*Witch*	Eileen Way
Banquo	Ian Hogg	*Witch*	Anne Dyson
Macduff	Tony Doyle	*Gentlewoman*	Denyse Alexander
Seyton	Eamon Boland	*Porter*	James Bolam

The New York Shakespeare Festival, The Public Theatre, 1990

Director: Richard Jordan   Set design: John Conklin
Costume design: Jeanne Button   Lighting design: Brian Gale
Fight director: Peter Nels   Music: Daniel Schreier

Macbeth	Raul Julia	Lady Macbeth	Melinda Mullins
Duncan	Mark Hammer	Lady Macduff	Harriet Harris
Malcolm	Thomas Gibson	Witch	Mary Louise Wilson
Donalbain	Scott Allegrucci	Witch	Jeanne Sakata
Banquo	Larry Bryggman	Witch	Katherine Hiler
Macduff	William Converse	Gentlewoman	Mary Louise Wilson
Seyton	Rene Rivera		Roberts
Porter	Harry S. Murphy		

Japan, 1980; USA, 1990

Director: Yukio Ninagawa   Set designer: Kappa Senoh
Lighting designer: Sumio Yoshi   Costume designer: Jusaburo Tsujimura
Fight director: Masahiro Kunii   Music arrangement: Masato Kai
Sound effects: Akira Honma   Choreography: Kinnosuke Hanayagi
Translation into Japanese: Yushi Odajima
Producers: Tadao Nakane and Noriko Sengoku

Macbeth	Masane Tsukayama	Lady Macbeth	Komaki Kurihara
Murderers	Hiroshi Atsumi	Old Women	Yoko Haneda, Sachiko
	Shigeru Harihari		Ishimaru
Macduff	Haruhiko Joh	Lady Macduff	Hitomi Kageyama
Witch	Tokusaburo Arashi	Witch	Matanosuke Nakamura
Witch	Goro Daimon		

Ninagawa Macbeth Videotape 1985 Japan

Television direction: Ryuzo Matsumoto   Technical: Kurosu Terebi
Producer: Keiji Yabuki   Production Toho
No subtitles

New York, Theatre for a New Audience, 1999

Director: Ron Daniels   Artistic director: Jeffrey Horowitz
Set design: Neil Patel   Costume design: Constance Hoffman
Lighting design: Donald Holder   Composer/musical director: Akin Atoms
Choreographer: Kimi Okada   Fight choreography: B. H. Barry

1st Weird Sister	Rajika Puri	Macduff	Stephen Pelinski
2nd Weird Sister	Starla Benford	Fleance	James Yaegashi
3rd Weird Sister	Careena Melia	Porter	Reg E. Cathey
Duncan	Graham Brown	1st Murderer	Stephen Pelinski
Malcolm	Daniel J. Shore	2nd Murderer	Daniel J. Shore
Donalbain	T. R. Knight	Lady Macduff	Starla Benford
Lenox	Tom Hammond	Boy	Kyle Russell
Sergeant	James Farmer	Messenger	T. R. Knight
Ross	Jonathan Hammond	Gentlewoman	Rajika Puri
Macbeth	Bill Camp	Doctor	Reg E. Cathey
Banquo	Reg E. Cathey	Siward	Graham Brown
Lady Macbeth	Elizabeth Marvel	Young Siward	James Yaegashi
Seyton	James Farmer		

Sources of information: For productions at Stratford-upon-Avon: Mullin, *Theatre at Stratford-upon-Avon*. For film and television productions: Rothwell, *Shakespeare on Screen*. For London productions: TQ, p. 12. Also, reviews, playbills, and promptbooks. The Theatre on Film and Tape (TOFT) Archive of the New York Public Library at Lincoln Center for tapes of some productions, including Daniels's, in New York and elsewhere.

C Some significant recordings of Verdi's *Macbeth*

Macbeth is available in several fine CD versions. Although Riccardo Muti's 1976 EMI recording is now rather ancient, it might still have been my first recommendation, if only EMI understood the value of its own archives: the original LP and CD issues had included, as a kind of appendix, the three arias in the 1847 *Macbeth* that Verdi removed or replaced in his 1865 revision. Since EMI's current reissue no longer includes this invaluable appendix there is no pressing reason to recommend the Muti recording rather than that of Claudio Abbado, on DG, or the late Giuseppe Sinopoli's recording for Philips. All are very fine. Sinopoli's would be my first choice, and includes a riveting performance of the brilliantly scored 1865 ballet music, which modern productions (and Sinopoli's video version) usually, and in my view quite rightly, omit.

For some, the choice may well depend on the singers, even when the recording is deficient in other respects. For example, admirers of Fischer-Dieskau would want to hear his powerfully nuanced Macbeth in the 1971 Decca recording conducted by Lamberto Gardelli, with a youthfully ardent Pavarotti as Macduff – even though Elena Souliotis's Lady Macbeth is too squally. Similarly, lovers of Birgit Nilsson would certainly want to hear the later Decca recording, with Giuseppe Taddei's fine Macbeth – even though Thomas Schippers's conducting is underwhelming, and Schippers was allowed to cut the score in atrociously insensitive ways. So far as Lady Macbeths are concerned, Maria Callas would probably have been Verdi's own first choice, and the live recording of her La Scala performance is still available. But EMI's remastering sounds worse than the LPs, with intolerable distortion and pre-echo in Act I; moreover, the rest of the La Scala cast and the conductor were all (on this occasion) undistinguished. Those who want to hear Callas singing Lady Macbeth's three main arias would do better to buy the 'Verdi Arias' recital that she recorded with Nicola Rescigno and the Philharmonia Orchestra in 1958 (also for EMI). RCA's old (1959) recording, by Erich Leinsdorf, with Leonard Warren as Macbeth, Leonie Rysanek as an incandescent Lady Macbeth and Carlo Bergonzi's superb Macduff, is musically fine; it includes Macbeth's final aria in the 1847 version, and is usually very cheap.

There are two commercial videos of Verdi's *Macbeth*, and the contrast between them might be compared with the contrast between performances of Shakespeare's play in the Globe and in the Theatre Royal. One, very intelligently directed for videogram by Brian Large, presents an enthralling visual record of the Berlin Deutsche Oper production in June 1987. The staging was dark and minimalist, and the few sequences that provide a view of the whole stage quite predictably involve the chorus, most notably at the end of Act I and the beginning of Act IV. Most of the camerawork is in closeup, but is faithfully attentive to the stage director's blocking: to see where Renato Bruson – probably the finest Verdi baritone since Tito Gobbi – and Mara Zampieri draw together or apart in the Macbeths' great Act I duet is no less exciting than watching the interplay between McKellen and Dench in the video of Trevor Nunn's RSC production. The result is one of the most thrilling video performances of an opera that I have ever seen. The other video is an ambitious (or pretentious) French film version directed by Claude D'Anna (London POVL-2031). This has its moments, but can't be recommended. Samuel Ramey is a wonderful Banquo, but Shirley Verrett's performance as Lady Macbeth is lacklustre when compared with her rivals or her own earlier performance in the Abbado recording, and the intelligent Leo Nucci isn't at his best as Macbeth. The busy, fussy visuals cannot compensate for these musical limitations, and even distract from the music – whereas the editing of the Deutsche Oper video quietly directs attention to Verdi's musical structures, not least when it includes sequences showing the conductor. These audio and screen recordings empower anyone anywhere to learn from Verdi.

Graham Bradshaw

BIBLIOGRAPHY

Abbate, Carolyn, *In Search of Opera*, Princeton, 2001.
——, *Unsung Voices: Opera and Musical Narrative in the Nineteenth Century*, Princeton, 1991.
Account of the Terrific and Fatal Riot at the New-York Astor Place Opera House, On the night of May 10th, 1849: With the Quarrels of Forrest and Macready. (Including all the Causes which Led to that Awful Tragedy! Wherein an infuriated mob was quelled by the Public Authorities and Military, with the mournful termination in the Sudden Death or Mutilation of more than Fifty Citizens, With Full and Authentic Particulars. 'Let Justice Be Done Though The Heavens Fall!' New York, 1849.
Adelman, Janet, *The Common Liar: An Essay in* Antony and Cleopatra, *Yale Studies in English* 181, New Haven, 1973.
Aitchison, Nick, *Macbeth: Man and Myth*, Phoenix Mill, Gloucestershire, 1999.
Arai Yoshio, 'Nihon no Shakespeare Geki Joen' [Shakespeare Performance in Japan], *Bungaku* 54 (April 1986), 243–4.
Aston, Anthony, 'A Brief Supplement to Colley Cibber, Esq; His Lives of the Late Famous Actors and Actresses', in *An Apology for the Life of Mr. Colley Cibber ...*, ed. Robert W. Lowe, 2 vols, London, 1889, rpt 1966, II, 297–371.
Avery, Emmett L., and Arthur H. Scouten, *The London Stage 1660–1700: A Critical Introduction*, Carbondale, 1968.
Baldini, Gabriele, *The Story of Giuseppe Verdi: Oberto to Un Ballo in Maschera*, trans. Roger Parker, Cambridge, 1980.
Barish, Jonah, 'Madness, Hallucination and Sleepwalking', in David Rosen and Andrew Porter, eds, *Verdi's* Macbeth: *A Sourcebook*, Cambridge, 1984, pp. 149–55.
Barrett, Lawrence, *Edwin Forrest*, 1881, rpt New York, 1969.
Barroll, J. Leeds, 'A New History for Shakespeare and His Time', *Shakespeare Quarterly* 39, 4 (Winter 1988), 441–64.
Bartholomeusz, Dennis, *Macbeth and the Players*, Cambridge, MA, 1969.
Bate, Jonathan, *Shakespearean Constitutions: Politics, Theatre, Criticism 1730–1830*, Oxford, 1989.
The Beauties of Mrs. Siddons ... Letters from a Lady of Distinction to her Friend in the Country, London, 1786.
Beckerman, Bernard, *Dynamics of Drama: Theory and Method of Analysis*, New York, 1979.

——, 'Shakespeare's Dramaturgy and Binary Form', *Theatre Journal* 33 (March 1981), 5–17.

Bellenden, John, trans. 1531, *The Chronicles of Scotland Compiled by Hector Boece*, ed. Edith C, Batho and H. Winifred Husbands, 2 vols, Edinburgh and London, 1941.

Berger, Harry, Jr, 'The Early Scenes of *Macbeth*: Preface to a New Interpretation', *ELH* 47 (1980), 1–31.

——, *Revisionary Play: Study in the Spenserian Dynamics*, Berkeley, 1988.

Berkowitz, Gerald M., *David Garrick: A Reference Guide*, Boston, 1980.

Berlin, Normand, '*Macbeth*: Polanski and Shakespeare', *Literature/ Film Quarterly* 1,4 (Fall 1973), 292–8.

Billington, Michael, 'Macbeth' (Lyttleton Theatre, 19 September 1987), *One Night Stands: A Critic's View of British Theatre from 1971 to 1991*, London, 1993.

Bloch, Ernest, *Macbeth*, Vocal score, Milan, 1910.

Blumenthal, J., '*Macbeth* into *Throne of Blood*', *Sight and Sound* 34 (Autumn 1965), 190–5; rpt in Gerald Mass and Marshall Cohen, eds, *Film Theory and Criticism*, London, 1974.

Boaden, James, *Memoirs of Mrs. Siddons: Interspersed with Anecdotes of Authors and Actors*, London, 1827, rpt 1893.

——, *Memoirs of the Life of John Philip Kemble: Including a History of the Stage, from the Time of Garrick to the Present Period*, 2 vols, London, 1825.

Booth, Stephen, *King Lear, Macbeth, Indefinition, and Tragedy*, New Haven, 1983.

Bradley, A. C., *Shakespearean Tragedy: Hamlet, Othello, King Lear, Macbeth*, 1904, rpt Cleveland, OH, 1963.

Bradshaw, Graham, '*Othello* in the Age of Cognitive Science', *Shakespeare Studies* [Japan] 38 (2001), 17–18.

——, 'A Shakespearean Perspective: Verdi and Boito as Translators', in James A. Hepokoski, ed., *Giuseppe Verdi: Falstaff*, Cambridge, 1983, pp. 152–71.

——, *Shakespeare's Scepticism*, Brighton, 1987.

Brooke, Nicholas, ed., *Macbeth*, Oxford, 1990.

Brooks, Cleanth, '"The Naked Babe" and the Cloak of Manliness' (from *The Well-Wrought Urn: Studies in the Structure of Poetry*, New York, 1947), rpt in John Wain, ed., *Shakespeare: Macbeth, A Casebook*, Nashville, 1970, pp. 183–201.

Budden, Julian, *The Operas of Verdi, Vol. 1: From Oberto to Rigoletto*, rev. ed., Oxford, 1992.

Bullough, Geoffrey, *Narrative and Dramatic Sources of Shakespeare*, vol. VII, London, 1973.

Bulman, J. C., and H. R. Coursen, *Shakespeare on Television: An*

Anthology of Essays and Reviews, Hanover, NH, 1988.

Burckhardt, Sigurd, *Shakespearean Meanings*, Princeton, 1968.

Burnim, Kalman A., *David Garrick: Director*, Pittsburgh, 1961.

Calderwood, James L., *If It Were Done: Macbeth and Tragic Action*, Amherst, 1986.

Campbell, Thomas, *Life of Mrs. Siddons*, London, 1839, rpt New York, 1972.

Carr, Stephen Leo, and Peggy A. Knapp, 'Seeing Through *Macbeth*', *PMLA* 96 (1981), 837–47.

Celletti, Rodolfo, 'On Verdi's Vocal Writing', trans. Harold Barnes from 'Caraterri della vocalità di Verdi', 1974, in William Weaver and Martin Chusid, eds, *Verdi Companion*, New York, 1979, pp. 216–38.

Cone, Edward T., *The Composer's Voice*, Berkeley, 1974.

——, *Music: A View from Delft*, Chicago, 1989

David, Richard, 'The Tragic Curve', *Shakespeare Survey* 9 (1956), 122–31.

Davies, Anthony, *Filming Shakespeare's Plays: The Adaptations of Laurence Olivier, Orson Welles, Peter Brook and Akira Kurosawa*, Cambridge, 1988.

Dawson, Robert, *Scotsman* review, cited by Yuriko Akishima, 'Ninagawa Densetsu' [The Ninagawa Legend], in *Ninagawa Yukio no Chosen* [*Yukio Ninagawa's Challenge*], *Taiyo* special edition, Tokyo, 25 February 2001.

Deren, Maya. *Divine Horseman: The Living Gods of Haiti*, London, [1953], rpt New York, [1983].

Dommett, Sue, '*Macbeth* at The Other Place, 1976: A Commentary', expanded MA thesis, unpublished, Stratford, 1978.

Donaldson, Peter S., *Shakespearean Films/Shakespearean Directors*, Boston, 1990.

Donohue, Joseph, W. Jr, *Dramatic Character in the English Romantic Age*, Princeton, 1970.

——, '*Macbeth* in the Eighteenth Century', *TQ*, 1, 3 (September 1971), 20–4.

Downer, Alan S., *The Eminent Tragedian: William Charles Macready*, Boston, 1966; Oxford, 1967.

Eagleton, Terry, *William Shakespeare*, Oxford and Jackson, 1986.

Edwards, Geoffrey, and Ryan Edwards, *The Verdi Baritone: Studies in the Development of Dramatic Character*, Bloomington, 1994.

Estrin, Mark W., ed., *Orson Welles: Interviews*, Conversations with Filmmakers Series, Jackson, 2002.

Evans, G. Blakemore, with J. J. M. Tobin, eds, *The Riverside Shakespeare*, 2nd edn, Boston, 1997.

Evans, Gareth Lloyd, '*Macbeth*: 1946–80 at Stratford-upon-Avon',

John Russell Brown, ed., *Focus on* Macbeth, London, 1982, pp. 87–110.

——, 'Macbeth in the Twentieth Century', *TQ*, 1, 3 (September 1971), 36–9.

Evans, Maurice, *All This ... and Evans Too! A Memoir*, Columbia, SC, 1987.

Fiske, Roger, 'The "Macbeth" Music', *Music and Letters* 45 (April 1964), 114–25.

Forman, Simon, 'The Original Macbeth: A Contemporary Account', *TQ*, 1, 3 (September 1971), 13.

France, Richard, 'The "Voodoo" *Macbeth* of Orson Welles', *Yale/Theatre* 5,3 (Summer 1974), 66–78.

——, ed, with an introduction, *Orson Welles on Shakespeare: The W.P.A. and Mercury Theatre Playscripts*, Contributions in Drama and Theatre Studies 30, New York, 1990.

French, Marilyn, *Shakespeare's Division of Experience*, New York, 1981.

Furness, Horace Howard, ed., *Macbeth*, New Variorum Edition of Shakespeare, 1873, rpt New York, 1963.

——, *Macbeth* Scrapbook, 'Mrs. Siddons's Last Appearance as Lady Macbeth', Furness Library, University of Pennsylvania, II, 9–10.

Gallimore, Daniel, 'Ninagawa Yukio', in J. E. Hoare, ed., *Britain and Japan: Biographical Portraits*, vol. 3, London, 1999, pp. 324–37.

Garrick, David, *The Letters of David Garrick*, ed. David M. Little and George M. Kahrl, associate ed. Phoebe de K. Wilson, 3 vols, London, 1963.

Gentleman, Francis, *Theatre Quarterly*, I, 3 (September 1971), 19.

Goldman, Michael, *Acting and Action in Shakespearean Tragedy*, Princeton, 1985.

Gushurst, Bruna, 'Polanski's Determining of Power in *Macbeth*', *Shakespeare on Film Newsletter* 13, 2 (April 1989), 7.

Hawkes, Terence, 'Shakespeare and New Critical Approaches', in Stanley Wells, ed., *The Cambridge Companion to Shakespeare Studies*, Cambridge, 1986, pp. 287–302.

Highfill, Philip H., Jr, Kalman A. Burnim and Edward A. Langhans, eds, *A Biographical Dictionary of ... Stage Personnel in London, 1660–1800, Vol. 14: S. Siddons to Thunne*, Carbondale, 1991.

Hinman, Charlton, ed., *The First Folio of Shakespeare: The Norton Facsimile*, New York, 1968.

Hogan, Charles Beecher, *Shakespeare in the Theatre, 1701–1800*, 2 vols, Oxford, 1952, 1957.

Holinshed, Raphael, *Holinshed's Chronicles of England, Scotland, and Ireland*, 6 vols, rpt. from 1808 ed., New York, 1965.

Homan, Sidney, *Shakespare's Theater of Presence: Language, Spectacle, and the Audience*, Lewisburg, 1986.

Horwich, Richard, 'Integrity in *Macbeth*: The Search for the "Single State of Man"', *Shakespeare Quarterly* 29, 3 (Summer 1978), 365–73.

Houseman, John, *Run-Through: A Memoir*, New York, 1972.

Hughes, Ted, *Shakespeare and the Goddess of Complete Being*, London, 1992.

Hutton, Clayton, *Macbeth: The Making of the Film*, London, 1960.

Jenkin, Fleeming, 'Mrs. Siddons As Lady Macbeth' [G. J. Bell's notes, originals at Folger Shakespeare Library], *Papers Literary, Scientific, &c*, 2 vols, eds Sidney Colvin and J. A. Ewing, London, 1887, I, 45–66.

Jorgens, Jack J., *Shakespeare on Film*, Bloomington and London, 1977.

Keene, Donald, *No: The Classical Theatre of Japan*, Tokyo, 1966.

Kennan, Patricia, and Mariangela Tempera, eds, *Shakespeare from Text to Stage*, Bologna, 1992.

Kennedy, Dennis, *Looking at Shakespeare: A Visual History of Twentieth-century Performance*, Cambridge, 1993.

Kimbell, David R. B., *Verdi in the Age of Italian Romanticism*, Cambridge, 1981.

Kinney, Arthur F., *Lies Like Truth: Shakespeare, Macbeth, and the Cultural Moment*, Detroit, c. 2001.

Kliman, Bernice W., 'Gleanings: The Residue of Difference in Scripts: The Case of Polanski's *Macbeth*', in Jay L. Halio and Hugh Richmond, eds, *Shakespearean Illuminations: Essays in Honor of Marvin Rosenberg*, Newark, 1998, pp. 131–46.

——, 'The Nicholas Rowe *Macbeth* Illustration Corroborated', *The Shakespeare Newsletter* 42, 2 (Summer 1992), 23.

——, 'Rowe 1709 *Macbeth* Illustration Again', *The Shakespeare Newsletter* 48, 3 (Fall 1998), 59–60.

——, 'Setting in Television Productions', in Hamlet: *Film, Televison and Audio Performance*, Rutherford, NJ: Fairleigh Dickinson University Press, 1988, pp. 117–226.

——, 'Thanes in the Folio *Macbeth*', *Shakespeare Bulletin* 9,1 (Winter 1991), 5–8.

——, 'Welles's *Macbeth*, a Textual Parable', in Michael Skovmand, ed., *Screen Shakespeare*, Aarhus, 1994, pp. 25–37.

Knowles, John, 'The Banquet Scene from Verdi's *Macbeth*: An Experiment in Large-scale Musical Form', in David Rosen and Andrew Porter, eds, *Verdi's* Macbeth: *A Sourcebook*, Cambridge, 1984, pp. 284–92.

Kott, Jan, *Shakespeare, Our Contemporary*, trans. Boleslaw Taborski, London, 1966.

Latham, Alison, and Roger Parker, *Verdi in Performance*, Cambridge, 2001.

Levenson, Jill L., *Romeo and Juliet*, Shakespeare in Performance, Manchester, 1987.

Levine, Lawrence W. *Highbrow/Lowbrow: The Emergence of Cultural Hierachy in America*, Cambridge, MA, 1988.

McClosky, Susan, 'Shakespeare, Orson Welles, and the "Voodoo" *Macbeth*', *Shakespeare Quarterly* 36 (Winter 1985), 406–16.

Macready, William Charles, *The Diaries of William Charles Macready, 1833–1851*, ed. William Toynbee, 2 vols, New York, 1912.

Manvell, Roger, *Shakespeare and the Film*, New York, 1971.

Minami Ryuta, Ian Carruthers and John Gillies, eds, *Performing Shakespeare in Japan*, Cambridge, 2001.

Morris, Peter, 'Shakespeare on Film', *Films in Review* 24,3 (March 1973), 132–63.

Muir, Kenneth, ed., *Macbeth*, The Arden Shakespeare, 1951, rpt London, 1982.

Mullin, Michael, '*Macbeth* on Film', *Literature/Film Quarterly* 1 (Fall 1973), 332–42.

——, ed., Macbeth *Onstage: An Annotated Facsimile of Glen Byam Shaw's 1955 Promptbook*, Columbia, MO, and London, 1976.

——, compiler and ed, with Karen Morris Muriello, *Theatre at Stratford-upon-Avon: A Catalogue-Index to Productions of the Shakespeare Memorial/Royal Shakespeare Theatre, 1879–1978*, 2 vols, Westport, CT, 1980.

Mulryne, J. R., 'From Text to Foreign Stage: Yukio Ninagawa's Cultural Translation of Macbeth', in Patricia Kennan and Mariangda Tempera, eds, *Shakespeare from Text to Stage*, Bologna, 1992, pp. 131–43.

Nelson, Richard, *Two Shakespearean Actors*, London, 1990.

Nicoll, Allardyce, *The Garrick Stage: Theatres and Audience in the Eighteenth Century*, Athens, 1980.

Ninagawa Yukio, dir., *Ninagawa Macbeth*, video, Toho, 1985.

——, *Note 1969–1988*, Tokyo, 1989.

——, *Tatakau Gekijo* [Fighting Theatre], Tokyo, 1999.

Noske, Frits, *The Signifier and the Signified: Studies in the Operas of Mozart and Verdi*, Oxford, 1990.

Nouryeh, Andrea, 'Understanding Xanadu: An Alternative Way of Viewing Orson Welles's Shakespeare Films', *Shakespeare on Film Newsletter* 14,1 (December 1989), 3.

Odajima Yushi, trans., *Macbeth*, Tokyo, 1983.

——, and Yukio Ninagawa (in conversation), 'Shakespeare no uchi naru sekai e' [Into Shakespeare's World] *Shingeki* 422 (May 1988), 101.

Odell, George C. D., *Shakespeare from Betterton to Irving*, 2 vols, 1920, rpt New York, 1966.

Olivier, Laurence, *On Acting*, London, 1986.

Orgel, Stephen, 'Macbeth and the Antic Round', *Shakespeare Survey* 52 (1999), 143–53.

Orrell, John, *The Human Stage: English Theatre Design, 1567–1640*, Cambridge, 1988.

Paul, Henry N., *The Royal Play of Macbeth: When, Why, and How It Was Written by Shakespeare*, New York, 1950.

Pinciss, Gerald M., and Roger Lockyer, *Shakespeare's World: Background Readings in the English Renaissance*, New York, 1990.

Porter, Andrew, *A Musical Season*, New York, 1974

Raab, Felix. *The English Face of Machiavelli: A Changing Interpretation, 1500–1700*, London, 1964.

Rabkin, Norman, *Shakespeare and the Problem of Meaning*, Chicago, 1981.

Roberts, Jeanne A., 'Shades of the Triple Hecate in Shakespeare', *Proceedings of the PMR Conference*, Augustinian Historical Institute, Villanova University, vols 12/13 (1987–88), pp. 47–66.

Rosen, David, and Andrew Porter, eds, *Verdi's Macbeth: A Sourcebook*, Cambridge, 1984.

Rosenberg, Marvin, *The Masks of Macbeth*, Berkeley, 1978.

——, 'Trevor Nunn's *Macbeth*', *Shakespeare Quarterly* 28 (1976), 195–6.

Rothwell, Kenneth S., *A History of Shakespeare on Screen*, Cambridge, 1999.

——, 'Roman Polanski's *Macbeth*: The "Privileging" of Ross', *CEA Critic* 46 1 & 2 (Fall and Winter 1983–84), 50–5.

——, 'Shakespeare and the People: Elizabethan Drama on Video', *Shakespeare on Film Newsletter* 1, 2 (April 1977), 4, 7.

——, and Annabelle Henkin Melzer, *Shakespeare on Screen: An International Filmography and Videoography*, New York, 1990.

Sasayama Takashi, J. R. Mulryne and Margaret Shewring, eds, *Shakespeare and the Japanese Stage*, Cambridge, 1998.

Schlegel, Augustus William, *Course of Lectures on Dramatic Art and Literature*, 1808, rev. 1811, trans. into Italian by Giovanni Gherardini, 1817; trans. into English John Black and rev. J. A. Morison, London, 1846.

Schmidgall, Gary, *Shakespeare and Opera*, New York, 1990.

Scragg, Leah, '*Macbeth* on Horseback', *Shakespeare Survey* 26 (1973), 81–8.

Senda, Akihiko, 'The Rebirth of Shakespeare in Japan, from the 1960s to the 1990s', trans. Ryuta Minami, in Takashi Sasayama, J. R. Mulryne and Margaret Shewring, eds, *Shakespeare and the Japanese Stage*, Cambridge, 1998, pp. 15–37.

Shakespeare, William, *Macbeth*, The BBC TV Shakespeare, London, 1983.

——, *Macbeth* [Davenant?] Players Quarto. London, 1673.

——, *Macbeth* [Davenant] Players Quarto. London, 1674.

Shakspere Allusion-Book, The: A Collection of Allusions to Shakspere From 1591 to 1700, originally compiled by C. M. Ingleby, L. Toulmin Smith and F. J. Furnivall, re-ed. and rev. by John Munro, 1909, 2 vols, rpt London, 1932.

Shattuck, Charles H., *The Shakespeare Promptbooks: A Descriptive Catalogue*, Urbana, 1965.

Siddons, Sarah Kemble, *The Reminiscences of Sarah Kemble Siddons, 1773–1785*, ed. William Van Lennep [Curator, Harvard Theatre Collection], Cambridge, MA, 1942.

Somville, Marilyn Feller, 'Vocal Gesture in Verdi's *Macbeth*', in David Rosen and Andrew Porter, eds, *Verdi's* Macbeth: *A Sourcebook*, Cambridge, 1984, pp. 239–44.

Southern, Richard, *Changeable Scenery: Its Origin and Development in the British Theatre*, London, 1952.

Speaight, Robert, *Shakespeare on the Stage: An Illustrated History of Shakespearian Performance*, Boston, 1973.

Sprague, Arthur Colby, *Shakespearian Players and Performances*, Cambridge, 1953.

Stopes, Charlotte Carmichael, '*Hamlet* and *Macbeth:* An Intended Contrast', *Athenaeum* 3995 (14 May 1904), 666–8.

Tacitus, *The Annales of Cornelius Tacitus* ..., London, 1604–5.

Takahashi Yutaka, 'Gekimandala: My Life, Yukio Ninagawa', *Mainichi Newspaper* (series of 110 columns), 1 June to 28 December 2000.

Tatlow, Antony, *Shakespeare, Brecht, and the Intercultural Sign*, Durham, NC, 2001.

The Theatrical Review for the Year 1757 and beginning of 1758, Containing Critical Remarks on the Principal Performers of both the Theatres ..., London, 1758.

TQ: Theatre Quarterly, 'One Play in Its Time: *Macbeth*', 1, 3, September 1971, 12–53.

Tynan, Kenneth, *The Sound of Two Hands Clapping*, London, 1975.

Verdi, Guiseppi, letters in Italian and in English trans., in David Rosen and Andrew Porter, eds, *Verdi's* Macbeth: *A Sourcebook*, Cambridge, 1984, pp. 1–125.

Walker, Frank, *The Man Verdi*, London, 1962.

Weaver, William, 'The Shakespeare Verdi Knew', in David Rosen and Andrew Porter, eds, *Verdi's* Macbeth: *A Sourcebook*, Cambridge, 1984, pp. 144–8.

Wilkes, [Thomas], *A General View of the Stage*, London, 1759.

Williams, George Walton, *Shakespeare Newsletter* (Spring 1993), p. 3.

Wright, George T., *Shakespeare's Metrical Art*, Berkeley, 1988.

——, 'Troubles of a Professional Meter Reader', in Ross Macdonald, ed., *Shakespeare Reread: The Text in New Contexts*, Ithaca and London, 1994, pp. 56–76.

Wyntoun, Andrew, *Orygynale Cronykil of Scotland*, ed. F. J. Amours, *The Original Chronicle of Andrew of Wyntoun*, 6 vols, Edinburgh, 1903–14.

Zambrano, Ana, *'Throne of Blood*: Kurosawa's *Macbeth'*, *Literature/Film Quarterly* 2 (Summer 1974), 262–74.

INDEX

Note: page numbers given in *italic* refer to illustrations; 'n.' after a page reference indicates a note number on that page.

08 DEC 2023 S

Lightning Source UK Ltd.
Milton Keynes UK
22 December 2009

147825UK00001B/25/P